W9-BQJ-860

ADVANCES IN INTERNATIONAL MARKETING

Volume 7 • 1996

MARKETING IN ASIA PACIFIC AND BEYOND

ADVANCES IN INTERNATIONAL MARKETING

MARKETING IN ASIA PACIFIC AND BEYOND

Series Editor: S. TAMER CAVUSGIL
        The Eli Broad Graduate School
          of Management
        Michigan State University

Volume Editor: CHARLES R. TAYLOR
        Department of Marketing
        Villanova University

VOLUME 7 • 1996

 JAI PRESS INC.

Greenwich, Connecticut   *London , England*

CONTENTS

PART III.   INTERNATIONAL ADVERTISING

PART IV.   METHODOLOGICAL CONTRIBUTIONS TO THE INTERNATIONAL MARKETING LITERATURE

Contents

LIST OF CONTRIBUTORS

Hugh Cannon	Wayne State University
Seoil Chaiy	Korea University
Dae Ryun Chang	Yonsei University
Don Ryun Chang	Managing Director, DC&A Seoul, Korea
Steven R. Clinton	Michigan State University
M. Bixby Cooper	Michigan State University
George R. Franke	University of Alabama
James W. Gentry	University of Nebraska
Sungil Kim	Yonsei University
Gyungtai Ko	Chonbuk National University
Minhi Hahn	Korea Advanced Institute of Science and Technology
Sunkyu Jun	Han Nam University
Kyung Hoon Kim	Changwon National University
Jay L. Laughlin	Kansas State University
Dong Hwan Lee	State University of New York, Albany
Kwon Soo Lee	Yonsei University
Gordon E. Miracle	Michigan State University
David B. Montgomery	Stanford University
Young Sook Moon	Marketing Director, KORAD Seoul, Korea

Edward A. Morash	Michigan State University
Sejo Oh	Yonsei University
Sehoon Park	Sookmyung Women's University
Mary Anne Raymond	American University
William Rylance	President, Merit Communications Seoul, Korea
Charles M. Schaninger	State University of New York, Albany
Alan T. Shao	University of North Carolina, Charlotte
Changhoon Shin	Korea Advanced Institute of Science and Technology
Michael Stricklin	University of Nebraska
Charles R. Taylor	Villanova University
John C. Taylor	Wayne State University
Hans B. Thorelli	Indiana University
Julie Scott Wilcox	The Gallup Organization Irvine, CA
Attila Yaprak	Wayne State University
Heon Deok Yoon	Soong Sil University
Sung-Joon Yoon	Chief Researcher, Samsung Economic Research Institute Seoul, Korea
Shaoming Zou	Kansas State University

LIST OF REVIEWERS

Catherine Axinn — Ohio University

Peggy Chaudry — Villanova University

Sang T. Choe — University of Southern Indiana

Young-Won Ha — Sogang University

Minhi Hahn — Korea Advanced Institute of Science and Technology

Sang Lin Han — Chung Nam National University

Ronald Paul Hill — Villanova University

Sung-Tai Hong — Han Yang University

William Keep — University of Southern Mississippi

Jae Wook Kim — Korea University

Steve W. Kopp — University of Arkansas

Jay L. Laughlin — Kansas State University

Chol Lee — Hong Ik University

Doo Hee Lee — Korea University

Han Joon Lee — Western Michigan University

Moonkyu Lee — University of Colorado

Woo-Young Lee — Sogang University

Tiger Li — Florida International University

Chae Wun Lim — Sogang University

Jeen S. Lim — University of Toledo

Robert MacKoy — Butler University

Michael L. Maynard — Temple University

Gordon E. Miracle — Michigan State University

Sejo Oh	Yonsei University
Aysegul Ozsomer	Seattle University
Jong-Won Park	Korea University
Jeffrey Schmidt	Michigan State University
Geon-Cheol Shin	Kyung Hee University
John C. Taylor	Wayne State University
Daniel Wardlow	San Francisco State University
Jong Suk Ye	Han Yang University
Shaoming Zou	Kansas State University

PREFACE

Volume 7 of *Advances in International Marketing* is a special issue guest edited by Professor Charles Ray Taylor at Villanova University. The volume features selected essays presented at the conference on "Marketing in Asia Pacific: Challenges and Opportunities of Marketing in a Dynamic Region" held in Seoul, Korea, in May 1995. The conference was sponsored by the Korean Marketing Association in affiliation with the American Marketing Association.

Michigan State University's CIBER provided program support for this event, which brought together more than 400 marketing professionals from four continents.

We are grateful to Professor Taylor for his careful editing of the papers in this volume and his diligence in working with the authors from around the globe.

Our thanks also go to Gayle Jerman, Danielle Shaban-Turner, and Lindsay Claire at JAI Press Inc., who maneuvered the project through the production phase.

S. Tamer Cavusgil
Series Editor

INTRODUCTION

The past few decades have witnessed a substantial increase in the number of academic studies dealing with international marketing topics (Cavusgil & Li, 1992). In conjunction with this increase we have seen greater scrutiny of the quality of the research. As noted by Aulakh and Kotabe (1992), past reviews of the international marketing literature (e.g., Albaum & Peterson, 1984; Bradley, 1987) have cited a need for improvement in both: (a) the use of conceptual and theoretical frameworks to guide the research; and (b) methodological rigor. Cavusgil (1993) adds that there is a need for more research that either originates from a substantive managerial issue or integrates and builds on previous research.

The contributors to this volume have clearly taken heed of the above critiques of research in international marketing. This is evidenced by both the quality of the theoretical frameworks employed in the research and the number of papers in which advanced methodological techniques are used. Analytical techniques employed in the papers include: multiple regression (Oh and Kim; Shin, Hahn and Park); factor analysis (Wilcox, Ko, Gentry, Stricklin and Jun; Kim; Yoon, Cannon and Yaprak), conjoint analysis (Lee and Schaninger); and t-tests (Zou and Laughlin; Taylor and Miracle). It is notable that several of the studies go to great lengths to assess the reliability and validity of their results (e.g., Zou and Laughlin; Kim; Moon and Franke; Taylor and Miracle; Yoon, Cannon and Yaprak). Moreover, some of the papers explicitly set out to make methodological advancements (Kim; Zou and Laughlin; Yoon, Yaprak and Cannon).

The papers come from diverse theoretical perspectives, including game theory (Shin, Hahn and Park); industrial organization (Oh and Kim); and power and conflict management (Yoon, Morash, Cooper, and Clinton); as well as from cultural (Raymond and Rylance; Wilcox, Ko, Gentry, Stricklin, and Jun; Taylor and Miracle); and ecological perspectives (Thorelli). The Zou and Laughlin paper explicitly tests a previously developed conceptual framework, and several other papers clearly build on prior research (e.g., Moon and Franke; Shin, Hahn and Park). Thus, the papers exemplify recent advancements in theory building and methodological rigor in international studies.

Some of the papers are clearly motivated by issues facing managers, including: the need to employ state of the art logistics techniques in order to be competitive (Taylor); legal and environmental barriers facing global advertisers (Shao); issues in the selection of service providers (Raymond and Rylance); the need to develop and build a corporate identity (Chang, Chang and Lee); and the need to better understand partners in strategic alliances (Yoon, Morash, Cooper and Clinton). The output of these studies has clear implications for managers.

While this volume is not limited to issues associated with the Asia Pacific region, many of the papers focus on this growing region. Several of the papers focus on marketing issues in South Korea. Given the country's increased prominence in the world's economy, this attention is warranted. A strong case can be made for the notion that Korea has advanced beyond "newly industrializing country" status to become a country with a developed economy. Recently, Korea has eclipsed the $10,000 (U.S.) mark in per capita income and it now ranks as one of the world's top 10 countries in terms of advertising expenditures (Holstein & Nakarmi, 1995; Pruzan, 1995). Forecasts indicate that per-capita income may top $20,000 by the year 2000. Additionally, a recent *Business Week* article proclaimed that Korea is "Headed for High Technology's Top Tier" (Holstein & Nakarmi, 1995).

Clearly, there is a need for more studies focusing on marketing phenomena in economies that have achieved significant advances over the past few decades (e.g., Taiwan, Hong Kong, Singapore, Mexico, and Brazil), as well as those countries that comprise the new generation of "up and coming" economies (e.g., Malaysia, Indonesia, Chile). The studies on Korea in this volume exemplify the timely knowledge that can be gleaned from such projects.

The volume is organized into four sections. Papers in the first section examine corporate strategy in an international context. The papers in this section reflect the continued dynamism of global markets. Hence, it is titled, "Corporate Strategy in the 1990s." First, Yoon, Morash, Cooper and Clinton examine how channel integration between a company, its customers, and its supplier partners can be used to build a sustainable competitive advantage. The authors also compare channel integration approaches in Japan, Australia, Korea, and the United States. Chaiy and Montgomery investigate differences in perceptions of Korean and U.S. managers toward factors that lead to an effective strategic alliance. Next, Thorelli provides an analysis of key environmental forces facing today's global marketers by examining the relationship between marketing, authoritarian vs.

democratic rule, and economic development. The final paper in this section, by Chang, Chang, and Lee, explores the importance of corporate identity programs in global markets.

Part II includes papers that examine issues in global distribution and the marketing of services. Shin, Hahn and Park present an empirical test of the relationship between competitive intensity and reliance on indirect marketing channels. The next paper, by Taylor, examines the importance of international logistics in corporate strategy and explores the role of governments in facilitating improvements in logistical efficiency. This is followed by a study of negotiation processes and outcomes by Oh and Kim that offers insight on effective negotiation strategies. Finally, Raymond and Rylance analyze factors that influence the selection of professional service providers in Korea.

International advertising is the focus of the third section. Moon and Franke lead the section off with a longitudinal study of the information content of advertising in Korea. This study includes an analysis of how the Korean advertising environment has changed as the country has developed. Next, Shao compares the environment faced by advertisers in developing countries, NICs and developed countries by analyzing the results of a survey of affiliates of U.S. advertising agencies. Wilcox, Ko, Gentry, Stricklin and Jun then examine the influence of cultural factors in advertising in an experiment comparing the effectiveness of ads aimed at the independent vs. interdependent self. Finally, Taylor and Miracle compare the types of foreign influences present in Korean and U.S. advertising.

Part IV consists of papers that make methodological contributions to the international marketing literature. In a study reporting the results of a survey of European and Japanese managers, Zou and Laughlin propose and validate an expanded scale for measuring the extent to which a firm follows a global strategy. Support for the use of a scale developed to measure the degree to which consumers are cosmopolitan in orientation is found by Yoon, Cannon and Yaprak. The third paper, by Lee and Schaninger, proposes the use of a conjoint methodology to assess the effect of a new construct: country of production/assembly. The fourth paper in this section, by Kim, explores the number of response categories which should be used in studies examining Korea, and suggests implications for studies conducted in other Asian markets.

The fact that 50 percent of the papers in this volume are co-authored by authors of different national origin warrants mention. Such collaborations are of the type that bring diverse perspectives to the field and help to avoid exclusive reliance on U.S. literature and U.S. derived scales.

In closing, I would like to thank those who served as reviewers for this volume for their diligence and for the insight which they provided to the authors. I especially appreciate the assistance of Professor Minhi Hahn of KAIST during the review process. Special thanks are also due to Tamer Cavusgil of Michigan State

University and Jong Won Lim of Seoul National University for their encouragement and advice, and for their help in publicizing this volume.

Charles R. Taylor
Volume Editor

REFERENCES

Albaum, G., & Peterson, R.A. (1984). Empirical research in international marketing. *Journal of International Business Studies*, 15, 161-173.

Aulakh, P.S., & Kotabe, M. (1993). An assessment of theoretical and methodological development in international marketing. *Journal of International Marketing*, 1 (2), 5-28.

Bradley, F.M. (1987). Nature and significance of international marketing: A review. *Journal of Business Research*, 15 (4), 205-219.

Cavusgil, S.T. (1993). From the editor in chief. *Journal of Inernational Marketing*, 1 (4), 3-4.

Cavusgil, S.T., & Tiger Li. (1992). *International Marketing: An Annotated Bibliography*. Chicago, IL: American Marketing Association.

Holstein, W.J., & Nakarmi, L. (1995). Korea: Headed For high technology's top tier. *Business Week*, (July 31), 56-64.

Pruzan, T. (1995). Top global markets. *Advertising Age*, (February 20), I-9.

PART I

CORPORATE STRATEGY IN THE 1990s

GLOBAL COMPARISONS OF CHANNEL INTEGRATION STRATEGIES AND STRATEGIC ALLIANCES

Heon Deok Yoon, Edward A. Morash, M. Bixby Cooper
and Steven R. Clinton

ABSTRACT

Channel integration is an important contemporary concern for marketers. The integration of marketing relationships between a company and its external customers, internal customers, and supplier partners can be an important source of sustainable competitive advantage. The present research compares the channel integration approaches, including strategic alliances, used by approximately two thousand firms in the Pacific Basin countries of Australia, Japan and Korea as well as the United States. Differences are identified which have substantial implications for channel management theory and practice.

I. INTRODUCTION

Channel integration is an important contemporary topic for retailers, wholesalers, manufacturers, service providers, and other marketing participants (Anderson &

Advances in International Marketing, Volume 7, pages 3-20.
ISBN: 1-55938-839-0

Narus, 1990; Sonnenberg, 1992; Robicheaux & Coleman, 1994). The integration of marketing relationships means that external customer behavior and needs, a company's internal customers, and supplier activities must be coordinated and integrated so that all marketing relationships focus on the final consumers and create value for them (Johnston & Lawrence, 1988; Heide & John, 1990; Hendrick & Ellram, 1993; Hines, 1993).

A consumer focus ensures that marketing relationships reflect customer requirements and needs that are cascaded back or factored to sales requirements, distribution requirements, buyer requirements, and supplier requirements. These marketing relationships are relatively new in not emphasizing relationship power, negotiation for the lowest price, and adversarial relationships between a company and its suppliers and customers (Sonnenberg, 1992; Kanter, 1994; Robicheaux & Coleman, 1994). Rather, the emphasis is on partnerships and strategic alliance relationships that stress creating value for final consumers and that actively draw in supply partners and internal organizational customers to achieve that value.

For effective partnerships there is a recognition that excellence requires continuous improvement in levels of customer value. For example, the 3 S's of marketing thus far include customer service, satisfaction, and success (Bowersox & Cooper, 1992; Normann & Ramirez, 1993). Companies and their partner suppliers who have achieved the third customer success level continuously work toward ensuring that their customers are increasing their sales, market shares, and profitability. There is a growing recognition that if the customer succeeds, then the partners will succeed. From such a perspective, relationship partners increase mutual respect, loyalty, and trust; foster win-win opportunities; and link their destinies and roles. However, even achieving the third customer success level may not be sufficient in the future. Possibly, a future fourth "S" will be partnership synergy or relationship superiority where combined firm, customer, and supplier relationships will be so close, effective, and invisible that the integrated relationships become virtually inimitable and invincible to competitors.

A.   Internal and External Customers

Integrated relationship marketing also recognizes that there are both internal customers and customers external to the firm. For example, to buyers or logisticians, internal customers may include sales and production support. In turn, the organization as a whole will have its external customers and supply partners. However, it is not clear from relationship marketing literature whether all firms and indeed different countries will develop their internal and external relationship capabilities to the same levels and in similar forms. There is some suggestion in the relationship literature that companies and possibly countries evolve through stages to increasing levels of integration (e.g., Grosse & Kujawa, 1992; Bowersox & Closs, 1995). Thus, there may be a life cycle or natural progression of stages or steps in the creation of both internal and external relationship integration (Kanter,

1994). For example, some researchers believe that internal integration is a necessary first condition but not sufficient condition for marketing success (Bowersox & Closs, 1995). Such a perspective would postulate that firms must increasingly expand their integrated behavior beyond internal integration to incorporate external customers and suppliers which will become the heart of their future relationship marketing.

B.   Operational versus Behavioral Integration

It is also not clear from relationship marketing literature whether all companies and countries tend to use the same strategic approaches to achieving relationship integration. For example, external partnerships and alliances have already been mentioned and more will be said about them below. However, even for external partnerships, there are operational and technical relationships such as efficient JIT (just-in-time) network systems as well as behavioral and relational approaches (Gronroos, 1990). For example, technical network planning adds customer value by ensuring that products are available where and when needed in the correct assortments and at minimum total cost (Alderson, 1957; Bowersox & Closs, 1995). In essence, these networks represent efficient operating systems.

In turn, behavioral and relational approaches may stress visiting key customers or forming joint company/customer teams for opportunity development. They may even involve stationing resident company employees at customer premises for ordering and buying, pricing, providing consumer services, and problem recovery. But are operational versus behavioral approaches developed to the same degree and levels by different countries? And are there differences in relationship integration approaches which relate to cost versus customer service strategies? Finally, are company practices such as mission statements to integrate relationships equally evident in different countries?

The present research will address these questions as to whether there are international differences between the ways that each country's firms integrate marketing relationships. The research will focus on comparisons between three "models" or types of countries in the Asia Pacific region; Japan, Korea, and Australia; as well as comparisons with the United States. In total, the study will empirically investigate the relationship marketing practices of approximately two thousand firms. After providing a brief overview of relationship marketing, partnering, and strategic alliances, the study's methodology will be set forth. The empirical results will then be presented followed by conclusions and implications for marketing practice and theory including for international relationship marketing and global competition.

II.   RELATIONSHIP MARKETING AND PARTNERING

Traditional marketing relationships have stressed concepts such as relative buyer/ seller power, contractual obligations, conflict, centralized authority and responsibility, and specialization (Gaskin, 1984; Heide & John, 1990; Bowersox & Cooper, 1992; Heide, 1994). As already alluded to, external relationships can also exhibit operational and technical network excellence or stress behavioral and relational marketing (Gronroos, 1990; Larson, 1993). Newer relational types of partnerships have stressed greater relationship equality or egalitarianism, partner empowerment, freedom of choice, and voluntary cooperation and commitment in the partnership (Sonnenberg, 1992; Bucklin & Sengupta, 1993; Kanter, 1994; Morgan & Hunt, 1994). However, relational external integration must still remain instrumental in creating value for consumers. As such, partners must continuously measure their relationship and share performance results to increasingly improve the relationship over time. They may also stress joint and creative problem solving, opportunity recognition, and proactive planning. Further, mission statements to the extent that they are developed in participation and shared with or disseminated to partners, customers, and suppliers may also foster communication and proactively drive integrated planning (Pearce, 1982; Germain & Cooper, 1990). In essence, at the root of most of these integrative partnership initiatives is information sharing which can be viewed as a key to successful partnering and relationship building.

A.   Strategic Alliances

An especially important and contemporary form of marketing relationship is the strategic alliance (Bucklin & Sengupta, 1993; Heide & John, 1990). In a strategic alliance, two or more companies pool or exchange resources to achieve one or several well-defined business objectives. In an increasingly global and competitive world marketplace, firms in virtually every industry must cooperate with other firms in marketing, technology, and other areas. An alliance is a way of achieving these goals without resorting to mergers, acquisitions, or asset swaps. As such, companies may try to strengthen their global competitiveness by building the capabilities and competencies they need through alliances and by overcoming their weaknesses through collaboration (Ohmae, 1989; Schmitz, Frankel, & Frayer, 1994).

The strongest and closest collaborations are value-chain relationships in which companies with complementary skills link their capabilities to create value for ultimate consumers (Kanter, 1994). In this value chain form, commitments tend to be high and partners develop joint activities in many functions and operations.

B.   Motivations for Strategic Alliances

The present research will compare the motivations for strategic alliances between Australia, Japan, Korea, and the United States. Past research suggests that there are a variety of specific reasons for generally considering the formation of strategic alliances. These include access to or acquisition of new technologies and skills, improvement of a firm's technology and product competencies, conservation of scarce financial resources, and reduction in the costs and risks of entering new markets and businesses (e.g., Hamel, Doz, & Prahalad, 1989). The objectives of competing more effectively through greater asset utilization and leverage, faster customer responsiveness, and improved quality are also prime stimulants toward alliance collaboration. Further, increasingly global competitive environments force firms to do all they can to become the lowest cost, best service, or highest value competitors. Thus, in order to achieve these objectives and particularly for international companies, the use of qualified external expertise becomes essential.

C. Stages of Strategic Alliance Integration

Whatever the motivations for strategic alliances, the earlier discussion of stages of marketing relationships in general suggests that strategic alliances might also go through progressive stages of integration evolution including country evolution. For strategic alliances specifically, some prior research does hypothesize that relationships go through an evolutionary process, even before and after the formal agreements. One study indicates that as alliance relationships begin, grow, and develop or fail, successful alliances generally unfold in five different phases. These include courtship, engagement, setting up housekeeping, learning to collaborate, and changing within (Kanter, 1994). The present study's inter-country comparisons of strategic alliances may also shed light on relationship evolution.

D. Benefits of Strategic Alliance Integration

Alliance participating firms can exploit the strengths and competencies of the alliance partners to execute functions more efficiently and effectively; and to enhance the overall global competitive advantage of the market alliance. Integrative and cooperative marketing relationships can reduce duplications of time and effort and complement each partner's skills and resources (Harrigan, 1988; Bowersox, 1990; Prahalad & Hamel, 1990). Increasing competitive emphasis on customer satisfaction and customer service forces many firms to acquire the operations that deliver consistently high levels of performance and service. Alliance relationships can give to partnering firms the expected level of customer flexibility and responsiveness to handle their customers' needs and to adjust to the ever changing marketplace. The integrative and cooperative marketing alliance relationships can improve the long-term globally competitive market position of the participating firms.

III. METHODOLOGY AND SAMPLING

The present study is part of the continuing and larger global best practice research being conducted at Michigan State University. To compare the relationship marketing practices of Australia, Japan, Korea, and the United States, a questionnaire was first developed by the Michigan State research team. To ensure a valid and reliable instrument, the research team first reviewed all relevant marketing and global literature for concept definitions, prior marketing scales, and existing models. Expert panels were also used to validate construct measures. The initial survey instrument was then pretested for content validity and reliability with executives from numerous participating firms including representatives from foreign countries. Modifications were made based on these interviews. The research team's 16 member Advisory Board also made recommendations and suggestions for improving the validity and reliability of the instrument.

To test for construct reliability, the Cronbach coefficient alpha was calculated for each construct (Churchill, 1979). This test determines whether questionnaire items are consistently applied across respondents to measure the same underlying construct. The present tests produced coefficient alphas above .80—well above the threshold level of .50 to .60 recommended by Nunnally (1967).

The survey measurement scales are shown at the bottom of each Table and are of the five point Likert-type scales. Tests for measurement equivalence across cultures found no consistent pattern of cross-country equivalence bias in the use of these scales. For the last Table dealing with the importance of strategic alliance motivations, respondents were asked to rank each item from most important to least important for establishing alliances. Respondents were asked to consider alliances in general.

To ensure that questionnaire translations into foreign languages were accurate, native speakers and subject experts were used to translate the questionnaires. As recommended by Douglas and Craig (1983), the questionnaires were then back-translated using different native speakers to check for consistency.

The U.S. sample consisted of firms from a major national professional association that broadly represents firms from 13 major categories including manufacturers, wholesalers, retailers, service suppliers, and so on. These firms are from many different industries, geographically represent all parts of the United States, and are inclusive of most major U.S. companies. For each foreign country, the major analogous national professional association was selected. To help identify these similar leading professional associations, the Advisory Board to the research team was used to achieve "multiple source informant" agreement. The associations selected have group and industry memberships similar to the U.S. association and are broadly representative of national coverage, channel position, and industry types. The country-wide mailing list rosters of these associations were also checked for comparability. However, these are not perfectly matched samples since different countries have their own competitive advantages despite being diversified economies. Virtually all of these association members have a major presence in their countries and represent most significant firms in their respective industries.

The top level executives of each company were identified by the professional associations. The questionnaires were then sent to the entire membership of each professional association along with the association's own letter of support. The questionnaires were sent to 9,634 firms in Australia, Japan, Korea, and the United States. A total of 1,951 usable questionnaires were returned for an overall response rate of 20.1 percent in the Asia Pacific region and 20.4 percent in the U.S. Statistical analyses of nonrespondents and of possible systematic response patterns did not identify these as potential sources of survey bias.

To test for the possibility of covariates other than country sources of variation, on an aggregate questionnaire and regional basis, ANOVA was used to group firms by size, region, industry, location of headquarters and channel position. No significant between group differences were found other than those attributable to country.

IV.   RESULTS

A.   Internal Relationship Integration Tendencies

Table 1 shows a comparison of internal integration tendencies between Australia, Japan, Korea, and the United States. Korea is shown to have the greatest tendency of all countries toward increased internal organizational integration as evidenced by their significantly lower mean scores on all of the internal integration items. Specifically, Korea has significantly more interfunctional coordination than five years ago for the organizational areas of sales, marketing, logistics, manufacturing, and purchasing than Australia, Japan, and the United States. Korea also views their firms as having significantly more local operating presence than five years ago compared to all other countries. Job functions within the Korean firm are also becoming more specialized and internal integration of decision making is viewed as performing best when centralized. Again, these differences for Korea are all significant at the $p < .05$ level of significance and reflect increased internal organizational tendencies.

Finally, the strongest differences in Table 1 are for the possibly telling question of cost reduction being the primary motivation for improved information systems. The means for all countries are significantly different at the $p < .05$ level of significance with Korea again tending most strongly toward cost reduction motivations for information systems. The other countries were significantly lower than Korea, with the United States having the lowest relative cost motivation for information systems. Subsequent analyses will report the overall relative strategic cost emphasis across countries which will show that Korean firms also exhibit a strong cost emphasis for corporate strategy.

In total, Korea has the greatest tendency toward increased integration by internal organizational means such as interfunctional coordination, local operating presence, functional specialization, centralized decision making, and information systems for cost reduction. These survey measures appear to capture the strategic integration emphasis of Korea as using internal relationship integration primarily

Table 1.   Internal Organizational Relationship Integration

	Mean Responses[a]			
Internal Relationship Integration Tendencies:	*n=280* *AUS*	*n=324* *JAPAN*	*n=124* *KOREA*	*n=1223* *United States*
1. More Interfunctional Coordination Among Sales, Marketing, Logistics, Manufacturing, and Purchasing than Five Years Ago.	1.91	1.94	1.65[2]	1.86
2. More Local Operating Presence than Five Years Ago.	2.05	2.21	1.71[2]	2.45
3. More Specialization of Job Functions	2.24	2.20	2.02[2]	3.91
4. Internal Integration of Decision-Making Should Be Centralized	2.64	2.81	2.45[1]	2.67
5. Primary Motivation For Impoved Information Systems Is Cost Reduction	2.64	2.41	2.19[3]	2.82

Note: [a]SCALE: 1-Strongly Agree;   5=Strongly Disagree
[1]Korea is significantly different from Japan and the U.S. at $p \leq .05$.
[2]Korea is significantly different from Australia, Japan and the U.S. at $p \leq .05$.
[3]All means are significantly different at $p \leq .05$.

for cost reduction objectives. Perhaps, leveraging relationships internally for cost reduction serves as a substitute for past labor cost advantages. Such a competitive strategy would stress the "internal" customers of an organization as opposed to the "external" customers.

B.   External Relationship Integration:
Technical Network Solution Tendencies

Table 2 compares Australia, Japan, Korea, and the United States on external relationship integration tendencies. The emphasis is on technical network integration between a company and its suppliers and customers. It also focuses on external customers of the firm as opposed to internal organizational customers.

Technical Network Planning

The first four measures in Table 2 reflect external integration through technical network planning. These tendencies emphasize technical and physical network solutions for external relationship integration and responsiveness. For all four means, Japan shows a significantly greater tendency toward external relationship integration through technical network planning. First, Just-in-time (JIT) systems are rated significantly more important for superior performance by Japanese firms than by Australian, Korean, or U.S. firms. Second, Japan rates the currently timely and popular topic of network reengineering as significantly more important than other countries. This network variable also most strongly differentiates between

Table 2. External Relationship Integration:
Technical Network Solution Tendencies

		Mean Responses			
		$n=280$ AUS	$n=324$ JAPAN	$n=124$ KOREA	$n=1223$ United States
A.	TECHNICAL NETWORK PLANNING				
1.	Importance of Just-in-Time Systems for Superior Performance[a]	2.01	1.63[4]	1.83	2.04
2.	Importance of Network Reengineering[a]	2.19	1.59[5]	1.75	2.01
3.	General Importance of Network Planning for Recycling, etc.[a]	2.33	2.06[4]	2.28	2.44
4.	More Systems Planning or Problem Recovery than Five Years Ago[b]	2.27	2.00[4]	2.36	2.46
B.	TRADITIONAL RELATIONSHIP POWER				
5.	Strategic Alliances are Typically Dominated by Member with Greatest Power[b]	2.90	2.67[3]	3.00	2.74
6.	Effective Strategic Alliances Must be Supported by a Written Contract or Agreement[b]	2.78	2.15[4]	2.55	2.86
C.	LOYALTY				
7.	Employees are More Loyal to Their Organization than Five Years Ago[b]	3.25	3.15[2]	3.85	3.81
8.	Firms are More Loyal to Their Employees than Five Years Ago[b]	3.42	2.89[1]	2.95	3.93

Note: [a]SCALE: 1-Very Important; 5=Not Important at All
[b]SCALE: 1-Strongly Agree; 5=Strongly Disagree

[1]Japan is significantly different than Australia and the U.S. at $p \leq .05$.
[2]Japan is significantly different than Korea and the U.S. at $p \leq .05$.
[3]Japan is significantly different than Australia and Korea at $p \leq .05$.
[4]Japan is significantly different than Australia, Korea, and the U.S. at $p \leq .05$.
[5]All means are significantly different at $p \leq .05$.

all countries in Table 2. As such, all four means are significantly different at the $p < .05$ level of significance. Thus, Japan is followed by Korea, the United States, and finally Australia in the relative importance attached to network reengineering.

Next, Japanese firms attach significantly greater importance to environmental network planning for issues such as recycling. Similarly, Japan places significantly greater emphasis on systems planning for problems recovery. Both of these variables' means are significantly different from Australia, Korea, and the United States at the $p < .05$ level of significance.

In total, for external channel integration through technical network planning, Japan scores the highest on all four of the technical network measures as reported in the top portion of Table 2. Thus, Japan attaches greater importance to JIT systems, network reengineering, environmental network planning, and systems planning for problem recovery.

Traditional Relationship Power

The middle portion (B) of Table 2 is interesting in showing the use of traditional relationship power rather than the currently popular strategic alliances and partnerships. These latter strategic alliances involve greater partner equality or egalitarianism, greater information sharing, and greater relational integration between a company and its suppliers and customers. Strategic alliances will be reported later in the results section.

For the two measures of traditional relationship power, Japan displays the greatest tendency toward their use. Specifically, Japan is most likely to view logistical alliances as being typically dominated by the party with the greatest power. The mean for Japan is significantly different from Australia and Korea at the $p < .05$ level of significance. For the second relationship power survey item, Japan is significantly most likely to characterize effective logistics alliances as requiring the support of a written contract or agreement. Japan is significantly different than Australia, Korea, and the United States on this measure at $p < .05$. However, subsequent personal interview data indicate that these written contracts are broad in scope and do not attempt to specify all details.

In essence, Japan appears to attach significantly greater emphasis to the use of traditional relationship power. Viewed in light of the earlier finding that Japan attaches greater importance to external integration through technical network planning, it is possible to speculate that a technical network focus coincides very well with a traditional use of relationship power and possibly with greater organizational loyalty as will be discussed next.

Loyalty

The bottom section (C) of Table 2 is also interesting in showing that Japan displays the greatest tendency toward increased loyalty. In terms of employees being more loyal to their organization, Japan reports greater employee loyalty and is significantly different than Korea and the United States but not Australia. Korea displays the lowest loyalty in Table 2 which may reflect currently changing cultural and economic patterns where labor conflict has become more common and company paternalism more open to question. For firms being more loyal to their employees, Japan again scores highest on this dimension and is significantly different from Australia and the United States but not Korea. This latter result is interesting in that Korean managerial respondents see the decline in organizational loyalty as being one sided; that is, increased company loyalty to employees is not reciprocated by employees.

In total, Japan displays a possible competitive advantage over other relevant countries in terms of both greater loyalty to the organization and to employees. Korean labor issues appear to be a concern. In terms of respondents from the United States, the overall loyalty scores are lacking and very disconcerting. It is also informative to note that the mean U.S. responses differ from the midpoint by almost a full point, possibly suggesting a particular competitive disadvantage. It is interesting to speculate that the U.S. trends over the last decade toward increased mergers and acquisitions, leveraged buyouts, corporate downsizing, employee buyouts, temporary employment, early retirements, and so on have possibly taken their toll on organizational loyalty.

C.   External Relationship Integration:
Relational & Behavioral Solutions

Table 3 compares Australia, Japan, Korea, and the United States also on external relationship integration tendencies of the firm. However, these survey items primarily emphasize relational and behavioral integration of a company with its suppliers and customers. The focus is again on external customers of the firm rather than internal organizational customers.

Customer Relationship Integration

Table 3 shows that Australia has the greatest tendency in the Asia Pacific Region toward relational integration of a company with its suppliers and customers. All of the Australian comparisons are significantly different from Japan and Korea at the $p < .05$ level of significance. Australia has a significantly greater incidence of managers contacting customers than Japan and Korea. In a possibly telling question, Australia is also significantly more likely to have senior level executives actually visit their key customers.

Supplier Relationship Integration

For supplier relations as an external focus, Australia is more likely than Japan and Korea to report increased measurement of suppliers' performance. In another particularly telling relational question, Australia more often shares these performance results with suppliers. This survey item also most strongly differentiates between all countries in Table 4 since all means including the United States are significantly different from each other at $p < .05$. As such, Australia trails only the United States in sharing performance information with suppliers. Finally, internal measurement of performance is most likely to accompany external performance measures for Australia compared to Japan and Korea. Again, this comparison is statistically significant at the $p < .05$ level. In essence, Australia is more likely than

Table 3. External Relationship Integration:
Relational & Behavioral Solution Tendencies

	Mean Responses[a]			
Relational Integration Tendencies:	n=280 AUS	n=324 JAPAN	n=124 KOREA	n=1223 United States
A. CUSTOMER RELATIONSHIP INTEGRATION				
1. Managers Contact Customers More than five years ago	2.02[1]	2.20	2.77	2.00
2. Most Senior Executives Visit Key Customers	2.56[1]	2.88	3.23	2.66
B. SUPPLIER RELATIONSHIP INTEGRATION				
3. More Measurement of Suppliers' Performance Over Past Five Years	1.87[1]	2.16	2.82	1.85
4. More Sharing of Performance Results with Suppliers than Five Years Ago	2.13[2]	2.34	2.98	1.90
5. Internal Measurement Firms More Likely To Extensively Use External Measurement	2.08[1]	2.37	2.50	2.18
C. STRATEGIC ALLIANCES AND RELATIONSHIP MARKETING				
6. More Strategic Alliances With Suppliers than Five Years Ago	2.05[1]	2.53	3.28	2.09
7. More Strategic Alliances With Customers than Five Years Ago	2.07[1]	2.39	3.24	1.98
8. Key to Strategic Alliances is Information Sharing	1.70[1]	1.98	1.87	1.63
9. General Importance of Strategic Alliances and Relationship Marketing[b]	1.71[1]	2.29	2.51	1.60

Note: [a]SCALE: 1-Strongly Agree;   5=Strongly Disagree
[b]SCALE: 1-Very Important;   5=Not Important at All

[1]Australia is significantly different than Japan and Korea at $p \leq .05$.
[2]Australia is significantly different than Japan, Korea, and the U.S. at $p \leq .05$.

Japan and Korea to pursue relational and behavioral solutions for achieving external relationship integration with both suppliers and customers.

Strategic Alliances and Relationship Marketing

Table 3 also compares Australia, Japan, Korea, and the United States on the incidence of strategic alliances as a major and contemporary means to achieve the external integration of marketing relationships. Subsequent analyses later in this results section will also analyze strategic alliance motivations and in much greater depth. Table 3 shows that Australia is much more likely to form strategic alliances with both material suppliers and customers. In a possibly telling question, Australia is also significantly more likely than Japan or Korea to view information sharing as the key to strategic alliances. However, it is also interesting to note that all four countries rank information sharing at the highest level of all items in Table 3. Finally, as a summary question, Australia is more likely to attach greater overall importance to strategic alliances and to relationship marketing in general.

Relationship Integration through Mission Statements

An additional relational means of attempting to achieve relationship integration is through the development and dissemination of organizational mission statements. Although Australia, Japan, and Korea do not significantly differ on having a mission statement (Table 4, Section D), Australia is significantly more likely than Japan, Korea, and the United States to widely disseminate their mission statement both internally and externally. Similarly, in a particularly strong statistical difference, Australia is also more likely to share their mission statements with customers.

Service vs. Cost Strategy

In a final and possibly indicative strategy comparison, Australian firms place a significantly greater strategic emphasis on the provision of service rather than cost reduction. In turn, Japan and Korea place a significantly greater emphasis on cost reduction than Australia. It is also interesting to note the very large divergence for this question between Australia on the one hand versus Korea and Japan on the other, almost a full point on the cost-service scale. It is possible that a relational and behavioral integration emphasis conforms best with a service strategy while the previously discussed technical operational network emphasis is more consistent with a cost reduction strategy.

In total, Australia is most likely to achieve external relationship integration through relational and behavioral solution tendencies. These relational tendencies include customer and supplier behavioral integration, the formation of strategic alliances with customers and suppliers, the dissemination of mission statements beyond the organization, and the provision of services.

V. STRATEGIC ALLIANCES

Strategic alliances are a major contemporary form of marketing relationship. Table 5 compares Australia, Japan, Korea, and the United States on the relative importance of strategic alliance motivations. Each country's mean ranking for each item is shown with one being the most important motivation and ten being the least important. These rankings provide insights and explanations for strategic marketing alliances which could serve as a strategic guideline for engaging in cooperative relationships.

Table 4.   External Relationship Integration:
Relational & Behavioral Solution Tendencies

	Mean Responses[a]			
Relational Integration Tendencies:	n=280 AUS	n=324 JAPAN	n=124 KOREA	n=1223 United States
D. MISSION STATEMENTS FOR RELATIONSHIP INTEGRATION				
1. Company Has Written Mission Statement	39.0%[1]	42.8%	41.8%	60.1%
2. Mission Statement Widely Disseminated Internally and Externally	78.3%[3]	57.6%	65.8%	65.2%
3. Mission Statement Shared with Customers	60.3%[3]	22.4%	25.0%	53.5%
E. CUSTOMER SERVICE VS. COST STRATEGY				
4. Relative Strategic Emphasis of Company (cost = 1, service = 5)	3.73[2]	2.85	3.04	3.46

Note: [1]Australia is not significantly different from Japan and Korea but is significantly different from the U.S. at $p \leq .05$ using the Chi Square Test.

[2]Australia is significantly different than Japan, Korea and the U.S. at $p \leq .05$.

[3]Australia is significantly different than Japan, Korea and the U.S. at $p \leq .05$ using the Chi Square Test.

Table 5 shows that the Australian and U.S. respondents have almost identical rankings of motives for establishing marketing strategic alliances. This finding does not necessarily imply that Australian and U.S. respondents are facing the same current situations and problems. Rather, the possible explanations for this pattern could be: (1) Active involvement of Australians and the U.S. in the same professional associations leading to similar concerns for strategic alliances; (2) Cultural similarities leading to preferences for certain strategic alliance solutions; (3) Greater similarity in geographical size and less density; and (4) Similarities in terms of product and customer marketing requirements.

Australian and U.S. respondents perceive Competitive Advantage and Improved Quality as the prime motivations for establishing strategic marketing alliances. These high rankings may possibly reflect a particularly strong strategic focus on external marketing relationships for relational integration. Korean respondents also perceive improved quality as a prime motive for strategic alliance formations. Since quality improvement is presently almost a national Korean obsession, this might be reflected in their high first place ranking of quality.

For Japanese respondents, leadtime performance improvement is the highest ranking motive for strategic alliances, and a similar level of ranking can be seen for Korea. Thus, for both countries, speed is considered as a crucial element of operations. Closely related to leadtime performance improvement, inventory reduction is perceived by Japanese firms as the second most important motive for strategic alliances. For Australians and the United States, it is also considered important, but not as highly as for Japan while Korea shows the lowest ranking for inventory reduction. These stronger leadtime and inventory reduction motivations

Table 5. Motives for Establishing Strategic Alliances[a]

Motives:	Country Rank[b]			
	AUS	JAPAN	KOREA	United States
Competitive Advantage	1	5	7	1
Improved Quality	2	4	1	2
Leadtime Performance Improvement	3	1	2	3
Inventory Reduction	4	2	6	4
Increased Customer Involvement	6	7	8	5
Exploiting Core Competency	7	8	9	6
Supply/Demand Stability	5	3	5	7
Technological Access	8	6	10	8
Market Access/Globalization	9	9	3	9
Leveraging Capital	10	10	4	10

Note: [a]Respondents were asked to consider strategic alliances in general for ranking the relative importance of motivations for forming strategic alliances.
[b]Ranked by Mean

for Japan may possibly reflect the primacy of external relationship integration for efficiency and cost improvements.

Increased customer involvement and exploiting core competencies are motives relatively less important across countries. Interestingly however, they receive their highest rankings by the U.S. firms. For Japanese respondents, the supply/demand stability motive is perceived as the third highest reason for strategic alliances. Specifically, supply stability is strongly emphasized by Japanese firms possibly due to their heavy reliance on JIT which requires less variation and less leadtime. Again, these results for Japan possibly indicate a particularly strong focus on external integration for efficiency and cost improvements.

The technological access motivation for strategic alliances is not perceived as a major motivation for any of the four countries. However, the market access/globalization motive is perceived by Korean respondents as significantly important, while other countries indicate otherwise. This finding might be due to the dominant market position held by a few major players in each target market which could force Korean firms to search for an "alliance" in order to obtain market accessibility both domestically and globally. In essence, strategic alliances may be a means for Korean firms to overcome market barriers to entry.

Similarly, leveraging capital is perceived by the other three countries as the lowest motivation for alliances while Koreans consider it one of the major motivations. General scarcity of Korean resources, including low land availability along with skyrocketing land prices (although presently stabilized), may force Korean firms to find alternatives for better use of their scarce resources. For example, subsequent firm interviews indicate the general trend among Korean firms to close private warehouses located near urban areas where land prices have appreciated tremendously in the last several years. The firms then outsource their warehousing needs and the "freed up" urban land is used to build apartments, offices, or shops. Once again, Korean firms appear to use strategic alliances as a means to overcome market barriers.

Based on firm interviews, the strategic alliance concept is still unfamiliar to some respondents in Japan and Korea. However, strategic alliances are perceived as the coming future reality and interest in forming alliances has recently increased. Across countries, there are no strong perceptions that strategic alliances are disguised ways for the more powerful party member to maintain power/control and to shift inventory responsibility (although there are some relative differences between countries).

In total, Japanese and Korean respondents appear to emphasize strategic alliances for the improvement of operational efficiency, either for internal customers or for external customers. Koreans also use strategic alliances to overcome market barriers. In contrast, Australian and U.S. firms appear to concentrate more on external relational alliances which may increase perceptions of external marketing effectiveness.

CONCLUSIONS

The present study investigates and compares relationship marketing for approximately two thousand firms from the three Pacific Basin countries of Australia, Japan, and Korea as well as the United States. In terms of marketing relationship integration, Korea shows the greatest tendency to internal relationship integration which stresses the internal customers of the organization. In contrast, Japan and Australia show the greatest current tendency to external relationship integration which stresses the external customers of the firm. However, while the external emphasis of Japanese firms is on operational and technical network excellence, Australian firms increasingly emphasize behavioral and relational integration solutions. An investigation of strategic alliances as an especially important and contemporary form of marketing relationships also finds significant differences in alliance motivations between the four countries which parallel the previous results.

Although strategic alliance activity is generally increasing, the implementation of external alliances and effective relationship integration is lagging expectations in all four of the participating countries. Strategic alliances with suppliers, customers, and service suppliers are more common today than five years ago in Pacific Basin countries. However, managers report difficulty in operationalizing cross-boundary arrangements. This might be expected since strategic alliances are in some cases serving as alternatives to horizontal or vertical integration. The real and actual collaboration takes place when companies jointly develop appropriate structures, processes, and skills. In this way, companies can achieve full collaboration and real consumer value from the integrated relationship.

Japanese and Korean managers generally believe that alliances require written contracts or agreements, although they do feel alliances are compatible with a bid process. Interestingly, the majority of respondents feel the key to successful strategic alliances is information sharing.

In total, the study results confirm that different countries employ different prevailing strategies for relationship marketing. Although the current research is suggestive, future research might investigate if there is a natural progression or life cycle of integration strategies. The degree of substitutability between integration strategies should also be researched.

REFERENCES

Alderson, W. (1957). *Marketing behavior and executive action.* Homewood, IL: Richard D. Irwin.

Anderson, J.C., & Narus, J.A. (1990). A model of distributor firm and manufacturing firm working partnerships. *Journal of Marketing*, 54, 1 (January) 42-58.

Bowersox, D.J. (1990). The strategic benefits of logistics alliances. *Harvard Business Review*, 68, 4 (July-August), 36-45.

Bowersox, D.J., & Cooper, M.B. (1992). *Strategic marketing channel management.* Hightstown, NJ: McGraw-Hill Publishing Company.

Bowersox, D.J., & Closs, D.J. (1996). *Logistical management*, fourth ed. Hightstown, NJ: McGraw-Hill Publishing Company.

Bucklin, L.P., & Sengupta S. (1993). Organizing successful co-marketing alliances. *Journal of Marketing*, 57, 2 (April), 32-46.

Churchill, G.A., Jr. (1979). A paradigm for developing better measures of marketing constructs. *Journal of Marketing Research*, 16 (February); 64-73.

Douglas, S.P., & Craig, S.C. (1983). *International marketing research.* Englewood Cliffs, NJ: Prentice-Hall.

Gaski, J.F. (1984). The theory of power and conflict in channels of distribution. *Journal of Marketing*, 48, 3 (Summer), 9-29.

Germain, R., & Cooper, M. B. (1990). How a customer mission statement affects company performance. *Industrial Marketing Management*, 19, (1), 47-54.

Gronroos, C. (1990). *Service management and marketing.* Lexington, MA: Lexington Books.

Grosse, R., & Kujawa, D. (1992). *International business: Theory and managerial applications*, Second ed. Homewood, IL: Irwin Publishing Company.

Hamel, G., Doz, Y.L., and Prahalad, C.K. (1989). Collaborate with your competitors and win. *Harvard Business Review*, (January-February), 133-139.

Harrigan, K.R. (1988). Strategic alliances and partner asymmetries. In F.J. Contractor & P. Lorange (eds.), *Cooperative strategies in international business.* Lexington, MA: Lexington Books.

Heide, J.B. (1994). Interorganizational governance in marketing channels. *Journal of Marketing*, 58, (January), 71-85.

Heide, J.B., & John, G. (1990). Alliances in industrial purchasing: The determinants of joint action in buyer-seller relationships. *Journal of Marketing Research*, 27, (February), 24-36.

Hendrick, T., & Ellram, L. (1993). *Strategic supplier partnering: An international study.* Tempe, AZ: Center for Advanced Purchasing Studies.

Hines, P. (1993). Integrated materials management: The value chain redefined. *The International Journal of Logistics Management*, 4, 1, (July), 13-22.

Johnston, R., & Lawrence. P.R. (1988). Beyond vertical integration—the rise of the value-adding partnership. *Harvard Business Review*, 66, (July-August), 94-101.

Kanter, R.M. (1994). Collaborative advantage: The art of alliances. *Harvard Business Review.* 72, (July-August), 96-108.

Larson, A. (1993). Network dyads in entrepreneurial settings: A study of governance of exchange Relationships. *Administrative Science Quarterly,* 37, (July), 76-104.

Morgan, R.M., & Hunt S.D. (1994). The commitment-trust theory of relationship marketing. *Journal of Marketing,* 58 (July), 20-38.

Normann, R., & R. Ramirez (1993). From value chain to value constellation: Designing interactive strategy. *Harvard Business Review,* 71, (July-August), 65-77.

Nunnally, J. (1967). *Psychometric theory.* New York: McGraw-Hill.

Ohmae, K. (1989). The global logic of strategic alliances. *Harvard Business Review,* 67, (March-April); pp. 143-154.

Pearce, John A. (1982). "The Company Mission as a Strategic Tool." Sloan Management Review; 23 (Spring), 15-24.

Prahalad, C.K., & Hamel, G. (1990). The core competence of the corporation. *Harvard Business Review,* (May-June), 79-91.

Robicheaux, R.A., & Coleman, J.E. (1994). The structure of marketing channel relationships. *Academy of Marketing Science,* 22, (July), 38-51.

Schmitz, J.M., Frankel, R., and Frayer, D.J. (1994). Vertical integration without ownership: The alliance alternative. *Association of Marketing Theory and Practice Annual Conference Proceedings,* (Spring), 391-396.

Sonnenberg, F.K. (1992). Partnering: entering the age of cooperation." *Journal of Business Strategy,* 13, (May-June), 49-52.

STRATEGIC ALLIANCES:
CONTRASTING KOREAN AND U.S. PREFERENCES

Seoil Chaiy and David B. Montgomery

ABSTRACT

This study examines several contrasts and similarities between Korean and U.S. exec-utive approaches to certain aspects of strategic alliances. The underlying research premise is that better understanding of the typical similarities and differences in stra-tegic alliance approaches between executives from different countries should facili-tate more harmonious and successful cross border alliances. Specifically a sample of Korean and U.S. executives were asked to consider a potential future alliance which they would expect to pursue. In this context they were asked to identify the time frame they would expect, to prioritize results such as profits, market share, and learning, and to make conjoint trade-offs between six attributes of the potential alliances: (1) what they must give, (2) what they will get, (3) the home area of a prospective partner, (4) the time frame of the prospective alliance, (5) the degree of competitive overlap between the partners, and (6) the firm's equity position in the partnership.

I. INTRODUCTION

Strategic alliances are increasingly becoming a vital part of global competitive marketing strategy (Bleeke & Ernst, 1993; Yoshino & Rangan, 1995). Bleeke and

Advances in International Marketing, Volume 7, pages 21-31.
Copyright © 1996 by JAI Press Inc.
All rights of reproduction in any form reserved.
ISBN: 1-55938-839-0

Ernst (1993) in their introductory chapter note in particular that differences between countries in alliance objectives, backgrounds, and strengths are equally important with industry structure and regulatory environment in impacting the development of strategic alliances across borders. The premise underlying the current research is that better understanding of the typical similarities and differences in strategic alliance approaches between executives from different countries should facilitate more harmonious and successful cross border alliances. This research seeks to examine empirically differences and similarities between Korean and U.S. executive preferences relating to several selected aspects of strategic alliances. While no claim for completeness may be made, hopefully this will be a useful beginning in better mapping the interface between Korean and U.S. firms engaged in cross border alliances.

This paper first reviews several a priori expectations concerning contrasts between Korean and U.S. executives in the domain of strategic alliances. Some rationale from both the literature and experience will be offered for these prior expectations. Next the research procedure will be presented followed by the results and discussion.

II. ANTICIPATED KOREAN/U.S. CONTRASTS

Based on the literature and the experience of the authors in cross cultural environments, several a priori expectations were developed. Further, several more informal expectations contrasting the Korean and U.S. alliance responses were examined as were several empirical observations for which no strong prior expectations were established.

Before stating the a priori expectations some background issues which have served as input to these expectations will be discussed briefly. Usunier (1991) suggests that differences in behavior in relation to time often generate misunderstandings, particularly in relation to international business negotiations such as transnational strategic alliances. These behavioral differences in relation to time emanate in large measure from cultural differences. Frank, Hofstede, and Bond (1991) empirically suggest that South Koreans have a much more long term view of time than do Americans. Similarly, Kang (1989, p. 13) suggests that Korean's have a planning horizon at least as long as Americans. In another domain, that of preference for licensing over direct foreign investment, another of Hofstede's cultural dimensions, the power distance index, has been found to explain national differences (Shane, 1992).

An important reason for senior U.S. managers to have a short term perspective relates to the system of professional management. American companies are largely run by professionals whose job security can depend on their ability to produce profitable quarterly returns which will govern the price of the stock. Much of their income, aside from their base salary, comes from stock options and bonuses of publically held shares. Jacobs' (1991) analysis supports the view that the commoditization of corporate ownership and the concommitant separation of ownership and management have helped create the conditions for more short term decision making by U.S. managers.

In contrast, in most Korean companies the current managers are actual owners or members of the founder's family which owns a substantial stake (Steers, Shin, & Ungson, 1989). They do not need to be as sensitive to the quarterly returns that would govern the price of shares on a short term basis. They can afford to view their stockholding as a long term investment in which they have control and may benefit from a longer term investment perspective.

Korean executives might also be expected to have greater concern for learning from a strategic alliance than their U.S. counterparts. In the first place, Confucian cultures, such as Korea, have a profound reverence for learning. By contrast, in the United States one hears discussion of "do it yourself" and the "not invented here" syndrome. In addition, Korea has a relatively shorter industrial and business history than the United States. Relative to the tremendous success that Korea has thus far achieved, there is an inherent insecurity in most Korean companies who understand that their "Han River Miracle" resulted from what may prove to be short term advantages of low labor and infrastructure cost in Korea prior to the mid-1980s. They believe that to continue their success, they will need to have value added technology, which they currently do not have, that can enhance their products. They also understand the changing environment in which they operate. The globalization of industry seems certain to substantially reduce the protection of local industry by the Korean government. Also furthering the Korean desire to learn from strategic alliances is the realization that partners are needed to avoid costly and time consuming in company developments which may cost them the strategic opportunity to participate in the rapid changes in the global marketplace.

It was also expected that Korean executives would have greater preference for domestic Korean market share while U.S. executives would have greater preference for foreign market share as an objective for a strategic alliance. Relatively slower growth in the U.S. domestic market both incentivizes U.S. executives to seek growth in international markets and makes it more difficult and risky for Korean firms to seek a U.S. position. The higher growth rate of the Korean market and their linguistic and cultural familiarity make domestic Korean market position particularly attractive to Korean executives.

More formally, the a priori expectations were:

Expectation 1.   In relation to an anticipated future alliance, U.S. executives will have a shorter definition of:

  a.   Short term
  b.   Medium term
  c.   Long term

Expectation 2.   Korean executives will be relatively more concerned that U.S. executives with learning from a future strategic alliance. This will be particularly true for learning technology.

Expectation 3.   U.S. executives will have a greater preference for profits than will Korean executives in relation to a future strategic alliance. This will be particularly true for short term profits.

Expectation 4.   Korean executives will have greater preference for enhanced domestic market share resulting from a strategic alliance than will their U.S. counterparts.

Expectation 5.   U.S. executives will have greater preference for enhanced foreign market share resulting from a strategic alliance than will the Korean executives.

Expectation 6.   Korean executives will have different preferences for alliance attributes from their U.S. counterparts.

III.   METHOD

The research instrument used in this study first asked each executive respondent to choose as a focus the area of potential alliance in which the company is most likely to participate in the future. They were then asked to allocate 100 points to the potential results of a strategic alliance, with the number of points reflecting their evaluation of the relative importance of each aspect of alliance results. There were eight categories of potential alliance results to which an executive could allocate points:

1.   My firm learns technology from the alliance.
2.   My firm learns markets from the alliance.
3.   My firm learns manufacturing/operations from the alliance.
4.   My firm gains domestic market share from the alliance.
5.   My firm gains foreign market share from the alliance.
6.   The alliance enhances my firm's near-term profits.
7.   The alliance enhances my firm's longer-term profits.
8.   Other (specified by the respondent).

Each executive was then asked to assess what he/she would consider to be the short, medium, and long term time frame in relation to the alliance area they had chosen as their focus.

Finally, the executive respondents were asked to complete a conjoint task relating to six alliance attributes. See Montgomery (1985) for a discussion of the use and validity of conjoint analysis in industrial marketing situations. Again each executive was asked to complete this task in relation to the potential alliance area they had chosen as most likely for their firm. The conjoint attributes were presented in pairwise tradeoff tables and were as follows along with the subcategories of each attribute:

1. Partner's Main Contribution
   a. Marketing/Distribution
   b. Research & Development/Technology
   c. Manufacturing/Operations
   d. Capital
2. My Firm's Contribution
   a. Marketing/Distribution
   b. Research & Development/Technology
   c. Manufacturing/Operations
   d. Capital
3. Home Area of the Partner (where partner is headquartered)
   a. United States/Canada
   b. Europe
   c. Japan
   d. Other (This was specified as Korea for the Korean respondents.)
4. Partner Competitiveness with My Firm
   a. High (Significant degree of overlap, as between direct competitors)
   b. Moderate (Moderate degree of overlap, as between firms in related industries)
   c. Low (little overlap, as between firms in unrelated industries)
5. Time Frame (How long the partners will be bound to the relationship)
   a. less than four years
   b. Four to seven years
   c. More than seven years
6. My Firm's Equity (The amount of equity my firm holds in the strategic alliance)
   a. None (My firm holds no equity in the alliance)
   b. Minority (My firm holds a minority stake in the alliance)
   c. Equal (My firm holds an equal stake in the alliance with our partner)
   d. Majority (My firms holds a majority stake in the alliance)

The U.S. executive respondents were senior and upper middle level executives who attended executive programs at Stanford University. The Korean executives were contacted directly and reflected a similar level of executive positions. Naturally, the U.S. executives responded to an English version of the questionnaire, while a Korean version was developed for the Korean executives. Aside from language, the primary difference between the questionnaires was that in the Korean version, Korea was specified as the "Other" category in the conjoint task.

Table 1.   Time Frame Definitions
(Years)

Time Frame	U.S. Mean (Std. error)	Prediction	Korea Mean (Std. error)	Difference in means (Std. Error of Diff.)	t-ratio of difference Significance
Short	1.26 years (.077) n = 147	<	1.78 years (.161) n = 45	−0.52 years (.178)	t = −2.91 < 0.005
Medium	3.62 years (.159) n = 145	<	4.71 years (.313) n = 45	−1.09 years (.351)	t = −3.10 <0.005
Long	7.05 years (.332) n = 149	<	8.33 years (.599) n = 36	−1.28 years (.685)	t = −1.87 <0.035

IV.   RESULTS

A.   Time Frame

The expectation, for reasons of culture and corporate ownership, is that Korean executives will have longer definitions of short term, medium term, and long term with respect to prospective alliances than will U.S. executives. The results are reported in Table 1. All three sub-hypotheses are confirmed at p levels well beyond the 0.05 level. Thus, there does indeed appear to be a statistically significant shorter term orientation by U.S. executives, at least with respect to strategic alliances and in contrast to Korean executives.

Further, the U.S. long term average of 7.05 years is also substantively, not just statistically, different from the Korean average of 8.33 years. That is, the shorter U.S. views of the long run in a prospective alliance, is likely to substantially impact financial evaluations of potential alliances by lowering their value. However, it should be noted that the difference of 1.28 years in the long run definition, while both statistically and substantively significant, is not overwhelming. Thus, these results suggest that the view of short term U.S. executive thinking is both valid and important, but by no means overwhelmingly large, as sometimes implied by management journalism.

B.   Desired Alliance Results

Desired alliance results are first examined in terms of the macro categories of overall learning, total profits, and total market share. Each of these macro categories is the sum of the point allocation to the relevant subcategories (e.g., the sum of the points allocated to learning technology, markets, and operations comprises

Table 2. Desired Alliance Results: Macro

	U.S. Mean points (Std. error of mean) n=150	Prediction	Korean Mean points (Std. error of mean) n=45	Difference in means (std. error of diff.)	t-ratio of difference Significance
Overall Learning (Sum)	37.9 (1.78)	<	44.0 (3.12)	−6.1 (3.59)	t=−1.70 <0.05
Total Profits (Sum)	30.9 (1.39)	>	25.9 (2.08)	5.0 (2.50	t=2.00 <0.05
Total Market Share (Sum)	31.0 (1.46)	≠	26.7 (3.98)	4.3 (4.24)	t=1.01 not sig.

Table 3. Within Country Sample Desired
Alliance Results: Macro Comparisons

Desired Alliance Result First Result minus Second Result	U.S. n=150 Prediction (sign)	Mean (std. error) t-ratio significance	Korea n=45 Prediction	Mean (std. error) t-ratio significance
Overall Learning minus Overall Profit	< (−)	7.00 (2.67) 2.62 <0.005	> (+)	18.07 (4.62) 3.91 <0.04
Overall Learning minus Overall Market Share	≠ (?)	6.90 (2.82) 2.45 <0.02	> (+)	17.33 (5.03) 3.45 <0.001
Overall Market Share minus Overall Profit	< (−)	.08 (2.08) .04 not sig.	> (+)	.73 (5.03) .15 not sig.

the macro category of overall learning). The results are presented in Table 2. Recall that it is expected that Korean executives will place greater emphasis on overall learning (as indicated by a greater point allocation to the learning subcategories) than will their U.S. counterparts. This expectation is confirmed in Table 2 at the 0.05 level of significance.

Second, it is expected that U.S. executives will place greater emphasis on profits than will Korean executives due in large measure to the differences in ownership structure. This expectation was also confirmed in the data reported in Table 2. The total market share expectation was ambiguous due to directionally opposite expec-

Table 4. Desired Alliance Results: Subcategories

Desired Alliance Result	U.S. Mean points (Std. error) n=150	Prediction	Korea Mean points (Std. Error) n=45	Difference of means (std. error of diff.)	t-ratio Significance
Learn Technology	13.4 (1.28)	<	21.1 (2.24)	-7.7 (2.58)	t=-2.98 0.005
Learn markets	16.1 (1.16)	≠	14.1 (1.55)	2.0 (1.94)	t=1.03 not sig.
Learn Mfgr./Operations	8.4 (1.00	≠	8.8 (1.13)	-0.4 (1.50)	t=-.27 not sig.
Near Term Profit	11.7 (.94)	>	8.6 (1.10)	3.1 (1.45)	t=2.14 <0.02
Long Term Profit	19.2 (1.17)	≠	17.4 (1.58)	1.8 (1.97)	t=.92 not sig.
Home Market Share	15.1 (1.25)	<	19.8 (2.18)	-4.7 (2.51)	t=-1.87 0.04
Foreign Market Share	15.9 (1.24)	>	6.9 (1.52)	9.0 (1.96)	t=4.59 <0.001

tations of its two sub components—domestic and foreign market share. The data show that the U.S. executives were somewhat more concerned with market share, but the difference was not statistically significant.

Thus Korean executives place greater emphasis on learning from an alliance and less emphasis on profits than do the U.S. executives. It should be noted that although these country contrasts exist the Korean executives do place substantial weight on profits while the U.S. executives consider overall learning to be very important— in fact overall learning is the most important of the three macro categories of alliance results for the U.S. executives as well as for the Koreans. Overall the rank order of the marco categories is identical for the U.S. and Korean executives.

Thc differences stem from the relative emphasis on the three macro categories. The results suggest that the US priority across the macro categories is quite close with a range of 7.0 (from 37.9 for learning to 30.9 for profits). In contrast, the Koreans are far more prioritized with about 2 1/2 times the range (a range of 18.1 from 44.0 for learning to 25.9 for profits).

Within country contrasts between the macro categories are given in Table 3. As expected, the Korean executives substantially and significantly preferred overall learning to both profits and market share. There was no difference between overall market share and profit for the Koreans. Surprisingly, the expectation that U.S. executives would prefer profits to learning was not confirmed. In fact, the results suggest just the opposite at a very high level of significance. Although no directional prediction was made, the results indicate that U.S. executives give greater priority to learning than they do to market share ($p < .02$). The expectation that

U.S. executives would prefer profits to market share was not confirmed. In sum, the expected Korean desired alliance results were confirmed in two of three cases with the third being insignificant, whereas the US results were surprisingly strong in support of learning and not profits.

Results for the subcategories of desired alliance results are given in Table 4. It was expected that the Koreans would place greater emphasis on learning technology and home market share than would the U.S. executives, while the U.S. executives would emphasize short term profit and foreign market share more. All four of these directional expectations were confirmed at beyond the .05 level of significance. None of the three subcategories of alliance results for which there was no directional expectation were found to be significant. Thus the results do not provide support for Korean/U.S. differences in the weights attached to alliance results for long term profit, learning markets, and learning manufacturing/operations. The Pearson correlation between the Korean and the U.S. executive results between the seven categories in Table 4 is 0.4. To be significant at the 0.05 level for $n = 7$ the correlation would have to exceed 0.666. Hence, there is no statistical support for a similarity of desired results between the Koreans and the U.S. executives. To the extent executives from the two countries are different in their priorities, it would suggest that projection of one's own culturally bound priorities on others could well lead to misunderstandings or naive bargaining in the course of alliance negotiations.

C.   Alliance Attribute Importance

Conjoint analysis was used to calibrate the importance weights Korean and U.S. executives give to the six alliance attributes included in the study. Recall that these attributes are: time frame of the alliance, competitiveness of the partner with the firm, home country of the partner, the firm's equity position in the alliance, the main contribution of the partner to the alliance, and the firm's contribution to the alliance. For a discussion of industrial applications of conjoint analysis and its validity, see Montgomery (1986). The results are reported in Table 5. The importance weights are rescaled to sum to 1.00. It was generally expected that there would be differences in the importance weights between the two countries. The tests reported in Table 5 are thus two tailed tests. While there were no formal hypotheses about the contrasts, informal analysis conducted prior to data analysis suggested the following with the associated results:

1.   Korean executives will be more concerned that U.S. executives with what the partner will contribute to the alliance. Directionally this expectation was correct but the result was not statistically significant.

2.   Korean executives will be less concerned than U.S. executives with the home area of the prospective partner. The results show a trivially small difference, thus this expectation was not confirmed.

3. Korean executives will be more concerned than U.S. executives with the home area of the prospective partner. This conjecture was disconfirmed and is statistically significant at the 0.01 level in the opposite direction. That is, U.S. executives are significantly more concerned about the home area of a prospective partner than are Korean executives.

4. U.S. executives will be more concerned than Korean executives with competitive overlap with a prospective partner. This expectation was confirmed at the 0.05 level of significance.

5. Korean managers will be less concerned with the alliance time frame. This contrast is statistically insignificant and the sign is in the opposite direction.

6. Korean executives will be more concerned than U.S. executives with their firm's equity position in a prospective alliance. This expectation was supported at beyond the 0.01 level.

In sum, two of the prior expectations were upheld (Koreans more concerned with equity, U.S. more concerned with partner competitive overlap), one was significant in the opposite direction (U.S. executives are more concerned with home area of a partner), and three of the attributes importance weights showed no differences between the two countries. Interestingly, the Pearson correlation between the two countries across the six alliance attributes is 0.704 which is statistically significant at about the 0.05 level ($p = 0.707$). Thus, despite the difference discussed above, the Korean and U.S. executives demonstrate significant similarity in their evaluation of the importance of these alliance attributes.

Table 5.   Alliance Attribute Importance Weights

Alliance Attribute	U.S. Mean (Std. error) n=151)	Prediction	Korea Mean (Std. error) (n=35)	Difference of means (std. error of diff.)	t-ratio Significance
Partner's Main Contribution	0.141 (.020)	≠	0.191 (.030)	−.050 (.036)	t=−1.39 not sig.
My Firm's Contribution	0.153 (.021)	≠	0.159 (.027)	-.006 (.034)	t=−.18 not sig.
Home Area of Partner	0.261 (.028)	≠	0.124 (.038)	.137 (.047)	t=2.90 <0.01
Partner Competitiveness	0.124 (.021)	≠	0.045 (.030)	.079 (.037)	t=2.16 <0.05
Time Frame	.043 (.011)	≠	.053 (.009)	−.010 (.014)	t=−.70 not sig.
My Firm's Equity	.278 (.028)	≠	.429 (.045)	-.151 (.053)	t=−2.85 <0.01

IV. SUMMARY

Korean executives were found to have a statistically and substantively significantly greater time horizon for strategic alliances than their U.S. counterparts. The differences, although real and important, are not overwhelmingly large. Somewhat surprisingly, U.S. executives prefer learning from alliances to both profits and market share. However, their Korean counterparts have significantly greater preference for learning and lesser preference for profits. Although the Korean and U.S. executives differ in the importance attached to alliance attributes—Koreans are very sensitive to holding an equity position in any alliance and U.S. executive care much more about the country origin and competitive overlap with a partner—the Korean and U.S. executive importance weights for alliance attributes are fairly strongly positively correlated.

Again, this research has as its basic premise that a better understanding of similarities and differences in strategic alliance preferences will facilitate more harmonious and successful cross border strategic alliances. Although this paper does not prove the premise, it does provide a step toward enhanced mutual understanding in this vital and growing aspect of globalization.

REFERENCES

Bleeke, J., & Earnst D. (Ed.s) (1993). *Collaborating to compete: Using strategic alliances and acquisitions in the global marketplace*. New York: Wiley.

Franke, R.H., Hofstede G., & Bond M.H. (1991). Cultural roots of economic performance: A research note." *Strategic Management Journal*, 12, 165-173.

Hall, E.T. (1993). *The dance of life: The other dimension of time*. New York: Anchor Books.

Hofstede, G. (1980). *Culture's consequences*, Abridged edition, Vol. 5. Cross-Cultural Research and Methodology Series. New York: Sage.

Hofstede, G. & Bond M.H. (1988). The Confucius connection: From cultural roots to economic growth. *Organization Dynamics*, 16, 4, 4-21.

Hofstede, G., Neuijen B., Ohayv, D.D. & Sanders G. (1990). Measuring organizational cultures: A qualitative and quantitative study across twenty cases. *Administrative Science Quarterly*, 35, 2: 286-316.

Hofstede, G. (1991). *Cultures and organizations: Software of the mind*. London: McGraw-Hill.

Jacobs, M.T. (1991). *Short-term America: The causes and cures of our business myopia*. Boston: Harvard Business School Press.

Kang, T.W. (1989). *Is Korea the next Japan?* New York: Free Press.

Montgomery, D.B. (1985). Conjoint calibration of the customer/competitor interface in industrial markets. In K. Backhaus & D. Wilson (Eds), *New developments in industrial marketing: A German/American perspective*. Frankfurt: Springer Verlag.

Shane, S.A. (1992). The effect of cultural differences in perceptions of transaction costs on national differences in the preference for licensing. Management International Review, 32, 4: 295-311.

Steers, R.M., Shin, Y.K. & Ungson G.R. (1989). *The chaebol*. New York: Harper and Row.

Usunier, J-C.G. (1991). Business time perceptions and national cultures: A comparative survey. *Management International Review*, 31, 3: 197-217.

Yoshino, M.Y., & Rangan U.R. (1995). Strategic alliances: An entrepreneurial approach to globalization. Boston: Harvard Business School Press.

MARKETING, OPEN MARKETS AND POLITICAL DEMOCRACY:
THE EXPERIENCE OF THE PACRIM COUNTRIES

Hans B. Thorelli

ABSTRACT

Marketing is the generation, execution, and evaluation of transactions. Transactions implement the division of labor in an economy. Thus, marketing is universal, although its character differs from one place and time to another. The motivational aspects of marketing are the key to sustained economic development. The relationship between marketing, development and authoritarian/democratic government is examined in an ecological perspective.

I. THE UNIVERSALITY OF MARKETING

Every marketing person with any self-respect—and marketing people tend to have a lot of self-respect—has their own definition of what marketing is all about. My definition is not terribly original. It is unusual only in one respect: it varies from day to day, and from one place to another. I call it the human ecology (Thorelli, 1995) view of marketing. Here it is:

Advances in International Marketing, Volume 7, pages 33-46.
Copyright © 1996 by JAI Press Inc.
All rights of reproduction in any form reserved.
ISBN: 1-55938-839-0

Marketing is the generation, execution, and evaluation of transactions.

Transactions constitute *exchange* between two (or more) parties. We tend to think of marketing as involving arms-length exchanges, but transactions may also be instigated by third parties, such as government, or even the little girl who asks her mom to buy her a piece of chewing-gum. Evaluation is an indispensable part of our definition, as evaluation is a key determinant of future transactions (Did the little girl like the gum? And does she want a piece of the same gum next time?).

Marketing is a dynamic social process conditioned by the economic, social and political environment and, in turn, changing that environment. Marketing is also *universal*. Marketing *systems* differ by types of society around the PACRIM, and some day we shall have a full-blown theory of comparative marketing systems. But note that as long as all societies are based on economies of scale and specialization, the *division of labor* is implemented by means of exchange, that is, by transactions. If you are a shoemaker I will buy a pair of shoes from you. If I am a taxi driver, you buy a ride from me. Whether the price and other terms of trade are determined by the parties to the exchange or by the overwhelming power of one of them, or by higher authorities, is irrelevant here. The point is that a non-marketing society simply does not exist.[1]

II.   COMPARING MARKETING SYSTEMS

To begin understanding the relationship between marketing, open markets, and political democracy, we may make a vastly simplified comparison of marketing systems in different societies around the Rim. This comparison will focus around a few figures. The figures emphasize the relative roles played by three types of decision-makers in different types of societies. These decision-makers are the Government (G), the Sellers (S) and the Buyers. There is reason to distinguish between two kinds of buyers: industrial buyers, including distributors (I), and end consumer buyers (C).

The government exercises its power in the form of regulation. The regulation may apply to all transactions economy-wide, or at least to an entire industry, in which case we call it macro-regulation. But regulations may apply to individual firms or particular transactions (or both), in which case it is micro-regulation. It is convenient to think of decision-making in any marketing system on two levels: the government level and the transaction level, where the sellers and buyers are (see Figure 1). Note that governmental bodies may also be sellers and buyers, although these bodies generally will be separate from the regulators.

A full-drawn line beginning at the government means that the government exercises the primary authority over sellers. A full-drawn line between sellers and buyers indicates that the two parties in most transactions decide the terms of trade pretty much independently of the government. A line of dashes emanating from

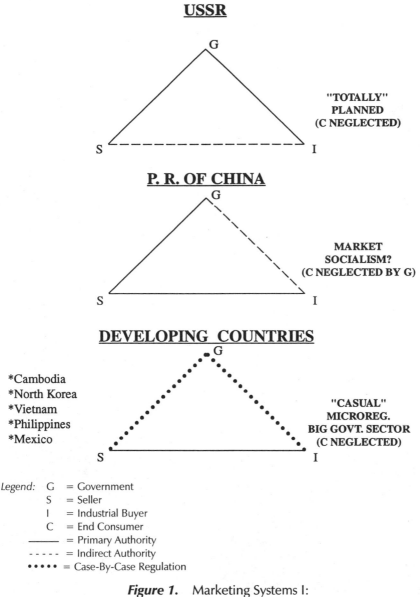

Figure 1.   Marketing Systems I:
Role of Decision-makers

the government suggests macro-regulation; again we should expect that the government then stays out of influencing individual transactions between sellers and

buyers. When a line of points originates from the government we have an unpredictable range from no government influence over individual firms and transactions all the way to case-by-case micro-regulation, which then typically is exercised on firms more than on individual transactions.

When a seller and a buyer are both government-owned and operated, we have, at least in theory, a totally planned system, as in the former Soviet Union. The plans involved all firms, whether sellers or buyers, and entailed incredibly detailed delivery schedules and planner-set prices. That is, there was, at least officially, no real transaction freedom at the firm level, the parties might perhaps be allowed to move a particular delivery date a week or two, or decide whether a piece of machinery should be black or blue (or why not red!). End consumers were not only neglected, they did not even have *any* legal rights.

In the People's Republic of China governments at various levels still practice a great deal of regulation of sellers. However, institutional buyers and sellers are nowadays relatively free to transact among themselves. The government takes little interest in end consumers.

There are some 100 Developing Countries in the world, making it difficult indeed to generalize about their marketing systems. Relatively few are in the PAC-RIM area. Typically, we find a big government sector, regulating sellers, and to some extent buyers as well to varying degrees. Regulations are often unpredictable and volatile in individual cases. The private sector tends to be characterized by what we have labeled *cryptocapitalism* (Thorelli & Sentell, 1982), rather than by open markets. End consumers are of little interest, except for price controls and subsidies on bread and/or rice in the capital and maybe a few other urban areas.

Among the Tigers so characteristic of the PACRIM, central Government typically exercises a strong influence over selected major industries, sometimes extending even to individual transactions of these industry sellers with their industrial buyers. Small business and service industries are generally left to their own devices (as indicated by the inside triangle in Figure 2). End consumers are basically underprivileged in Tiger societies, but thanks to rising standards of living they are slowly gaining some authority relative to both sellers and government (as indicated on the second Tiger figure).

The Post-Industrial countries, of which the world's two largest—the United States and Japan—are in the RIM, are characterized by indirect and macro-regulation setting a general framework essentially facilitating open market transactions, freely engaged in by sellers and buyers. Nonetheless, it is clear that the Japanese elitist civil service bureaucracy continues to exercise an influence on the economy unparalleled in Western democracies, often in close cooperation with the *keiretsu*. In the United States, American end consumers play a greater role, and have more rights, and a more powerful position than in any other country.

We should finally add a note on the global scene. Thanks to initiatives originally taken by the United States, the global marketing system has been based on a basically liberal trade philosophy for almost half a century, symbolized by the GATT

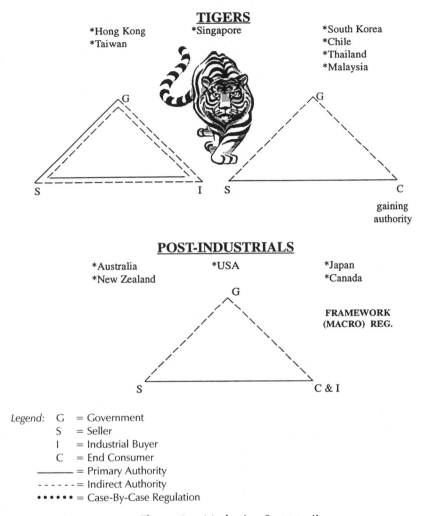

TIGERS

*Hong Kong	*Singapore	*South Korea
*Taiwan		*Chile
		*Thailand
		*Malaysia

gaining
authority

POST-INDUSTRIALS

| *Australia | *USA | *Japan |
| *New Zealand | | *Canada |

**FRAMEWORK
(MACRO) REG.**

Legend: G = Government
S = Seller
I = Industrial Buyer
C = End Consumer
——— = Primary Authority
- - - - - = Indirect Authority
• • • • • = Case-By-Case Regulation

Figure 2.   Marketing Systems II

agreements and the new World Trade Organization. As we have seen, within this overall framework nations are pursuing an amazingly broad range of policies with regard to their own domestic marketing systems (indicated by the question marks in Figure 3). But it is important to note that without a liberal world marketing system, one may well doubt that there would have been a Japanese (or German) "Economic Miracle." And the Tigers would likely only be cubs by now—hemmed in by the protectionist fences of other nations.

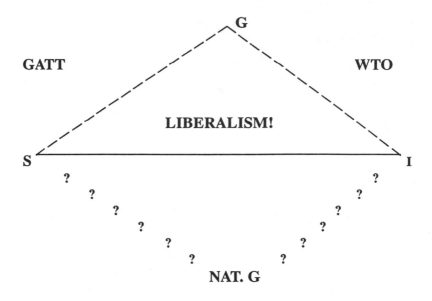

Without a liberal world marketing system, one may doubt there would have been a Japanese (or German) "economic miracle." And the tigers would likely only be cubs by now!

Legend: G-S-I   = Global Trading System
          GATT   = General Agreement on Tariffs and Trade
          WTO   = World Trade Organization
          NAT. G   = National Governments
          The question marks (?) indicate the vast variety of local trade policies.

Figure 3.   Global Marketing System

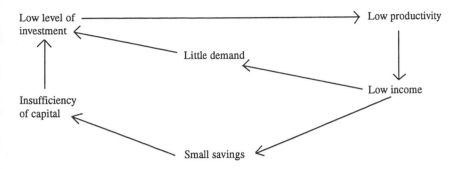

Figure 4. The LDC Syndrome: Orthodox View

III. THE DYNAMICS OF DEVELOPMENT

Let us now return to the problem of generating growth in the Less Developed Countries (LDC). We first present a capsulation of the economic assumptions on which the national and international efforts to emancipate the LDC have been based during the last half century. Taken together these assumptions form a model of what may be called the orthodox view of the LDC syndrome (see Figure 4). By contrast, we then introduce a human ecology view in which marketing emerges as the very engine of economic development (Figure 5). The role of government is then briefly commented on and the need for balance among the various elements of the development process is emphasized.

A.   Orthodox View of the LDC Syndrome

The model presented in Figure 4 is essentially a static one. Development economists and the policymakers influenced by them have concluded essentially that the key to breaking out of the vicious circle is the injection of a stream of outside capital. Hundreds of billions of dollars later this view is essentially bankrupt: we know (or certainly should know!) by now that no amount of wealth transfer in and of itself will fuel the development process.

B.   Emancipating the LDC: The Human Ecology View

Not surprisingly, considering the discipline, development economists (with the notable exception of P.T. Bauer & B.S. Yamey [1963] and a handful of others) have shied away from behavioral science variables. Thus, they have overlooked the key ingredient igniting and sustaining the development process: human motivation. The level of motivation in the LDC is typically low, due to the presence of one, or generally several of these phenomena:

1. *The dual economy-domestic colonialism constellation.* The great majority of the population are in effect secondary citizens.
2. *A sellers' market.* This is due to cryptocapitalism (don't rock the boat, cartel-type philosophy) and/or to the presence of an enormous public sector. Capitalist savings are often hoarded abroad.
3. *Fatalism.* "There is little I can do to improve my lot in life, as my fate is predetermined."
4. *Little circulation among social groups* (e.g., Middle East and India).
5. *Corruption.* Removes the causal relationship between honest effort and outcome (Thorelli & Sentell, 1982).
6. *Failure of the demonstration effect.* What people in the LDC see of Western TV and other media under circumstances above, they will literally ascribe to "another world."

The thesis here is that modern marketing is the key transformer of such motivational nihilism into an irresistible development-oriented value structure. This has already been demonstrated in such countries as South Korea and Chile, and other Tiger nations. Most people associate "marketing" with what we may call physical aspects, that is, delivering the right product, to the right customer at the right place and at the right time. Without denying the importance of these things, and of the infrastructure of transportation, communication and distribution that they require, we contend that the role of marketing as a primary actor in economic development is not physical. It is *psychological.* Modern marketing is first and foremost a *motivational force.*

Being based in human needs and wants, modern marketing in one form or another will emerge automatically in any society with a large open market sector,

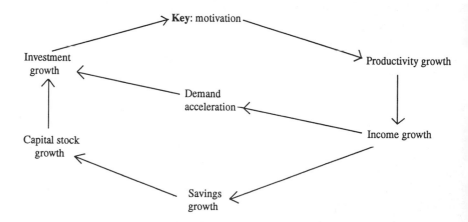

Figure 5.   Emancipating the LDC: The Human Ecology View

that is, a society based largely on individual initiative (even if not necessarily on private property). To understand the motivational impact of modern marketing you need to think only about marketing's first challenge, namely to generate transactions. To generate business, rival sellers are led to present opportunities to make our life more comfortable and enjoyable. Modern marketing does this by introducing *choice*, or discretion. In a sense, therefore, *all* personal income becomes discretionary! Recognizing the availability of choice and of discretion has two extremely important consequences: the first is the reduction, if not elimination, of fatalism—the notion that everything is preordained. The second consequence is that discretion conveys power—or at least a sense of it—which stimulates self-confidence. Self-confidence pretty soon will generate a degree of individualism (regardless of how collectivist the traditional culture may be). The most outstanding characteristic of an individual is that she/he makes their own decisions.

When the process has gone this far, it makes sense for the citizen to think of improving his lot, by working a little harder, or improving his firm by working more creatively. Individuals also begin to realize the value of *information* in making their decisions in the marketplace, forcing most sellers to provide more factual information, (though, inevitably, some of them will also supply exaggerated and misleading information). Interestingly, both competition and cooperation become more intense as the open market grows, replacing lethargy and fatalistic pessimism. Both competition and cooperation are strong motivational factors activated or enlarged by modern marketing.

The combination of choice, competition and cooperation leads to that self-perpetuating process in the marketplace which we call economic development.[2]

C.   Government in Early Stages of Development

As we have stated, the single most important, and the single most delicate task politically, of governments in the transformation from Developing Country to Tiger status, is to learn to liberate marketing, as it is the key to mobilizing the enthusiasm and the energy of the population for sustained economic development.

But clearly, other, more traditional measures are also needed. As they are well-known, we will just summarize some of these factors here, somewhat in order of their importance.

1.   *Birth Control/Family Planning.* Economic development is growth in output and productivity. But in Africa, India, and perhaps Indonesia, too, population still grows faster than the production of food and other necessities. Conditions in these parts of the world have made many of us believe that family planning is the world's biggest marketing challenge (whether or not contraceptive devices are in fact given away). Related to family planning is the world-wide issue of women's emancipation.

2. *Popular Education.* In economic development education has at least three major benefits:

   a. It reduces child-bearing as a perceived means of economic assurance.
   b. It increases the competence, mobility and understanding of individuals as *workers*.
   c. It increases the competence of individuals as *consumers* and their understanding of how the market system works.

These benefits are well documented, whether or not the subjects are explicitly taught in the schools. (By the way, remember that TV generally is not for education, but is a substitute for education!)

3. *Agriculture.* Unfortunately, most conventional development literature tends to have but modest interest in agriculture. Yet farmers should be looked upon as *entrepreneurs*, in need of information about both market conditions and how to increase productivity. They also need infrastructure (below), storage, and credit facilities. Last, but certainly not least, they must be free to sell their produce at open market prices. This is the crux of eliminating "economic dualism." Do not let us forget that a key factor in the startup of economic development in the PRC was the introduction of the open market system in agriculture in 1978.

4. *Infrastructure.* Mobility of people, mobility of products, and mobility of information is a crucial prerequisite to development. Roads, public transport facilities, telecommunications and other means of in- and out-bound information to rural areas are indispensable.

5. *Savings.* Research has demonstrated that even in the poorest countries some savings take place. However, they are typically not put to productive use. Note again that the small class of rich people often hold (or invest) their savings in foreign countries. Productive, domestic use of savings will accelerate with growing credibility in the sincerity and integrity of government as leader of the development effort, and with the broader scope for private initiatives.

6. *Inflation and Currency Stability.* The toughest test of successful development is the ability of a government to hold back inflationary pressures inevitably arising from investments in education, infrastructure, and private entrepreneurship. Inflation must be kept within such bounds that the credibility of the local currency is not lost either in the shape of uncontrollable increases in prices at home, or decreases in the value of the national currency abroad, or both.

7. *Import Substitution vs. Export Promotion.* Research in recent years has demonstrated the fallacy of one-sided protection of so-called virgin industries to allow for the substitution of imports. One-sided reliance on subsidies and other artificial means of export promotion presumably is equally dangerous from the point of developing long-term competitiveness in the global arena. A delicate balance of such measures, keeping in mind the ultimate goal of abandoning both types, is in order.

D. Balance Is a Mainspring in Development

Impatient to push progress, many Developing Countries emphasize one or two of the areas just mentioned at the cost of the others. For instance, certain primary industries or infrastructure may be accelerated at the cost of agriculture and monetary stability. Mexico is a case in point. Unfortunately, such one-sided development also tends to suppress the vital motivational aspects of modern marketing. Indeed, in a fatally misguided belief that marketing is essentially a parasitical activity, the open market sector may be suppressed in various ways by official disdain or unwarranted taxes on consumption, which directly counteract individual motivation.

Available evidence strongly suggests the wisdom of *balance* in the development effort. However, experience also indicates that the self-discipline called for to maintain such a balance is difficult to attain at individual levels. It is also difficult to attain by a weak government. Unfortunately, democratic governments in developing countries tend to be weak, and plagued by internal conflict. Balanced development in the pre-Tiger phase calls for *strong* government, which, given the weakness of democracy in such societies, will tend to call for a more or less authoritarian government (though by no means for fascist or communist dictatorship, neither of which ever showed the capability of *sustained* popularly motivated economic development). What we have in mind is rather the quasi-democratic strong governments characteristic of most of the Tigers around the RIM.

IV. FROM TIGERS TO POST-INDUSTRIALS

It is almost an axiom that mankind's needs/wants are limitless. As most of the Tigers want to move on to become what we are calling Post-Industrial countries, several aspects of the development process are likely to change. Marketing will become a more important part of the Value Added chain, and the urge of average citizens to improve their economic lot will be strengthened. In the marketplace, customer satisfaction, and meeting increasingly individualized demand, becomes ever more important. With consumer emancipation comes demands for government-enforced consumer rights and protection.

In many post-industrials we see a drive toward privatization of state industries in favor of open markets. There will also be a relative shift from heavy industry to information-intensive industries and, not least, to services of all kinds. The role of governments will tend to shift from the ever-present regulator toward becoming the ultimate umpire and standard-setter in the play of open market forces. Governments will find less and less need to make decisions in the area of import substitution and export promotion, as markets become increasingly capable of resolving these matters on their own. Family planning will also tend to take care of itself, and so, in most countries, will agriculture. Infrastructure and environmental protection become more important aspects of public policy, as does lifelong learning and education.

V.   MARKETING, DEVELOPMENT AND DEMOCRACY: ECOSYSTEM DYNAMICS

In summary, we have seen that *marketing is universal*, though its characteristics will vary from one time and one place to another. For *rapid* progress from Developing Country to the status of a Tiger nation we are claiming that modern marketing, operating in a large open market sector, is indispensable. This is because of the psychological fact that modern marketing is an unparalleled *motivator* of human enthusiasm and energy. We have also observed the vital need for a *balanced* view of development policy.

We come now to the final question: the relationship between marketing, development and political democracy. Marketing activates the universal human urge for self-improvement and higher standards of living that provides the popular engagement without which sustained development has proved impossible. We have also found that in the transition from less developed to Tiger status government has several crucial functions, some of which may not be popular. For instance, the release of marketing forces at first may set up unrealistic expectations among citizens, as recently typified by many East European nations. Many people will not see the need for family planning or formal education, and so on. In this kind of environment (eco-setting) democratic government is likely to prove too weak—especially in nations which have had no prior experience with the self-discipline democracy necessarily calls for. For the kind of rapid growth Developing Countries expect these days, some degree of authoritarian government seems unavoidable.

If our eco-logic reasoning is correct, it also follows that it is natural for rapid economic development to *precede* political democracy. The fatal mistake of Mikhail Gorbachev was to mobilize *glasnost* (freedom of speech and some other aspects of democracy) before he ever was able to follow through with his *perestroika* (that is, the necessary economic reforms to increase the standards of living of the Russian people).

By contrast, Deng-Xiaoping had a vision of "market socialism," which began with the introduction of open markets in agriculture, followed somewhat later by modest privatization of small business and a loosening up of central government regulation of the economy, and an invitation to foreign companies to form joint ventures with Chinese firms, albeit on restrictive terms (Thorelli, 1987). The Tiananmen episode made it crystal clear that the Chinese leadership feels that it is still premature to have a certain degree of economic freedom be accompanied by any real political freedom.

From an ecological perspective it is instructive to draw on the collective experience of the PACRIM countries in considering the relationship between marketing, economic development and political democracy. It would appear that freeing up a substantial sector of the economy, such as agriculture and small businesses, is a logical starting point in the long odyssey from economic underdevelopment and political volatility to post-industrial democracy. That free sector of modern marketing can be counted on to generate powerful motivational effects in favor of accelerated development. To live up to these expectations demands a public policy in a variety of areas which under these "hothouse" conditions seems to require a more or less authoritarian government, at least in countries which have not had a democratic heritage.

In the transition from Tiger to post-industrial society, there will be a tension between the economic freedom and aspirations of the population, and what will be perceived as lack of political freedom. Ecologic probabilism implies that economic freedom will eventually result in political freedom as well. But there is no automaticity in this process. Also, open markets as well as political democracy are not absolute concepts, both are matters of degree.

It is true that all post-industrial societies are also democracies. Postwar Japan is, and seems likely to remain, the only case where relatively open markets and democracy have developed simultaneously, possibly due to unique historic circumstances; among them not least following American examples. But the Japanese central bureaucracy exercises an influence unparalleled in any other democracy, including even France. Most other post-industrial societies than Japan have taken centuries, rather than decades, to reach their present status. The longer the process, the greater the interplay between economics and politics over time, including setbacks in one area or the other—or, sometimes, even in both. Of course, developing countries, as well as the Tigers, are in the fortunate, and enviable, position of being able simply to take over 200 years of technological development.

In fine: open markets, economic development and political democracy are somewhat, and somehow, intertwined. But we must realize that history, strong personalities, political and religious ideologies, wars and other catastrophes, make the correlation less than hard and fast. Nevertheless, the mere fact that such a correlation seems to exist might well serve as an inspiration to mankind—or, at least, to a great many of us.

ACKNOWLEDGMENT

This paper is based on the keynote address delivered by the author at the conference on Marketing Theory and Practice, co-sponsored by the Korean and American Marketing Associations in Seoul, Korea, May 14-16, 1995.

NOTES

1. Given our definition, this is a valid assertion, some Marxist writings to the contrary notwithstanding (see also Thorelli, 1983).

2. It is a sad reflection indeed that the World Bank's *World Development Report* 1994 does not even mention the word "Marketing!"

REFERENCES

Bauer, P.T., & Yamey, B.S. (1963). *The economies of underdeveloped countries*. London: Cambridge University Press.

Thorelli, H.B. (1983). Concepts of marketing: A review, preview and paradigm." In P. Varadarajan (Ed.), *The marketing concept: Perspectives and viewpoints*, (pp. 2-37). College Station, TX: Texas A&M University Marketing Department.

Thorelli, H.B. (1995). The ecology of organizations. In H. B. Thorelli (Ed.), *Integral strategy*, (pp. 415-442). Greenwich, CT: JAI Press.

Thorelli, H.B. (1987). What can third world countries learn from China? *Journal of Global Marketing*, 1, 69-83.

Thorelli, H.B., & Sentell, G.D. (1982). *Consumer Emancipation and Economic Development: The Case of Thailand*. Greenwich, CT: JAI Press.

A COMPARISON OF THE PERCEPTIONS OF CLIENTS AND DESIGN CONSULTANTS TOWARD CORPORATE IDENTITY PROGRAMS

Dae Ryun Chang, Don Ryun Chang and
Kwon Soo Lee

ABSTRACT

This paper examines the perceptions of clients and designers of corporate identity (CI) programs. The clients of CI are corporate managers who belong to the strategic planning and marketing departments. CI is being used as a tool to reengineer the corporate culture of a firm within the firm and to establish a new corporate image outside the firm. In the marketing context a specific subarea of CI is Brand Identity (BI) and the latter is being implemented to establish a coordinated marketing identity at the level of the individual product. In Korea both areas are gaining widespread attention because of the emerging need to reflect a more globalized and competitive identity both at the corporate and brand levels. The motivation of this study is to assess what are the conceptualized benefits of CI as perceived by two separate groups: cli-

Advances in International Marketing, Volume 7, pages 47-59.
ISBN: 1-55938-839-0

ents and designers of these programs. More specifically we compare the perceived strategic, organizational, marketing and communication effects of CI between clients and designers. A survey will be conducted among a sample of clients and designers to perform the comparative analysis.

INTRODUCTION

Although much attention has been given to the importance of developing and using corporate and brand identity programs (hereafter essentially combined and referred to as CI), in the business literature in contrast academic treatment is less abundant and in particular there is little research on their actual implementation. In Asia in particular CI has enjoyed enormous popularity among business ever since the concept was imported from the United States into Japan (Far Eastern Economic Review 1987; Asian Business 1991). Recently CI has become an important growth area in South Korea. While accurate statistics are not available, casual observation would indicate that the top 50 chaebols (Korean conglomerates) have commissioned a CI program. The more visible examples of this trend would be the well known cases and new logos of Samsung and Lucky Goldstar, now known as LG. This growth can be easily understood in these chaebols' attempts to reengineer and reorganize their operations and in so doing reflect a "new face" to the various external publics including their international consumers.

While the motivation for the emergence of CI is easily understood, what is not clear is how effective these programs are after implementation. In this paper we focus on two communities responsible for the creation and implementation of identity programs, the clients and the designers. Even within client corporations of CI programs confusion still remains over what these programs are and why they are needed (Marketing, 1988). This problem will be more accentuated in countries like Korea because identity programs have had a very short history. One of the major sources for this confusion may be the wide scope of CI. A well known guru of CI, Wally Olins argues that CI encompasses not only marketing but also behavior, communications, strategy, structure, advertising, and public relations. In that context different people in different parts of the organization may be looking at limited aspects of CI. It could be the proverbial problem where various blind men are touching different parts of the elephant and concluding different things. Moreover, outside the organization people are exposed to only the visible results of the CI, namely the logo and signage. They may easily conclude that the costs associated with these programs are excessive without realizing that the process of research and creative development is long and that there are substantial material costs involved (Marketing, 1989). Conversely, clients sometimes complain that designers are not sensitive enough about the marketing and strategic issues related to CI. Mistrust and misconception, therefore, may exist on both sides of the user-designer relationship. We propose in this paper that these perceptual barriers

inhibit the effectiveness of CI implementation. Do the clients and design consultants agree on what makes a good CI program? This is what we aim to determine
in this study.

What is corporate identity? In its present nomenclature this discipline sounds
esoteric and mysterious which adds to its appeal but also contributes to its misun-
derstanding. Olins (1989) keeps it simple:

> In order to be effective every organization needs a clear sense of purpose
> that people within it understand. They also need a strong sense of belong-
> ing. Purpose and belonging are the two facets of identity. Every organiza-
> tion is unique, and the identity must spring from the organization's own
> roots, its personality, its strengths and its weaknesses. This is true of the
> modern global corporation as it has been of any other institution in history,
> from the Christian church to the nation state. The identity of the corpora-
> tion must be so clear that it becomes the yardstick against which its prod-
> ucts, behavior and actions are measured. This means that the identity
> cannot simply be a slogan, a collection of phrases: it must be visible, tangi-
> ble and all-embracing. Everything that the organization does must be an
> affirmation of its identity..... Identity is expressed in the names, symbols,
> logos, colors and rites of passages which the organization uses to distin-
> guish itself, its brands and its constituent companies.

We see from the above description that while corporate identity does include
visible elements which we can call the "design," nonetheless corporate identity is
firmly rooted in the essential individuality of the organization. In fact the description of identity above is very consistent with the concept of "corporate mission"
found in marketing and, in this context, lacking an identity, just like lacking a mission, leads companies to make poor strategic decisions such as "make inappropri-
ate acquisitions, diversify into blind alleys, make inferior copies of other
companies "products" (Olins, 1989). The relationship between corporate identity
and portfolios of businesses can be understood with the General Electric example
where the design and names were changed to GE and a new logo was created to
reflect the wider spectrum of businesses. At the broad level, identity is very consistent with brand equity (Schmitt & Pan, 1994) and brand positioning.

Given the relevance of corporate and brand identity to business and especially to
marketing, it is somewhat surprising then that there is limited academic research in
this area. A recent computer-aided search of the business literature listed very few
academic studies related to corporate identity in the last 4 years. Part of the lack of
interest may stem from the common perception that "identity" and "image" are
interchangeable concepts. Kotler (1994) categorizes symbols such as logos and
signs as "image differentiation" which is one of his main positioning strategies.
While image is certainly part of identity, the term suggests a more restrictive

boundary than the identity process described above. Moreover, it puts more emphasis on the visible and creative aspects of identity management. This is analogous to the division in advertising agencies between "creative" people and marketing managers. Moreover, once a discipline becomes tagged with the "creative" label, managers and even academics seem to distance themselves from it perhaps because of their different background and training. In a different context, such an interdisciplinary gap may be observed in highly technology-intensive companies between managers and R&D personnel (Gupta et al., 1986). Recent managerial interest in cross-functional cooperation (e.g., Parker, 1994) suggests that resolving interdisciplinary differences leads to better organizational performance.

The objective of this paper therefore is to empirically examine the perceptions of two disciplines or "communities" involved in CI. One community is the clients of CI, who we define as the "client," and within this classification we include top, middle, and entry level managers belonging to the strategic planning and marketing departments. As mentioned above, the application of these programs is very broad but we limit the analysis to these two primary clients. The other community is the designers of CI, who we define as "design consultants" which include top is managers, project directors, and entry level designers. Thus within each community we have a fairly homogeneous group which is differentiated within only by managerial position. Between the two communities we have a differentiation in terms of not only corporate affiliation but also disciplines, the client being managerially oriented whereas the consultants are design oriented.

The use of such a dyadic approach is common in organizational buying behavior research in marketing. Other areas employing this method include the policy sciences area (Caplan, Morrison, & Stambaugh, 1975) where information use and perception were demonstrated to be significantly different between social scientists, the information producer, and policymakers, who were the information users. Because the two groups operated in different subcultures with different norms and reward systems this divergence lead to a mutual mistrust and a resultant lower information usage by the policy makers. A marketing application of such a "two-communities" framework is found in the area of marketing research. Deshpande and Zaltman (1984) compared the factors affecting researcher (information producer) and manager (information user) perceptions of market research use. They established that the factors perceived as influencing use of market research information were different between researchers and users. For researchers the most important influences were, in order or priority, interaction between researchers and managers, political acceptability, exploratory research purpose, technical and presentation quality of research report, confirmatory research purpose and actionability, surprise, and stage of product life cycle when the research was conducted. In comparison for managers the influences were degree of formalization of organizational structure (inversely related), technical quality of the research, extent of researcher-manager interaction, surprise, exploratory research purpose, and degree of centralization (inversely related). Among the notable differences was the political acceptability of the research findings which was perceived as being more instrumental by the researchers. Because researchers assume the position of information suppliers they realize that the results will impact either favorably or unfavorably the corporate commitment to products. This is a relevant issue to CI (and more specifically to BI). The negative perceptions for the organizational variables of formalization and centralization are also relevant in Asian companies given the more rigid hierarchical structure in these cultures.

A related literature for this topic is the conceptualization of market orientation. Kohli and Jaworski (1990, 1993) argue that despite the frequency in which the word "market orientation" is used, a commonly accepted definition, theory development, and empirical research on the concept is lacking. This implies that even though CI clients may complain that designers do not have a market orientation the client's own orientation is comparatively higher and moreover, that the concept is well established. Combining a review of extant theory with field-based research Kohli and Jaworski (1990) posit that market orientation can be operationalized as "the organization wide generation of market intelligence pertaining to current and future customer needs, dissemination of the intelligence across departments, and organization wide responsiveness to it." The definition is relevant to CI since the need for both entail elements of customer need/trends analysis, interdepartmental dissemination, and organization-wide response. The paper also points to the antecedents of market orientation as being senior management factors, interdepartmental dynamics, and organizational systems. Again all of these constructs and many of their specific measures can be linked with CI. For example one of the measures of the first factor is risk aversion. Changing the CI certainly entails a great deal of risk for a company especially when the existing market situation is positive. Nevertheless a "face-lift" may be recommended by designers in view of the likely future environment forecasted for the company. Another measure which is related to interdepartmental dynamics is interdepartmental conflict. If this is high it is plausible that not only market intelligence dissemination will be negatively impacted but also the dissemination and implementation of CI programs.

A third area of literature inquiry is the existing work on national culture and corporate culture. National culture is relevant to the extent that symbolism, a key component of identities, is subjective and somewhat culture-bound. For example, Schmitt and Pan (1994) demonstrate the uniqueness of Asia-Pacific languages and cultural characteristics which necessitates adjustments in corporate and brand identities. For example, monolithic identities are instances where a corporation uses one name and visual style (e.g., IBM). Olins (1989) argues that while monolithic identities are not unique to Japanese companies, nevertheless the acceptance of them are higher in Japan even though the range of activities and products are sometimes quite varied. One example cited is Mitsubishi whose products include aircraft, automobiles, a bank, and tinned salmon. Also corporate culture is important because it is synonymous with corporate identity as used by both academics and practitioners. This notwithstanding, examination of culture, especially corporate, in the marketing literature has been relatively limited as compared to the organizational behavior fields. Some of the few studies in marketing are those by Deshpande and Webster (cf. 1989, 1990) who examined the concept of corporate culture in non-marketing fields and defined it as "the pattern of shared values and beliefs that help individuals understand organizational functioning and thus provide them with the norms for behavior in the organization." Given the many paradigms of culture they selected one of them, labeled organizational cognition which views organizations as knowledge systems and uses a managerial information processing perspective. In that context it is consistent with the market intelligence approach used by Kohli and Jaworski (1990). An application of this framework is Deshpande et al. (1993) where the authors examined the effect of corporate culture, customer orientation, and innovativeness in various Japanese firms on business performance. While the body of such studies is still limited, nevertheless, they suggest the need to study corporate identity in context-specific domains.

Research on corporate culture of Korean companies, especially that in English, is fairly limited. The few studies which do exist (e.g., Steers et al. 1989) discuss characteristics which are common to Korean conglomerates also known as "chaebols": family control and management, paternalistic management, centralized planning and coordination, the wide range of business activity sometimes which are unrelated, a high entrepreneurial orientation, close business-government relations, and school-ties in hiring. Lee's (1989) survey of these companies found similar ideological themes: harmony and unity, family, sincerity and diligence, creation and development, business credibility, productivity and quality, work responsibility, progressiveness, social responsibility, scientific management, and sacrifice and service. A comprehensive work by Janelli (1993) used an ethnographic approach to study one of the largest chaebols in Korea disguised in the book as "Taesong." The author uses the term "bourgeois ideology" as the corporate culture prevailing in this large corporation. Some of the themes repeated in the work are: Korean corporations' emphasis on sales maximization (as opposed to profit maximization), the corporate cultural emphasis of harmony, and the linkage of corporate success to national success (evocation of patriotism). The most interesting suggestion offered by the book is that there is great dissonance between the cultural norms and actual employee attitudes. Some of the notable ones are company's emphasis on the company as a family and the employees' resistance to it, maintaining harmony by obscuring public expression of conflict, the negative general attitudes held by entering employees about the economic concentration of the chaebols, and disapproval of owner family management. These findings are tempered, as alluded to by the author, by changes taking place in Korean corporations in recent years which suggest new generations may be different from those described in the study. Although it is beyond the scope of this present paper, some interesting linkages between Korea's national and corporate culture may be applicable to CI management. For example, does the unrelated nature of many Korean conglomerates make achieving a single identity more difficult? Does the family ownership structure facilitate or impede effective CI implementation? These and other issues may be studied in future research.

RESEARCH QUESTIONS

Given the lack of research on the integration between identity management with marketing, this study is exploratory in nature and aims to guide future research which will be more formalized and theory based. Given the review of the literature above, the main research questions to be asked and empirically examined are essentially fourfold:

1. Are CI clients and designer consultants in agreement with respect to the usefulness of these programs?
2. Are there differences between companies in terms of their perceptions and attitudes toward CI?
3. What is the relationship between organizational characteristics such as corporate culture, centralization, formalization, interdepartmental relations and CI attitudes?
4. Are prevailing CI attitudes related to perceived CI effectiveness in the client firms?

III. METHOD

For the empirical examination of clients and design consultants of CI we administered a survey to two groups of respondents. The first group consisted of CI client managers in selected companies which recently implemented CI programs. These managers were selected from the marketing and strategic planning departments. Because of the potential for different perspectives by managers at different levels of the organization, a sample was drawn from the top, middle, and entry-levels, as indicated by their job titles. The second group consisted of CI design consultants from three top firms which specialize in corporate and brand identity development programs. For comparison purposes, we collected a sample for top, middle, and entry-level designers. The questionnaire was developed by using and modifying existing scales to measure market orientation and some of its key organizational antecedents and consequences (Jaworski & Kohli, 1993; Deshpande et al., 1994). We conducted field interviews to develop and refine a complementary set of questions to measure attitudes toward CI and its implementation. The final usable sample for the clients was 160 and 60 for designers.

Table 1.   Mean Scores for CI Perceptions and Attitudes

	Variable Name	Client	Designer
A1.	CI is a tool for adapting to environmental change	5.77	5.78
A2.	CI must start with marketing analysis	4.99	4.73
A3.	The creativity of the designer is most important for CI	4.39	5.00
A4.	Consumer is unable to discern the quality of CI	2.24	2.98
A5.	The designer operates without soliciting client opinion	2.26	2.13
A6.	CI must obtain approval from many people in the client's organization	4.64	3.70
A7.	The most important consideration in CI is top managers' intention for the CI	3.55	3.56
A8.	The value of design is difficult to measure	3.83	4.10
A9.	The cost of CI is groundlessly expensive	4.39	2.81*
A10.	The measurement of CI fees is difficult	4.39	3.44*
A11.	CI contributes to the enhancement of sales	5.15	5.69
A12.	CI must begin with analysis of the corporate culture	5.69	5.50*
A13.	CI unifies the minds and actions of corporate members	5.49	5.49
A14.	If the intention of the CI is clear then the actual form of the CI is not important	2.84	1.92*
A15.	The CI logo can be made by anyone	2.40	1.69
A16.	The color of the corporation can be any color	1.91	1.27*
A17.	The corporate logo is most important and implementation is not as important	3.25	3.33*
A18.	Word logo is more effective than a symbol logo	3.11	3.32
A19.	Ten years is a long time for a logo to last	3.06	3.06
A20.	Corporate logos should be changed frequently	5.28	5.72
A21.	CI is related to corporate diversification strategy	5.60	5.92
A22.	CI is related to corporate internationalization	4.53	3.41*
	strategy	4.08	4.44*
A23.	Foreign CI firms have better design sense vs local	5.35	5.06*
	ones	4.88	4.90
A24.	Korean CI firms have better sense of local aesthetics	6.01	5.20
A25.	There should be no "political problems" with CI	6.30	6.07
A26.	CI must be consistent with the corporate mission		
A28.	The client must be able to understand the CI's concepts and terminology		
A29.	The rationale of the CI must be communicated widely within the client organization		

Note: $*p < .05$.

RESULTS

The Likert 5 point items used to compare perceptions of design consultants and managers and their respective group means are show in Table 1.

The surprising result of this study is that by and large there is a convergence between designers and clients in terms of their perceptions and attitudes toward corporate identity. We had expected greater disparity between the two communities but this was not empirically shown to be the case in our sample. We posit some possible explanations in the discussion section. Nonetheless some important differences between the two groups remain. The significant differences based on a paired *t* test at the .05 significance level (indicated by asterisks) are in areas such as the accounting of CI fees (items A8-A10). There is a general perception on the part of clients that CI is not worth as much as the fees charged would imply. Of course we would expect designers to have an opposing view of those perceptions. Also we see significant differences in the relative utility perceptions of foreign versus local design firms. Here again, clients perceive a higher utility for foreign firms, a view not shared by local design firms. In contrast, the justification of using local firms, namely that they have a better feel for local aesthetics, is not as strongly felt by clients. Both areas had emerged as important points of contention between clients and designers in the fact finding stage of the research. Thus these results confirmed those prior expectations.

To increase the parsimony of the analysis we reduced the data using principal components with varimax rotation.[1] This resulted in 6 factors which we named CI over-simplicity, CI corporate communication, CI process requirements, CI-related strategic benefits, designer-related negative perceptions, and CI cost perceptions. Using these 6 factors we compared the means of the three client organizations. As shown in Table 2, differences in perceptions were found only in CI over-simplicity and designer-related negative perceptions. Firm 2 is the most recent adopter of a new CI program, and therefore it is interesting to note that it has the highest perception that CI is a simple activity. The other significant difference is in the negative perceptions of CI, which is the highest for Firm 3 and the lowest for Firm 2. At first glance the findings appear to be inconsistent since it would be reasonable to expect that companies which view CI in a simplistic way would also have generally negative perceptions about designers. That was, however, not the case here. One explanation might be that Firm 2 managers generally have a positive view of CI but within a limited range of uses. Also consistent with

Table 2. Factor Score Means of Perceptions Across Different Firms

	Simplicity	*Corp. Comm.*	*CI Process*	*CI Strategy*	*Neg. Percept.*	*Costs*
Firm 1	.014	−.089	.099	−.027	.080	−.165
Firm 2	.412	.101	-.178	−.001	−.290	.022
Firm 3	-.411	.015	.046	.042	.177	.185
F-Statistic 2, 138	8.021	.492	.978	.061	2.701	1.521
sig. level	.001	.643	.379	.941	.071	.222

Table 3.   Correlations between Factor Scores and Organizational Variables

	Simplicity	Commun.	Process	Strategy	Negative	Costs
CENTRAL	.0265	.0843	.0076	−.0969	.0353	.0388
COMMIT	.1221	.0482	−.0377	.0802	.0917	.0113
CONFLICT	.1104	.0144	.0502	−.0438	−.0540	.0147
CONNECT	.1096	.1809*	.0151	.0486	.0000	.2131*
FORMAL	.1090	−.1419*	.0859	.0119	.2091*	.0198

Note: *p < .05.

that could be that other firms who hold negative perceptions do so because they think the process of CI is too complex. There were no significant differences in the other three factors.

The third research question dealt with the relationship between the CI perceptions and attitudes and organizational characteristics. We show in Table 3 a correlation matrix of the 6 factors with the key organizational characteristics of centralization, formalization, interdepartmental conflict, and interdepartmental connectedness.

Because we only sampled three companies, the variation in these key variables were limited. The pairwise correlations between the factor scores and the organizational variables are generally low and insignificant. The only relationships that we see are between connectedness and corporate communications and also cost perceptions, and between formalization and corporate communications and also negative perceptions. Again some of these results are not intuitively clear. For example, the positive correlation between interdepartmental connectedness and cost perception is difficult to explain. Nevertheless, the other results such as the negative correlation between formalization and communication, and the positive correlation of formalization and costs perception are consistent with the findings of previous research (e.g., Deshpande & Zaltman, 1985). Collectively they imply that CI is less likely to be adopted and communicated widely in firms which are highly formalized.

The last research question dealt with the relationships between CI perceptions/ attitudes and perceived CI effectiveness. Table 4 shows the results of regressions of a composite CI effectiveness scale against the 6 factor scores of CI perceptions/ attitudes and also the composite measure of market orientation.[2]

The results show that the overall perceived CI effectiveness is significantly predicted by only two variables, CI process requirements and customer orientation. The former implies that in order to have effective CI, managers must also pay attention to the various procedural requirements of this activity. In other words, implementation must be strong to have an effective CI. Also the results suggest that it helps to have a strong customer orientation.

Table 4. Regression of CI Effectiveness and CI Perceptions/Attitudes

R Square	.24597				
Adjusted R Square	.20473				
Standard Error	1.03914				
F = 5.96495, Sig. = .0000					

Variable	B	SE B	Beta	t	Sig t
CUSTOR	.648327	.121843	.443230	5.321	.0000
Simplicity	.092195	.089923	.079441	1.025	.3072
Commun.	.026560	.092591	.022899	.287	.7747
Process	.162238	.090509	.138363	1.792	.0754
Strategy	.086659	.088572	.075193	.978	.3297
Negative	−.078913	.092866	−.067423	−.850	.3970
Costs	−.049784	.090081	−.042533	−.553	.5815
(Constant)	1.378671	.566814		2.432	.0164

V. DISCUSSION

The motivation for this study was to examine whether differences in perception and attitudes existed between two important groups involved with an understudied area of marketing, namely corporate identity programs. Our results, while tentative, suggest that even though there are many similarities in the perceptions and attitudes between the two groups some differences do remain. We think these differences deserve attention since they emerged despite an upward bias toward convergence between the two groups. We only included recent adopters of CI and therefore we expected managers to have more positive evaluations. The remaining disparities, however, underscore important points of contention between the two groups which are not necessarily general perceptions or stereotypes but, given the nature of the sample, related to specific aspects of CI procedures. Most specifically, the accounting of CI fees appears to be a major source of disagreement. It is imperative that CI firms work to instill a constructive perception of fees accounting on the part of clients. We also saw differences between client firms in the summarized factors. Most notably, the firm which most recently adopted a CI program had the most positive perspective on CI despite their perception that the it is a simple activity. In this context we inferred that the negativity of CI can be abated by removing the mystery which sometimes masks the many benefits CI can actually provide. We attempted to relate the many perceptions and attitudes of CI to organizational variables. Given the lack of variation in the client sample we found very few significant correlations. Nonetheless, consistent with previous studies on market research use, we found formalization to be negatively related to internal CI communication and positively related to negative perceptions. This implies that CI will be adopted and implemented more effectively in informal organizations. The last point of inquiry was to determine potential predictors of a composite index of CI effectiveness. Here we found two significant predictors, CI process requirements and market orientation. Collectively they suggest that companies have to strive to be fundamentally market-driven and within that context adopt and implement a consistent CI program. In short, cosmetic changes in something like a corporate logo will not be effective. Given the exploratory nature of this study, future work should elaborate on the influence of organizational characteristics on designers and clients interaction patterns. Also, from an international marketing perspective, the national and corporate cultural constructs should be incorporated to assess their impact on how CI is perceived and implemented.

NOTES

1. Specific details of the factor analysis are omitted for the sake of brevity but will be sent upon request.
2. The composite scale used the items of (1) employees are generally aware of the new CI, (2) our CI is very special as compared to other CIs, (3) our CI reflects our company's essential characteristics, and (4) our CI reflects our company's long term vision.

REFERENCES

Asian Business. (1991). Making up a face to fit, 55-56.

Caplan, N., Morrison, A., Stambaugh R.J. (1975). *The use of social science knowledge in public policy decisions at the national level.* Ann Arbor, MI: Institute for Social Research.

Deshpande, R., & Webster, Jr., F.E. (1989). Organizational culture and marketing: Defining the research agenda. *Journal of Marketing*, 53, 3-15.

Deshpande, R., Farley, J.U., & Webster, Jr., F.E. (1993). Corporate culture, customer orientation, and innovativeness in Japanese firms: A quadrad analysis *Journal of Marketing*, 57, 23-37.

Deshpande, R., & Zaltman G. (1984). A comparison of factors affecting researcher and managerial perceptions of market research use. *Journal of Marketing Research*, 21, 32-38.

Far Eastern Economic Review (1987). Volume 49, 118-119.

Gupta, A.K., Raj, S.P. & Wilemon D. (1986). A model for studying the R&D-marketing interface in the product innovation process. *Journal of Marketing*, 50, 7-17.

Janelli, R. (1993). *Making capitalism: The social and cultural construction of a South Korean conglomerate.* Stanford, CA: Stanford University Press.

Jaworski, B.J., & Kohli A.K. (1993). Market orientation: Antecedents and consequences." *Journal of Marketing*, 57, 53-70.

Kohli, A.K., & Jaworski B.J. (1990). Market orientation: The construct, research propositions, and managerial implications." *Journal of Marketing*, 54 1-18.

Kotler, P. (1994). *Marketing Management.* Englewood Cliffs, NJ: Prentice-Hall.

Lee, H.J. (1989). Managerial characteristics of Korean firms. In Chung Kae H. & Lee Hak Jong (eds.), *Korean managerial dynamics.* New York, NY: Praeger.

Marketing. (1988). Evolution of an idea, 39-42.

Marketing. (1989). Marketing guide 15: Corporate identity, 21-24.

Olins, W. (1989). *Corporate identity.* Boston, MA: Harvard Business School Press.

Olins, W. (1991). Corporate identity: Do we have it all wrong? *Across The Board*, 29-34.

Parker, G.M. (1994). *Cross-functional teams.* San Francisco, CA: Jossey-Bass Publishers.

Schmitt, B.H., & Pan Y. (1990). Managing corporate and brand identities in the Asia-pacific region. *California Management Review* 32-46.
Steers, R.M., Y.K. Shin, & Ungson G.R. (1989). *The chaebol*. New York, NY: Harper & Row.

PART II

ISSUES IN GLOBAL DISTRIBUTION AND THE MARKETING OF SERVICES

COMPETITIVE INTENSITY AND CHANNEL STRUCTURE IN KOREAN CONSUMER GOODS INDUSTRIES

Changhoon Shin, Minhi Hahn and Sehoon Park

ABSTRACT

Manufacturers may distribute their products to their customers directly through integrated channels or indirectly through decentralized channels. In this study, we present an empirical test on the relationship between intensity of competition a strategic business unit (SBU) faces and its reliance on indirect channels using data collected from Korean manufacturers of consumer products. Also investigated are the effects of product substitutability, market predictability, and the number of competitors on the competitive intensity. Our test hypotheses are mainly based on predictions of game theoretic studies of channel competition as well as those presented by studies of transaction cost analysis of channel structure. The competitive intensity, defined as intensity of short term competitive interactions among competing SBUs, is derived from estimates of linear advertising reaction functions of 71 SBUs in 21 consumer product categories to their competitive advertising. Other perception data on market and channel characteristics, as well as reliance on indirect channels were collected by a mail survey. One of main results is that SBUs relying on indirect chan-

Advances in International Marketing, Volume 7, pages 63-81.

nels face lower competitive intensity. It suggests that SBUs facing high competitive intensity have a legitimate reason to rely more on indirect channels as predicted by game theoretic channel studies. Implications of this and other empirical results are discussed.

I. INTRODUCTION

Manufacturers may distribute their products to their customers directly through integrated channels or indirectly through independent intermediaries, that is, decentralized channels. There is an impressive number of studies in marketing and economics that pinpoint certain environmental and channel characteristics as determinants of channel structures. Typically, studies based on the transaction cost analysis (TCA) framework (Williamson, 1975, 1985) have not only identified important determinants of channel structures but also have supported their predictions using empirical data. While game theoretic studies have found some equally important determinants (Coughlan, 1985; McGuire & Staelin, 1983; Moorthy, 1988) of channel structures, attempts to empirically confirm the predictions have been almost negligible.

An important proposition in the game theoretic literature is that decentralized channels mitigate competitive interactions among manufacturers. In this study, our focus is to empirically investigate this strategic motive of decentralization using real world advertising competition data from Korean manufacturers of consumer products.

Our study is a significant departure from other related literature in two major respects. First, we consider both the results of analytical modeling literature and empirical TCA literature in generating our test hypotheses. Analysis will be never complete unless all the main determinants are considered together in the empirical investigation. Thus, although our focus is to test whether the analytically derived game theoretic results are supported by real world data, the determinants identified in the TCA literature are also considered in the analysis. If the proposed effects of these determinants are replicated, it will enhance the validity of the propositions as well as that of our study.

Second, we use a measure of competitive intensity drawn from actual real world competitive advertising data. Weitz (1985, p. 231) emphasizes that we need research on "how and to what degree the structural properties postulated by Porter (1980) are related to actual conduct, competitive reactions, and performance and how the level of competitive intensity in a market influences the effectiveness of marketing activities." Our study is a significant attempt to address this research question.

In the following section, we review the literature on strategic motives of firms for employing indirect channels and present our research hypotheses. Next in the third section, we describe how the main variables including competitive intensity are measured and how the data are collected. After discussion of test results in the fourth section, implications are discussed and suggestions are made for further research in the fifth section.

II. RESEARCH HYPOTHESES

A. Strategic Motives for Decentralization

Channel studies in marketing and economics suggest that there are situations in which manufacturers have strategic reasons to prefer indirect channels over integrated channels. First, we focus on such strategic motives of manufacturers for decentralization.

When the products of competing manufacturers are highly substitutable, integrated channels may exacerbate the price war lowering the profitability of the competing firms. McGuire and Staelin (1983) in their seminal paper show that if the competing products are highly substitutable in demand, decentralization is a Nash equilibrium strategy for the manufacturers. In the equilibrium, both the manufacturers can expect higher profits compared to the case where both manufacturers use vertically integrated channels. They explain the analytical result as follows: "if the retail market is highly competitive (in the sense that the demands are sufficiently interdependent), manufacturers in a duopoly are better off if they can shield themselves from this environment by inserting privately-owned profit maximizers between themselves and the ultimate retail markets even though they lose control of retail price" (McGuire & Staelin, 1983, p. 175).

Consistently, the decentralized channels are found in other game theoretic studies to be working as a buffer against intense price competition between manufacturers in a highly substitutable product market, embedding more potential price competition (Coughlan, 1985; Coughlan & Wernerfelt, 1989). Furthermore, Shin, Park, and Hahn (1993), in analyzing a model with advertising and price competition in marketing channels, show that it is not only the price competition but also the advertising competition which is intensified when integrated channels are used.

Moorthy (1988) identifies more general conditions for the decentralization to be a Nash equilibrium: that is, the manufacturers' products are either (1) demand substitutes and strategic complements at the manufacturer or retailer level, or (2) demand complements and strategic substitutes at the manufacturer or retailer level. When products are strategic complements in price, an increase in a firm's price leads to an increase in the competitor's price. That is, aggressive behavior by a firm induces an aggressive response by its competitor. Strategic substitutability is just the opposite in that aggressive behavior by a firm induces a conservative response by its competitor. Moorthy emphasizes that "the necessary conditions for decentralization show that what is important for decentralization to be an equilibrium strategy is not how substitutable the manufacturers' products are in demand, but rather the nature of the coupling between demand dependence and strategic dependence" (Moorthy, 1988, p. 337).

Ultimately, all theoretical models should be subjected to empirical verification (McGuire & Staelin 1983). Most propositions of channel structure determination based on the TCA framework have been tested empirically (Erramilli & Rao, 1993; Klein, Frazier, & Roth, 1990). However, empirical tests of predictions from game theoretic studies have been typically neglected by marketing scholars.

Exceptions are the empirical studies by Anderson and Coughlan (1987) and by Slade (1992). Anderson and Coughlan (1987) empirically investigate antecedents of channel integration relying mainly on the predictions of the TCA framework (Williamson, 1985). Among the hypotheses are the effect of product differentiation on channel integration which is based on analytic results of McGuire and Staelin (1983) and Coughlan (1985). Product differentiation is operationalized such that general purpose industrial products are assumed to be less differentiated than special purpose industrial products. Their finding supports the proposition that highly differentiated products are more likely to be sold through integrated channels. Slade (1992) investigates strategic motives of decentralization in the Canadian retail gasoline market empirically. She shows that product substitutability, measured by the cross price elasticity of gasoline products, is related to the use of independent gas stations, that is, decentralized channels, empirically supporting the prediction of game theoretic studies.

Hypotheses 1, 2, and 3 below present the relationships among product substitutability, competitive intensity, and reliance on decentralized channels as proposed in game theoretic studies. As noted, the logic behind Hypothesis 1 is that use of decentralized channel mitigates the competitive intensity. Thus, companies facing high competitive intensity have incentive to rely on decentralized channels. Among the three hypotheses, Hypothesis 3 has been empirically tested by Anderson and Coughlan (1987) and Slade (1992).

Hypothesis 1.   The competitive intensity is lower for SBUs relying on decentralized channels than those relying on integrated channels.

Hypothesis 2.   The more substitutable a SBU's product is to its competitor's product, the higher is the competitive intensity.

Hypothesis 3.   The more substitutable a SBU's product is to its competitor's product, the higher is the reliance on decentralized channels.

B. Market Predictability, Number of Firms and Competitive Intensity

Studies by McGuire and Staelin (1983) and Moorthy (1988) are both based on the Nash equilibrium with zero conjectural variations. Amit, Domowitz, and Fershtman (1988) argue that analysis of conjectures adds a new dimension to the rigorous study of competitors and provides further substantiation for selection of a viable business strategy. Montgomery and Weinberg (1979) also note that knowledge on a competitor's intentions can be a primary determinant of any strategy.

Conjectures concerning competitors' behavior can affect the evaluations of reaction functions, and consequently the competitive intensity. Managers may have good intuition concerning their own reaction to competitors' actions. But, the estimation of rivals' conjectures may be too difficult to assess. Amit, Domowitz, and Fershtman (1988) suggest that two kinds of information are needed to assess competitors' reactions. The first is information on the structural characteristics of the market, rival's technical ability, and its desire to respond. The second is information on rivals' conjectures about the firm's behavior. Furthermore, Coughlan and Wernerfelt (1989) and Fershtman, Judd, and Kalai (1991) suggest that the benefit of using indirect channels in competitive markets is based on the assumption that intrachannel agreements are observable to competitors and channel members can offer credible guarantees that unobservable agreements do not exist. Thus, market predictability could be an important factor if channel decentralization is to be beneficial in this respect, too.

In this study, we use the concept of market predictability as that of short term reactions to competitive marketing activities. A manufacturer as a member of a marketing channel reacts to actions of channel intermediaries, as well as to those of competitors and customers. The market predictability in this context reflects the availability of information on the conjectures concerning behavior of competitors, channel intermediaries, and customers. If such information is available, a firm is in a position to react more easily and more immediately to the moves of its competitors. Hypothesis 4 describes this prediction.

Hypothesis 4. The more predictable a firm's product market is, the higher is the competitive intensity.

When the number of firms in a certain product category is small, it may be feasible for a firm to analyze the conjectures of other competing firms with respect to its own marketing behavior. In this case, each of the competing firms is likely to have influence over the total market price and share. Ramaswamy, Gatignon, and Reibstein (1994) argue and empirically confirm that, in such a situation, firms are not likely to be engaged in price wars which will dissipate high margins. Also, they are likely to be cooperative to their competitors' reduction of the marketing expenditure. However, the firms would retaliate to any increased spending in marketing activities. Thus, number of firms in a certain product category is likely to be related inversely to the competitive intensity which is a firm's reactive tendency to its comeptitors' advertising. Hypothesis 5 summarizes this prediction.

Hypothesis 5. The smaller the number of competing firms in a product market is, the higher is the competitive intensity.

C.   Replication Hypotheses from TCA Literature

Obviously, competitive intensity is not the only determinant of channel structures. Many channel studies identified and empirically tested key determinants of
channel structures mainly based on the transaction cost analysis framework (Williamson, 1975, 1985). The TCA framework predicts the situations when the in-
house transaction is better than the market transaction in terms of transaction
costs.

Williamson's approach is readily applicable to explain why vertically integrated
or decentralized channels are preferred in certain situations. Channel members are
assumed to be subject to bounded rationality. Also, some actors are assumed to be
opportunistic if they are given a chance. An imperfect or asymmetric information
situation may give such an exploitable advantage for opportunistic actors in dealing with other channel members.

Asset specificity is the extent to which nonredeployable physical and human
investments are specialized and unique to a task. For example, the distribution of
a certain product may necessitate unique physical facilities or professional handling know-how and skills. The level of specialized assets required to support the
exchange is identified as one of the principal factors that make market mediated
exchange (decentralized channel) inefficient and cause a market failure (John &
Weitz, 1988). When a market fails, firms face the situation in which intermediaries
are fewer and not readily available. The market safeguard against opportunism is
no longer effective. Under such conditions, firms are unlikely to use decentralized
channels. This prediction has been confirmed in empirical studies on entry mode
choice in foreign markets (John & Weitz, 1988; Klein, Frazier, & Roth, 1990), on
service firms' international entry-mode choice (Erramilli & Rao, 1993) and on
integration of the salesforce (Anderson 1985; Anderson & Schmittlein, 1984). The
following hypothesis summarizes the finding:

Hypothesis 6.   The greater the specificity of assets is, the lower is the reliance
on decentralized channels.

Market uncertainty is also a necessary factor for a vertical market failure,
according to the TCA framework. High uncertainty, that is high heterogeneity in
the market, given bounded rationality, renders writing and enforcing contracts
with external channel intermediaries quite difficult. That is, the opportunistic
behavior from mutual contracts, the cost for monitoring performance, and the cost
from switching to a new relationship with other intermediaries become less prominent in a homogeneous market than in a heterogeneous market. Thus, in a homogeneous market, firms are more likely to prefer decentralized channels. There
appeared a few empirical studies that supported the predicted effect of a homogeneous market on the channel decision (Anderson, 1985; Klein et al., 1990).

Hypothesis 7. The more homogeneous is the market, the higher is the reliance on decentralized channels.

The prediction of Hypothesis 3 is also suggested by the TCA framework. Typically, high product substitutability reduces the need for transaction specific assets. Thus, as predicted by Hypothesis 6, the reduced need for transaction specific assets is likely to make decentralized channels more cost effective.

III.   MEASUREMENT AND DATA COLLECTION

A.   Competitive Intensity

The most important dependent variable in this study is competitive intensity. Competitive intensity is a construct that play a crucial role in the research focusing on the impact of competition on marketing decisions (Weitz, 1985, p. 229) and formulation of business strategies (Porter, 1979, 1980).

Competitive intensity is defined here as the intensity of exchange in competitive moves between firms in a market. The competitive intensity can be operationalized as the magnitude of strategic complementarity with respect to marketing variables (Moorthy, 1988). The strategic complementarity can be measured by estimating the firms' reaction functions with respect to some marketing variables. In a duopoly market, the competitive intensity (CI) is:

$$\tag{1}$$

where p_j is firm j's marketing variable and $R_i(p_j)$ is firm i's reaction function with respect to p_j. Reaction functions depict what a firm would do if it were to learn of a change in its opponent's actions (Tirole, 1988, p. 208).

To investigate the competitive reactions, systems of equation models have been estimated (Lambin, 1976; Wildt, 1974). Some authors have employed the competitive interactions of advertising and other marketing activities in their estimation models (Gatignon, 1984; Gatignon, Anderson, & Helsen, 1989; Hanssens, 1980; Leeflang & Wittink, 1992). Our measurement process of competitive intensity is in the same spirit of these past studies.

Unlike other studies which investigate the cross price elasticities or perceived competitiveness of managers, the competitive intensity is derived from actual advertising reactions among competing firms in our study. In Korean consumer markets, firms are hardly involved in intensive price competition. They typically use advertising, salesforce activities, and trade promotion as their main competitive means.

Our measurement of competitive intensity proceeds as follows: First, we standardize the competitive advertising expenditures to account for the relative market share effects of competing brands. The standardization also correct the heteroskedasticity in the data (see Pindyck & Rubinfeld, 1981, pp. 140-146).

Second, we eliminate the effects of seasonalities and trends by OLS estimations of the regression equations in (2). The residuals represent the prewhitened series of the advertising expenditures.

$$(2)$$

where

SA_{it} = standardized advertising expenditures of firm i at time t,
X_{jt} = monthly dummy variable; 1 if $t = jth$ month, and otherwise 0,
T_t = linear trend variable,
γ_{i0}, γ_{ij}, and β_i = regression coefficients,
a_{it} = error term of regression.

Third, competitive reaction equations as shown in (3) are estimated using the seasonality and trend free series of advertising data. The seemingly unrelated regression (SUR) model (see Johnston, 1984, pp. 337-341) is adopted for the estimation of reaction equations of SBUs in the same product categories.

$$a_{it} = \delta_i + \sum_{k=1, k \neq i}^{N} \mu_{ki} a_{kt} + \phi_{it}, \text{ for } i = 1, \ldots, N \tag{3}$$

where

a_{it} = prewhitened competitive advertising expenditures of firm i at time t,
δ_i = advertising scale for firm i,
μ_{ki} = pseudo reaction elasticity of firm i to firm k,
ϕ_{it} = disturbance term,
N = number of leading competitive firms in a certain product category.

Fourth, competitive intensity of a SBU i is calculated by the following weighted average formula.

$$(4)$$

where
  $\Gamma(i)$ = competitive intensity of SBU i in a certain product category,
  $m(k)$ = average market share of SBU k over analyzed time periods in a certain
          product category.

The competitive intensity measure of advertising in equation (4) represents the weighted average of the pseudo reaction elasticities by average market shares of competing firms.

B.   Data Collection

The primary unit of analysis for this study is a strategic business unit (SBU) which makes all the important brand decisions. We rely on two sets of data. One is the real world advertising expenditure data collected from Cheil Communications' advertising data base.[1] We randomly sampled product categories among those for which advertising expenditures were spent almost incessantly during a three year span from January 1989 to December 1991. The other was a mail survey data collected from product managers of the sampled SBUs. Questionnaires were mailed and responded during the period from September 1994 to November 1994.

To minimize problems that could accrue from the timing gap that exists between the two sets of data, we checked whether the market environment of each of the sampled product categories was changed significantly in terms of market share, number of competitors, and main characteristics of competing groups, by including related questions in the survey questionnaire and by interviewing the responsible manager. All but one product category was found to be stable enough. In the exceptional product category, an important new entrant entered the market during the gap period. For this category, we included additional advertising data covering from January 1992 to July 1994.

Twenty-one product (7 durables and 14 nondurables) categories were selected. In total, 71 leading SBUs were chosen on the basis of advertising and market share. After verifying the addresses, identifying the product managers of the SBUs, and calling to draw attention to our mail survey, we sent out the mail questionnaires. Among the 71 sampled SBUs, complete and usable responses were received from 42 SBUs, showing a 59 percent response rate. Table 1 shows the product categories, number of sampled firms, and number of responding firms in each category. There is no significant difference in the response rates between durable and nondurable product categories.

Table 2 summarizes the average competitive intensity estimated from the real world advertising data. In the table, we see that competitive intensity is relatively high in the categories of sports drink, casual shoes, refrigerator, uwhang-chung-simwhan (a medicine originating from China), facsimile, and beer. Categories showing relatively cooperative advertising interactions are those of instant coffee and laundry detergent.

Table 1.   Description of Product Categories

Product Category	Number of Leading SBUs (Advertising Share)		Number of Completely Responding SBUs
Durables (7 products, 24 SBUs, 16 completely responding SBUs)			
Gas ranges	5	(100%)	4
Electronic ranges	3	(100%)	2
Refrigerators	3	(99%)	2
VCR	3	(99%)	2
TVs	4	(99%)	2
Fax Machines	4	(64%)	3
Digital pianos	2	(85%)	1
Nondurables (14 products, 47 SBUs, 26 completely responding SBUs)			
Business suits	5	(65%)	3
Casual shoes	2	(80%)	2
Men's shoes	2	(95%)	2
Cosmetics	5	(76%)	1
Digestive (liquid)	4	(95%)	3
Digestive (pill)	4	(91%)	1
Uwhang-chungsimwhan*	4	(81%)	2
Chocolate	4	(97%)	2
Crackers	4	(98%)	2
Instant coffee	2	(99%)	2
Beer	2	(100%)	1
Salad oil	2	(71%)	2
Laundry detergent	5	(95%)	2
Sports drinks	2	(90%)	1
Total (21 products)	71		42

Note: *Uwhang-chungsimwhan is a Chinese medicine.

Table 3 shows an example of competitive intensity estimates for a product category. For each firm, the left part of the table shows the pseudo reaction elasticities toward its competitors' advertising. In the refrigerator market, there are three leading companies. According to the table, firm A is very reactive to firm C's advertising, while firm B and firm C are very sensitive to the advertising of firm A. Firm B is showing a cooperative gesture to firm C in terms of advertising behavior. In the right part of the table, there are estimates of competitive intensity of the firms. We weight the pseudo reaction elasticities by competitors' market shares to get the estimates of the competitive intensity for each firm. It turned out that firm A and firm B are highly sensitive to its competitors' advertising, showing high competitive intensity scores . Relatively, firm B is less sensitive to others' advertising.

Table 2.   Average Competitive Intensity of Product Categories

Product Category	Number of Leading SBUs	Competitive Intensity	Average per Group
Durables (7 products, 24 SBUs)			
Gas ranges	5	0.0150	
Electronic ranges	3	0.0325	
Refrigerators	3	0.5596	
VCR	3	−0.0240	
TVs	4	0.1160	
Fax Machines	4	0.2954	
Digital pianos	2	−0.0540	0.1343
Nondurables (14 products, 47 SBUs)			
Business suits	5	0.2305	
Casual shoes	2	0.6976	
Men's shoes	2	0.3098	
Cosmetics	5	0.1014	
Digestive (liquid)	4	0.3896	
Digestive (pill)	4	0.2121	
Uwhang-chungsimwhan*	4	0.5162	
Chocolate	4	0.2566	
Crackers	4	0.0222	
Instant coffee	2	−0.4402	
Beer	2	0.4624	
Salad oil	2	0.1467	
Laundry detergent	5	−0.1283	
Sports drinks	2	0.6251	0.2430

Note: *Uwhang-chungsimwhan is a Chinese medicine.

C.   Measurement of Reliance on Decentralized Channels

Another dependent variable we use is the reliance on decentralized channels. The data was collected from the mail survey. Because no SBUs are distributing through a single type of channel, we use a dichotomous variable to represent the reliance on decentralized channels, assigning 1 if SBUs rely mostly on decentralized channels, and 0 otherwise, following the operationalization of Hahn, Shin, and Kim (1995).

D.   Independent Variables and Covariates

Four independent variables have been measured in the mail survey using multiple items as shown in Table 4. Substitutability refers to the degree to which cus-

Table 3.   SUR Results, Market Share and
Competitive Intensity for the Refrigerator Industry

	Firm A	Firm B	Firm C	Market Share	Competitive Intensity
Firm A	0	0.2818	0.8452	45.3%	0.7279
		(0.0936)	(0.1085)		
Firm B	0.87472	0	−0.4679	11.3%	0.2209
	(0.2906)		(0.2913)		
Firm C	0.9546	−0.1703	0	43.0%	0.7300
	(0.1226)	(0.1060)			
System Weighted R-square: 0.7895					

Note: *The number in the parentheses stands for the standard error.

tomers perceive a firm's product to be substitutable (undifferentiated) for the competing products (Anderson & Coughlan, 1987; Coughlan, 1985). Asset specificity is the degree to which durable, transaction-specific assets are needed to market products. The items for this construct were selected, in part, from those used by Klein, Frazier, and Roth (1990). Homogeneity means that of customers and channel strategies of competing firms. Market predictability refers to the predictability of reactions to marketing activities by competitors, customers, and channel intermediaries. The responses for each construct were summed and averaged to obtain an overall score. In general, the multi-items show adequate levels of reliability as shown in Table 4 (Nunnally, 1978).

Another independent variable is number of competitors, that is, the number of competitors perceived to be significant rivals in the market. A single question was included in the questionnaire to measure this variable.

We also have three additional covariates. One is the relative importance of advertising for an SBU as a means to secure competitive advantage. Another is a dummy variable showing whether a product is a durable or not. The third is the relative importance of marketing channels among marketing variables. These covariates are used to eliminate the firm or product specific effects not related to our independent variables.[2]

IV.   ANALYSIS AND RESULTS

Our hypotheses are tested using three stage least square (3SLS) estimation of the following model.[3]

$$DC = \lambda_{10} + \lambda_{11} SB + \lambda_{12} AS + \lambda_{13} HM + \lambda_{14} DD + \lambda_{15} RC + \varepsilon_1 \tag{5}$$

$$CI = \lambda_{20} + \lambda_{21} SB + \lambda_{22} MP + \lambda_{23} DC + \lambda_{24} NC + \lambda_{25} RA + \varepsilon_2 \tag{6}$$

Table 4. Multi-Item Scale[a]

Substitutability[b] (Coefficient α=0.70)

1. Brand loyalty to our products is high relative to competitors.
2. Customer satisfaction with our products is high relative to competitors.
3. We receive a higher price from retailers relative to competitors.
4. In dealing with our retailers, we take the initiative relative to competitors.
5. We deal more with our retailers on credit relative to competitors.

Asset Specificity (Coefficient α=0.79)

1. A large investment in equipment and facilities is needed to market our products.
2. Specialized facilities are needed to market our product.

Homogeneity (Coefficient α=0.70)

1. We have a similar channel structure to our competitors.
2. We have homogeneous customers.
3. We manage our distributional channel similarly to our competitors.

Market Predictability (Coefficient α=0.55)

1. It is easy to predict competitors' reaction to our marketing efforts.
2. It is easy to predict customers' reaction to our marketing efforts.
3. It is important for us and retailers to follow existing rules and procedures in dealings.

Note: [a]All items use 5-point Likert scales.
[b]The items for the measure of substitutability are reverse-coded.

where the λ parameters are used to test the hypotheses and ε's represent random error terms. The variables in the equations, (5) and (6), are.

DC = reliance on decentralized channels,
CI = competitive intensity,
SB = substitutability,
AS = asset specificity,
HM = homogeneity,
DD = durables (dummy variable),
RC = relative importance of distributional channel,
MP = market predictability,
NC = number of leading competitors,
RA = relative importance of advertising.

Although we have covered most of important SBUs in a wide range of consumer product categories, we do not have a large enough sample size to apply more robust estimation techniques such as logistic regression, which has some advantage in handling binary type data (e.g., Anderson, 1985). Also, we note that the estimation could be biased due to differences in the number of observations in different product categories. To check the robustness of our results, we run the regression models using not only SBU level data, but also product category level pooled data.

Table 5 shows the estimation results when SBU level data are used. Most of the estimated coefficients are consistent with the hypothesized direction. Reliance on decentralized channels is significantly and negatively related to the competitive intensity supporting Hypothesis 1. The result is consistent with the suggestion of McGuire and Staelin (1983). It is also partly consistent with the prediction by Moorthy (1988) in that products in the same product categories are demand substitutes. To our knowledge, this empirical result is the first to empirically support the theoretical argument of retailers' buffering role in competitive situations.

The estimate of market predictability is also significantly related to the competitive intensity supporting Hypothesis 4. This result may be a hint that positive conjectures are actually functioning in the consumer product market.

Furthermore, product substitutability, asset specificity, and homogeneity are significantly related to the reliance on decentralized channels supporting Hypoth-

Table 5. Estimation Results (SBU data)

	Dependent Variables (N=42)	
Independent Variables	Reliance on Decentralized Channels	Competitive Intensity
Intercept	0.6670**[b]	−0.3263
Substitutability	0.0991*	0.0031
Asset Specificity	−0.0928*	
Homogeneity	0.1267*	
Durables (dummy)	0.4239***	
Relative Importance of Distribution Channel[a]	−0.1024***	
Market predictability		0.1707**
Reliance on Decentralized Channels		−0.2370**
Number of Leading Competitors		−0.0040
Relative Importance of Advertising[a]		0.0438
F-value	58.054***	20.972***
R-square	0.8897	0.7444
Adjusted R-square	0.8743	0.7089
System Weighted R-square		0.3819

Note: [a]The relative importance variables are ordinally scaled. A lower score indicates higher importance.
[b]***, **, and * stand for statistical significance at 1%, 5%, 10% (one-tail).

esis 3, Hypothesis 6, and Hypothesis 7. Thus, we have been successful in replicating the important findings from other TCA based channel studies, even though we used Korean data sets. Also, this may be a stronger finding because we have explicitly considered the effect of competitive intensity in addition to these determinants of channel structures simultaneously.

Our result further indicates that SBUs dealing with durables rely more on decentralized channels than on integrated channels. Also, interestingly, relative importance of marketing channels is significantly related to the reliance on decentralized channels. There may be two rival interpretations for this finding. One is that, on the average, it is true that SBUs rely more on indirect channels when they feel channel decisions are very important. We see that some large scale firms do integrate channels when they feel the channel decisions are important. However, the number of such firms may not be large. Another interpretation is that when SBUs feel channel decisions are important, they actually rely more on integrated channels. But, once they rely on integrated channels, the importance of channel decisions is reduced substantially. At present, we do not have sufficient information to know which of these interpretations makes better sense.

Unfortunately, Hypothesis 2 and Hypothesis 4 are not supported significantly. While substitutability is significantly related to channel structures, it is not related to competitive intensity. One reason for the failure may be due to the incompleteness of our comeptitive intensity measure. We have considered an important competitive activity in advertising in measuring the competitive intensity. Obviously it is not the only important competitive activity for a firm. Also, a certain firm may have its unique rivals. We have simply weighted the reactions by market shares. This measure does not incorporate the unique rivalries bctween specific competitors.

The expected relation between number of leading competitors and competitive intensity was not supported either. A conjecture is that there is an inverted U-shaped relationship between the two concepts. If the conjecture is true, there will exist a certain number when the competitive intensity is the highest. However, we need further studies to check this new hyphotheses.

The estimated model on competitive intensity shows relatively low r^2 and lower overall fitness than those on channel structure. It suggests that there may be other SBU-specific factors that contribute significantly to competitive intensity.

To check the robustness of the results, we re-estimated the same model with pooled data at product category levels. The result is presented in Table 6.

In general, the results are consistent to those analyzed with SBU level data. The hypotheses supported in SBU level are still supported except for Hypothesis 5. The small sample size (21 in this analysis) may have contributed to the lack of statistical significance. Also, aggregation of the market predictability over firms in the same product categories may have averaged out the firm-specific factors related to the market predictability. Hypothesis 1 is firmly supported in this analysis, too. The prediction of McGuire and Staelin (1983) that indirect channels can mitigate competitive intensity appears to be robust.

Table 6.   Estimation Results (pooled data)

Independent Variables	Dependent Variables (N=21)	
	Reliance on Decentralized Channels	Competitive Intensity
Intercept	0.8056*[b]	0.0292
Substitutability	0.1956*	0.0552
Asset Specificity	−0.2579**	
Homogeneity	0.2677**	
Durables (dummy)	0.3918**	
Relative Importance of Distribution Channel[a]	−0.1545***	
Market predictability		0.0854
Reliance on Decentralized Channels		−0.3835**
Number of Leading Competitors		−0.0033
Relative Importance of Advertising[a]		0.0492
F-value	55.910***	20.173***
R-square	0.9491	0.8705
Adjusted R-square	0.9321	0.8274
System Weighted R-square	0.5869	

Note: [a]The relative importance variables are ordinally scaled. A lower score indicates higher importance.
[b]***, **, and * stand for statistical significance at 1%, 5%, 10% (one-tail).

Compared to the SBU level analysis, product level analysis shows lower overall fit scores for the model of competitive intensity and higher fit scores for the model of reliance on decentralized channels. This implies that there may be the propensity for firms to sustain similar channel structures to others in the same product category. Thus, the relationship between competitive intensity and channel decentralization becomes more evident when analyzed at the product category level. On the other hand, the competitive intensity may be better explained by firm-specific factors.

V.   SUMMARY AND CONCLUDING REMARKS

In this study, we have investigated whether competitive intensity and channel decentralization show the relationship suggested in game theoretic literature. Several remarks can be made in testing and confirming the relationship. First, our competitive intensity measure was derived from real world advertising competition data on Korean firms. Furthermore, the competitive intensity captures how reactive a firm is to its competitors' moves. Thus, it incorporates the concept of rivalry suggested to be important by Weitz (1985) and Porter (1980).

Second, we studied the relationship between competitive intensity and channel decentralization, and the effects of determinants of these two variables in a unified framework. In the same model, predictors of channel decentralization suggested by game theoretical literature and those suggested by the TCA literature are tested simultaneously. Typically, findings from game theoretic studies have not been subject to rigorous empirical tests. Although game theoretic analysis is often based on too strong assumptions to be realistic (Chen et al., 1992; Kreps, 1990), we believe that empirical tests of the propostions should be encouraged if the findings are to be applied in reality. Our study is believed to be the first rigorous test of the main proposition suggested by McGuire and Staelin (1983), Moorthy (1988), and Shin, Park, and Hahn (1993).

Third, we have tested the hypotheses based on two different levels of analysis, that is, at the SBU level and at product category level. Such analysis enhances the robustness of the confirmed hypotheses. As noted, it may be that competitive intensity is affected significantly by firm specific factors, whereas channel structures could be affected significantly by product category specific factors.

Fourth, while most channel competition studies focused on price competition, we have focused on advertising competition. While it is only one of important competitive variables for competing firms, it is a much more important variable for Korean firms of consumer products than is price. The test result strongly supports that decentralized channels mitigate the competitive intensity in the market.

We also show that market predictability is positively related to competitive intensity. Thus, when rival firms are familiar with one another in terms of their strategies and competitive styles, they are likely to show higher competitive intensity. It has face validity in that most well-known Korean rival firms, such as LG electronics, Samsung electronics, and Daewoo electronics, are those who know one another extremely well.

Furthermore, predicted effects of asset specificity, product substitutability, and homogeneity on channel decentralization have been all confirmed, replicating other TCA based channel studies. Thus, our study enhances the validity of the predictions. In addition, the results enhance the validity of our study, too.

Clearly, our study has some limitations. First, competitive rivalry is measured using only the advertising competition data. In reality, there is the possibility that levels of one marketing instrument affect or are affected by levels of other marketing mix variables within the same firm, as argued by Hanssens (1980). Also, a firm's aggressive competitive advertising may be responded to a price cut by its competitor. Ramaswamy et al. (1994) suggest a research direction that can permit the joint marketing behavioral patterns. Clearly, it will be important to include more than one marketing variable in deriving competitive intensity in the future. Second, the sample size is relatively small in our study. Especially, the size is not large enough to perform a reliable analysis at the product class level. Although important product categories and most key firms are included in the sample, it will be desirable to increase the sample size, if possible. Also, a longitudinal data base is desirable to permit a dynamic analysis of competitive rivalries. In our static analysis, it was difficult to show causal directions between competitive intensity and the use of decentralized channels. Further studies which incorporate dynamic data are needed if the causality is to be analyzed clearly.

NOTES

1.   Cheil Communications is one of leading advertising agencies in Korea. It has been building a data base for advertising that encompasses monthly advertising expenditures in the four media of TV, radio, newspaper, and magazine. The expenditures in these four media accounted for 77.1 percent and 79.1 percent of total advertising market in 1992 and 1993, respectively (Cheil Communications, 1994).

2.   The correlations among the independent and control variables range from -0.34 to 0.38, indicating no serious problem of multicollinearity.

3.   The two dependent variables are correlated with the disturbances so that the ordinary least square (OLS) estimates of each regression could be biased and inconsistent. 3SLS involves the application of generalized least-square estimation to the system of equations, each of which has first been estimated using two stage least square (2SLS) estimation. The 3SLS procedure can be shown to yield more efficient parameter estimates than 2SLS because it takes into account the cross-equation correlation (Pindyck & Rubinfeld, 1981, p. 335).

REFERENCES

Amit, R., Domowitz, I., and Fershtman, C. (1988). Thinking one step ahead: The use of conjectures in competitor analysis. *Strategic Management Journal*, 9, 431-442.

Anderson, E. (1985). The salesperson as outside agent or employee: A transaction cost analysis. *Marketing Science*, 4, 234-254.

Anderson, E., & Coughlan, A. (1987). International market entry and expansion via independent or integrated channels of distribution, *Journal of Marketing*, 51, 71-82.

Anderson, E., & Schmittlein, D.C. (1984). Integration of the sales force: An empirical examination, *Rand Journal of Economics*, 15, 3, 385-395.

Cheil Communications. (1994). *The advertising yearbook '94*. Seoul: Cheil Communications Press.

Chen, M., Smith, K.G., & Grimm, C.M. (1992). Action characteristics as predictors of competitive responses. *Management Science*, 38, 3, 439-455.

Coughlan, A. (1985). Competition and cooperation in marketing channel choice: Theory and application. *Marketing Science*, 4, 110-129.

Coughlan, A., and Wernerfelt, B. (1989). On credible delegation by oligopolists: A discussion of distribution channel management. *Management Science*, 35, 2, 226-239.

Erramilli, M.K., & Rao, C.P. (1993). Service firms' international entry mode choice: A modified transaction-cost analysis approach. *Journal of Marketing*, 57, 19-38.

Fershtman, C., Judd, K., & Kalai, E. (1991). Observable contracts: Strategic delegation and cooperation. *International Economic Review*, 32, 3, 551-559.

Gatignon, H. (1984). Competition as a moderator of the effect of advertising on sales. *Journal of Marketing Research*, 21, 387-398.

Gatignon, H., Anderson, E., and Helsen, K. (1989). Competitive reactions to market entry: Explaining interfirm differences. *Journal of Marketing Research*, 26, 44-55.

Hahn, M., Shin, C., & Kim C.R. (1995). Channel selection control, and satisfaction of manufactures in Korean pharmaceutical market. *Journal of Marketing Channels*, forthcoming.

Hanssens, D.M. (1980). Market response, competitive behavior, and time series analysis. *Journal of Marketing Research*, 17, 470-485.

John, G., & Weitz B. (1988). Forward integration into distribution: Empirical test of transaction cost analysis. *Journal of Law, Economics, and Organization*, 4, 121-139.

Johnston, J. (1984). *Econometric methods*, 3rd ed. New York: McGraw-Hill Book Co.

Klein, S., Frazier, G.L., & Roth, V.J. (1990). A transaction cost analysis model of channel integration in international markets. *Journal of Marketing Research*, 27, 196-208.

Kreps, D.M. (1990). *Game Theory and Economic Modelling*. Oxford, England : Oxford University Press.

Lambin, J.J. (1976). *Advertising, competition and market conduct in oligopoly over time*. Amsterdam: North-Holland Publishing Co..

Leeflang, P.S.H., and Wittink, D.R. (1992). Diagnosing competitive reactions using (aggregated) scanner data. *International Journal of Research in Marketing*, 9, 39-57.

McGuire, T., & Staelin, R. (1983). An industry equilibrium analysis of downstream vertical integration. *Marketing Science*, 2, 161-192.

Montgomery, D.B., & Weinberg, C. (1979). Towards strategic intelligence systems. *Journal of Marketing*, 43, 31-52.

Moothry, S. (1988). Strategic decentralization in channels. *Marketing Science*, 7, 335-355.

Nunnally, J.C. (1978). *Psychometric theory*, 2nd ed. New York: McGraw-Hill Book Co.

Pindyck, R.S., and Rubinfeld, D.L. (1981). Econometric models and economic forecasts, 2nd ed. New York: McGraw-Hill Book Co.

Porter, M.E. (1979). How competitive forces shape strategy. *Harvard Business Review*, 137-145.

Porter, M.E. (1980). *Competitive strategy: Techniques for analyzing industries and competition*. New York: The Free Press.

Ramaswamy, V., Gatignon, H., & Reibstein, D.J. (1994). Competitive marketing behavior in industrial markets. *Journal of Marketing*, 58, 45-55.

Shin, C., Park, S., and Hahn, M. (1993). Price and communication competition in marketing channels. *Working Paper*, KAIST.

Slade, M. (1992). Strategic motives for vertical separation: An empirical exploration. University of British Columbia mimeo.

Tirole, J. (1988). *The theory of industrial organization*. Cambridge, MA: The MIT Press.

Weitz, B.A. (1985). Introduction to special issue on competition in marketing. *Journal of Marketing Research*, 22, 229-236.

Wildt, A. (1974). Multifirm analysis of competitive decision variables. *Journal of Marketing Research*, 11, 50-62.

Williamson, O.E. (1975). Markets and Hierarchies: Analysis and Antitrust Implications. New York: The Free Press.

Williamson, O.E. (1985), *The Economic Institute of Capitalism*. New York: The Free Press.

INTERNATIONAL MARKETING AND THE ROLE OF LOGISTICS:

LOGISTICS STRATEGIES AND THE IMPLICATIONS FOR MANAGEMENT AND GOVERNMENT

John C. Taylor

ABSTRACT

International logistics can play an important role in the firm's marketing strategy. New postponement based strategies in which inventories are centralized and distributed around the world with fast and reliable transportation can improve service and lower costs. However, such strategies require government policies and institutional innovations which facilitate fast and reliable transportation at low cost.

I. INTRODUCTION

International logistics and transportation have played a critical role in the growth of world trade and the integration of manufacturing on a global scale. In fact, the

Advances in International Marketing, Volume 7, pages 83-98.

level of world trade depends to a significant degree on the availability of economical and reliable international logistics services. Decreases in transportation cost and increases in performance reliability can expand the competitive trade area of a given manufacturing region and heighten the associated level of international trade and global competition (Dunning, 1988). Companies such as Federal Express and United Parcel Service, with their door to door international small package delivery services, point out the degree to which innovative transportation services can in effect create their own level of demand.

At the same time, international logistics capabilities can be critical to the individual firm's marketing program and competitive position in the marketplace (Anderson, 1985). One of the fundamental functions of marketing is to create time and place utility by overcoming time and space separations and quantity and assortment discrepancies between heterogeneous producers and consumers (Alderson, 1957). In a global marketplace the challenges and opportunities of overcoming these separations and discrepancies are great. Strong logistics capabilities can be used as an offensive weapon to help the firm gain competitive advantage in the marketplace by improving customer service and consumer choice, and by lowering the costs of both global components sourcing and finished goods distribution (Shapiro, 1984). These capabilities become increasingly important as the level of global integration increases, and as competitors move to supplement low cost manufacturing strategies in distant markets with effective logistics management strategies. However, what theoretical approaches and strategies should firms use in international distribution, and what are the government policy, logistics management and carrier services implications of those strategies?

This paper first examines why international logistics capabilities are critical to the firm, and discusses some of the complexities in international logistics not found in domestic operations. The paper then examines the two fundamental theoretical approaches to international logistics operations, speculation vs. postponement based systems, and the advantages of postponement based logistics. Finally, the public policy, logistics management, and carrier management implications of postponement based logistics are discussed.

II.   INTERNATIONAL LOGISTICS IMPORTANCE

International logistics capabilities have become increasingly important to the firm in recent years. This is in part due to the increasing level of world trade and the participation of firms in that trade, and the fact that international movements involve greater distances and more transportation cost than is the case in domestic operations. However, a number of other factors, such as varying levels of transportation infrastructure, customs barriers, and unfamiliar modes of transportation add to the complexity.

A. World Trade Levels and Manufacturing Strategy

While the world's total output of goods grew by 3.5 percent in 1994, trade in merchandise (excluding services) grew by 9 percent to a total of $4.06 trillion (Bahree 1995). World trade in merchandise totaled $3.7 trillion in 1992 (United States International Trade Commission, 1994). In North America, merchandise exports grew by 11.2 percent in 1994 while imports grew by 13.9 percent. In Asia, merchandise exports grew by 15 percent in 1994, with a 30 percent increase from China. Imports by Japan increased 14 percent in 1994, while South Korean imports were up by more than 20 percent.

The United States continued as the world's leading exporter of merchandise in 1994, followed by Germany and Japan. United States merchandise exports totaled $461.5 billion in 1993, while imports totaled $592.1 billion (U.S. Department of Commerce, 1994). Combined U.S. merchandise exports and imports now represent 16.5 percent of GNP, up from 14.0 percent in 1985, and just 8.5 percent in 1970. The United States also regained its position as the leading destination for foreign direct investment in 1994, while the United States continued as the world's largest foreign direct investor overseas, placing $56 billion dollars in foreign markets (Bleakley, 1995).

Together, the trade and foreign direct investment figures reveal the degree to which U.S. and foreign companies have increased their involvement in export marketing, foreign component sourcing and integrated international production activities. Exports and imports are growing at a much faster pace than total economic output, both globally and in the United States, and according to Richard Blackhurst of the World Trade Organization (WTO), this "is the handiest practical measure of the pace of globalization in manufacturing" (Bahree, 1995). The increasing levels of foreign direct investment also are indicative of the degree of product specialization and integrated production worldwide. In integrated global production systems, components are often sourced from the country with the greatest competitive advantage, assembled at dedicated plants in the country with the greatest assembly advantages, and marketed globally.

The impact of specialized production, global sourcing and worldwide marketing of standardized products on logistics and transportation systems can be illustrated by the North American automobile market (Fawcett, Taylor, & Smith, 1995; Taylor & Closs, 1993). Historically, barriers to trade required local production of a restricted range of models in each of the three North American countries. However, as trade restrictions have been liberalized, first in Canada and more recently in Mexico, auto manufacturers have specialized their plants in each country on a smaller number of models and dedicated those plants as the North American-wide source for those models. At the same time auto manufacturers have decreased the level of in-country component sourcing and increased global sourcing of components to improve quality and reduce cost. The end result is increased choice for consumers at lower cost with dramatic increases in the international movements of finished goods and components. This in turn has placed increased demand on logistics and transportation systems.

B.   International Logistics Complexity

Compared to domestic logistics operations in any one country, international logistics is considerably more complex, more costly, and as a result, more important to the overall success of the firm. This is in large part due to the great distances involved in international transportation, and the time required to overcome distance. Space, or distance between producers and buyers increases transportation costs, requires earlier commitments to forecasts and longer lead times, and potentially greater in-transit inventories (Bowersox & Sterling, 1982). Distance may also necessitate in-market inventories in order to achieve necessary customer service levels at acceptable costs.

Another complicating factor in international logistics is that shippers are often unfamiliar with the ocean and even air modes of transportation that are usually required. Nor are most shippers very familiar with containerized shipments and intermodal transportation methods, or the common international intermediaries and transportation specialists that may be required. There are also a number of legal issues, differing liability regimes, and pricing regulations that can effect transportation costs in a way not seen in domestic U.S. markets. For instance, under the Shipping Act of 1984, ocean carriers continue to have the right to form conferences and set prices and allocate freight on individual freight routes (Ferguson, 1994). This lack of familiarity can cause a number of problems and increase costs.

Trade barriers, and especially customs problems, along with the related customs paperwork, also create unique problems in international logistics and usually slow total order cycle times and reduce the reliability of the order cycle (Heaver, 1992). These barriers often result in a need for in-country warehousing in each country where the product is marketed, and can lead to extremely high safety stocks in order to cover replenishment uncertainty (Anderson, 1985). At the same time this need to position inventories in-country often reduces the amount of consumer choice possible because of the high costs of keeping inventory in each country. A lack of product standardization, and/or marketing decisions to market the same product under different brand names, can also lead to product proliferation and increased inventories. These problems have been especially common in Europe where until recently companies have had to warehouse product in each of the EC countries (O'Laughlin, Cooper, & Cabocel, 1993). Payment documentation, such as letters of credit, can also increase complexity, reduce options such as partial shipments of orders, and preclude channel separation options by requiring goods to physically flow to parties taking title in the sales channel (Davies, 1987).

A final complication in international logistics is often the lack of centralized control or visibility of channel flows and logistics costs both within and outside the manufacturing organization. In many multinationals sourcing decisions are unclear and there is often no centralized control over which plants serve which country markets. It is also quite common for international marketing personnel to manage the logistics function, as opposed to logistics specialists whose responsibilities may be limited to the United States (Picard, 1983). Often, manufacturers with separate home country and destination market operating subsidiaries do not coordinate logistics across the entire movement from origin to destination. It is very common for the shipping entity to control and pay for logistics costs to its border, and for the receiving entity to specify carriers and pay costs within its country. This can lead to a lack of coordinated door to door transportation, difficulty in tracing and diverting products en route, the need to deal with a greater number of carriers and freight bills, and suboptimization of the overall logistics flow. These problems are often seen in U.S.-Mexico flows where the U.S. shipper typically controls and pays freight costs to the Mexican border, and the Mexican subsidiary controls and pays all costs on the Mexican side (Fawcett, Taylor & Sheldon, 1995). Such arrangements often result in one carrier handing off to another totally independent carrier even though a through bill of lading and invoice with one set of strategically aligned carriers would be possible. Finally, there often is less cooperation and coordination across the overall channel of distribution, and this often leads to suboptimization of total logistics costs for the overall channel.

III. LOGISTICS STRATEGIES FOR INTERNATIONAL BUSINESS

Given the increasing importance of international logistics, and the challenges and opportunities presented, what are the theoretical options for accomplishing the logistics function while at the same time gaining differential advantage in the marketplace? Depending on the operating environment, companies will select the logistics strategy that maximizes customer service at the lowest possible total cost. The goal among leading edge firms is to position logistical capabilities to provide the greatest contribution possible to their offensive strategy for gaining competitive advantage (Stalk, Evans, & Schulman, 1992).

The traditional logistics strategy involves anticipatory demand management based upon forecasting and inventory speculation (Bucklin, 1965). An increasingly popular alternative strategy uses information and transportation technology to achieve inventory postponement. In effect, a postponement strategy substitutes information and transportation capabilities for forecasts, inventory, and forward positioning of product (Bucklin, 1965; Bowersox, 1982).

The strategy that the firm should chose for a given trade corridor depends in large part on the government policy, infrastructure and logistics services environment on that corridor. These external factors, and the industry and product in question, will in large part determine the nature of trade-offs between inventory related costs and transportation costs, and the level of total logistics costs related to each strategy. Speculative strategies rely on forward positioning of inventory commitments and typically result in higher warehousing and inventory carrying costs, but lower transportation costs. Postponement strategies often result in lower warehousing and inventory costs but higher transportation costs. If the right environment and product characteristics exist, the postponement based strategy has been found to offer the greatest potential for maximizing service while reducing logistics costs. Management must decide which strategy to use at any given time and place.

A.   The Speculation or Anticipatory Strategy

In international logistics, companies have historically relied on speculative strategies because of the lack of support services necessary for effective postponement. A speculative strategy seeks to position inventory in anticipation of customer requirements. In international trade, this means shipment to distant selling or manufacturing locations in advance of when the product or material is needed. Often, inventory must be positioned in warehouses within each destination country market. A speculation strategy relies on a firm's ability to forecast what will be required and where and when it will be needed. Speculation strategies proliferate when there is a lack of accountability for inventory costs and a failure to highlight the fact that total logistics costs are often higher than necessary, even though transportation expenditures are being minimized through large volume shipments on non-premium modes such as ocean and rail.

While the costs and risks of speculation strategies are high in domestic markets, they are even higher in world trade. In international markets, the distances are great and the activities required to move inventory through customs increase cost and increase uncertainty (Kearney, 1990). The nature of transportation demand in such a speculative system is for low cost, time insensitive services from manufacturing plants to warehouses in overseas markets. Traditionally, this strategy has led to minimal cooperation among channel members. As a result, the typical practice has involved an uncoordinated series of transportation movements. Emphasis is on low cost transportation with limited concern for order cycle time and reliability because inventory buffers are available to cushion any uncertainty. While transportation costs are minimized, total logistics costs are often higher than is the case in postponement based systems.

However, despite these shortcomings, a speculative approach may be the only strategy that can provide the necessary customer service levels and product availability at a reasonable cost. The great distances and time required to move many products internationally at reasonable cost may require speculation. Often, there is neither the infrastructure or the carrier institutions necessary to carry out postponement strategies.

B. The Postponement Based Strategy

Within the United States and other developed countries of the world, a revolution in logistics practice has begun. That revolution builds upon the rapidly emerging strategy of "inventory postponement." The objective of a postponement strategy is to maximize competitive advantage while at the same time minimizing the level of logistical expenditure. The strategy works best in marketing situations where there are minimal barriers to transportation and communications. This means that the primary applications to date have been in domestic markets and regional trading blocks where barriers are being reduced. The next natural frontier for such strategies is in intercontinental trade. In the international arena, the potential rewards for elimination of inventory and its related costs are significant.

"Postponers" don't guess or try to forecast demand, they wait for actual orders to be communicated instantaneously and then seek to respond quickly. Using flexible manufacturing systems and premium transportation services, firms can maximize competitive advantage and reduce overall system cost by eliminating inventory and forward warehousing and handling costs. In effect, postponers eliminate guesswork about the nature of demand in far flung markets and substitute real-time communications and high speed, reliable transportation for inventory on the inbound and outbound sides of their business.

There are two general categories of postponement—form and geographic (Bucklin, 1965). With form postponement, manufacturers delay production until an order is in hand, or produce the product to a limited point, awaiting an order to complete the final form of the product. This could mean delaying the final process of packaging until demand by package size is known, or delaying the application of private label brand names until orders are on hand for each private label. In an international setting the final processes related to application of safety warning labels, boxing with instructions and warranty materials, and so on, might be postponed until the orders by country are known. These final form processes could be completed at a central manufacturing facility, or might be completed at regional distribution centers if it is necessary to place inventory in distant foreign markets. Examples of form postponement can be found in the paint business, where the final color is mixed in the store after the customer's choice is known; in Burger Kings where hamburger toppings are not added until the customer order is taken, and in the greeting card business where customers are given the choice of producing their own Hallmark cards in-store.

Geographic postponement calls for centralization of inventories in one or a small number of distribution centers with direct shipping to customers, rather than speculating on which areas of the world to place inventory. While it is costly enough to make an incorrect guess on the amount of inventory to place in various distribution centers within a home market like the United States, it can be extremely expensive to make incorrect judgments about how much inventory to place in each country of the world. In addition to transportation costs, such deployments often result in the payment of duties and customs processing costs in international settings. If forecasts are accurate and products are especially expensive to ship by premium modes, it may be appropriate to geographically speculate. However, the centralization of international inventories, and the use of high speed order communications and premium transportation can often result in lower costs than would be the case if inventories were positioned in foreign distribution centers, while still meeting customer service order cycle time requirements (Quinn, 1987).

How does postponement save money when much higher transportation costs on premium service carriers are often necessary in order to meet customer service requirements? In the case of form postponement the savings come from reducing the number of stock keeping units (SKU's) for which forecasts and safety stocks are required in order to assure availability. By reducing the number of individual stock keeping units demand is consolidated against a smaller number of SKU's, and demand variability is decreased, allowing for smaller inventory safety stocks to achieve a given availability level. Reduced inventories lower the assets employed, improve inventory turnover, and reduce inventory carrying expenses, including the opportunity costs of money tied up in the inventory. Geographic postponement also reduces the amount of safety stock inventory and associated carrying costs that are needed to accomplish a given level of availability by reducing the number of locations at which safety stocks are required. However, geographic postponement also reduces costs by eliminating the fixed costs associated with field warehouses. At the same time, availability levels are higher with a given level of inventory commitment in centralized systems, and the customer can have an infinite choice of options if the product is not produced until the order is placed. The key is to have systems and services in place that provide the marketer with the maximum competitive advantage required, while minimizing the cost increases necessary for premium transportation, and maximizing the inventory and fixed cost savings that are possible.

Many companies utilize postponement strategies that take advantage of both form and geographic postponement. Perhaps the most extreme forms of international postponement involve catalog mail order suppliers that allow consumers to place orders from home computers with direct-to-home delivery by international small package services in a matter of days. Such services are growing quickly in Japanese and Latin American markets. A more advanced approach involves international distribution of software. Rather than committing specific versions of software inventory to an overseas foreign market, companies are now waiting for actual customer orders to be transmitted by electronic mail or Internet connections, and then downloading the actual software and any future updates directly to the user or retailers computer. Such systems rely on both types of postponement and eliminate all field inventory, storage and transportation costs while increasing customization options, choice and availability. An interesting question over payment of tariffs arises from these kinds of distribution systems. Such distribution systems may be feasible for domestic and international transmission of music, videos, computer based games, news publications and other products which can be transmitted as data.

Another example of international postponement based distribution involves Hewlett-Packard and their distribution of laser printers to Europe. Due to language differences and unique labeling requirements, printers were packaged individually in the United States for shipment to specific warehouses in a number of European countries. Forecast inaccuracies resulted in over-deployment of printers in some countries while stock outs existed in others. By utilizing a packaging/logistics postponement strategy, Hewlett-Packard was able to palletize printers into unit loads in the United States and ship them to a central European distribution center. Based on actual orders, printers could then be individually packaged and distributed. Cost savings were not only achieved through better demand management, but also through consolidated unit-load shipping from the United States. Throughout Europe, as trade barriers and border controls are minimized, companies are moving to implement geographic postponement strategies that eliminate country distribution centers and centralize inventory.

C.   Logistics Strategic Choice

The decision on whether to use postponement based or speculation based approaches to international logistics depends on which strategy can provide the maximum competitive advantage at the lowest desired cost. Speculation based strategies may be necessary in order to provide required availability levels at a reasonable cost. This is especially true of bulky low value products that would have high premium transportation costs. However, postponement based strategies can often provide increased customer choice with availability levels and order cycle times which are equal to or better than those available under speculation. Total logistics costs are often lower in postponement based systems, however, even if total costs are higher, the additional customer choice and availability may be worth the extra cost. What strategy will dominate in international distribution is highly dependent upon the quality of the transportation and communications institutions and the cost of transportation. Slow and unreliable customer clearance times can eliminate the postponement based option. In Eastern Europe, where transportation and communication infrastructure and institutions do not allow for fast and reliable transportation at a reasonable cost, the most effective logistics strategy for the foreseeable future may well continue to involve speculation and forward positioning of inventory to meet customer service requirements.

However, in regions where the environment offers state-of-the art communications and cost effective premium transportation services, the logistics system which utilizes postponement can lead to a competitive advantage in the market-place, and in many cases, a lower total cost. The necessary environment requires facilitation of transportation innovation and entrepreneurship, allowance for integrated door to door transportation services, elimination of customs barriers to reliability, and a cost environment which facilitates premium transportation.

IV. GOVERNMENT POLICY, LOGISTICS MANAGEMENT AND CARRIER SERVICES IMPLICATIONS

The benefits of postponement based international logistics strategies will result in firms making increasingly strong demands for the kind of policy environment necessary to support such systems. Firms that design and control international logistics systems will also place increasing demands on suppliers of logistics and transportation services, and are likely to seek the kinds of strategic alliances which have emerged in the domestic U.S. and European markets (Bowersox, 1990; Thomas, 1994). Such firms will also have to work towards development of integrated global logistics systems and organizational structures that can maximize the logistics function's contribution to competitive advantage and cost leadership.

A.   Government Policy

Government policy can either inhibit or help to develop postponement based logistics systems. A key requirement is for congestion free and reliable border crossing and customs processing at sea, air and land borders. Without quick and consistent processing times postponement based logistics strategies are unable to fulfill total order cycle time requirements for customer service (Heaver, 1992). For intercontinental trade it is also important for government authorities to reduce barriers to cross-border transportation on single carrier, through bill of lading services. This means allowing full cross-border trucking and rail rights, as well as domestic cabotage rights. The current restrictions on U.S.-Canada air freight services (Page, 1994), on U.S.-Canadian trucking cabotage, and on U.S.-Mexico cross-border trucking (Watson, 1994) are examples of the kinds of policies which must be changed. Recent efforts to change these rules as part of NAFTA and bilateral negotiations are encouraging.

It is also important for government policy to encourage the development of premium based international and domestic transportation services. Such systems will require increased public and/or private investments in transportation infrastructure (Ryan, 1994). Critical investments will be required in ports and waterways to accommodate larger, deeper draft and wider ships (Journal of Commerce, 1994). International airport and air traffic control systems in individual countries will also have to be enhanced in order to help eliminate congestion and assure reliable premium transportation services. There is also increasing roadway and rail congestion in both North America and Europe which will require public and/or private investment. Finally there is an urgent need for modernization of intermodal port/ rail/truck terminals and improved access to such terminals.

A number of government policies could also have a potential negative impact on the availability of premium transportation services and substantially increase their cost. Efforts to reduce fuel consumption through taxation and/or efforts to pay for government budget deficits through transportation taxes serve to increase transportation expense and favor inventory speculation strategies. Other impediments to expanded utilization of premium transportation include increased congestion resulting from bans on road and port construction under clean air policies (Mongelluzzo, 1994), restrictions on truck transportation, such as those contemplated by Switzerland (Zarocostas, 1994), limitations on the operating hours and number of stops allowed by package delivery services, and restrictions on air and seaport hours of service.

Restrictions on transportation competition could also reduce flexibility and innovation in a way which results in higher transportation cost. For instance, governmental efforts to restrict access of air package couriers to key airports, such as in Japan, have resulted in costly alternatives and sub-standard service. Cabotage and investment restrictions by non-nationals can also inhibit full competition and innovation in transportation services. Restrictions on ownership of multiple modes, and other restrictions on intermodal transportation can also be harmful to postponement based strategies. Finally, ocean shipping agreements providing for conference rates and other restrictions on services and competition can have a very negative effect on the introduction of innovative and reliable ocean services (Anderson, 1985).

B. Logistics Management

Postponement based international logistics operations have a number of implications for the managers of such systems. First, the development of such systems requires greater coordination and/or centralized management of logistics functions across the entire logistics channel and across individual country operating subsidiaries. Such control is necessary to assure maximum customer service and minimization of total logistics costs for the parent organization and the overall channel. Organizations must also be designed to facilitate the rapid and reliable movement of goods in a manner that will allow for the elimination of forward speculative inventories whenever possible. This control is much more difficult when individual country subsidiaries make logistics decisions for their portion of every logistics movement.

Logistics managers also must reevaluate their international logistics systems in light of potentially new opportunities to take advantage of postponement based systems. When government policies have been changed to facilitate freer and more reliable movement of goods, and premium transportation services with reasonable costs are available, management should consider system designs that eliminate forward warehouses and inventories. This is especially true today in Europe and North America where new trade agreements should facilitate postponement based international logistics.

Logistics managers also must examine the potential for new strategic partnerships with international carriers and other specialized international logistics services providers. While international carriers have generally not been oriented towards such business relationships in the past, many are now offering tailored, value added services that can help lower total international logistics costs while improving service reliability. These services specialists have the ability and the desire to help implement new systems that can improve logistics performance.

C. Carrier Services

International transportation providers will have to embark on an unprecedented wave of technology development and implementation if postponement based strategies are to come to full fruition. Such technology adoption will require new levels of capital commitment and institutional change.

Information processing technologies which can help tie transportation providers to their strategic partners will be especially important to the development of postponement based systems. Communications capabilities that allow for real-time tracing of shipments and diversion of consignments will also be important. Global electronic positioning systems for tracking container movements and monitoring power unit performance and reliability will become increasingly necessary. Real-time monitoring of equipment operating telemetry will also be necessary for assuring 100 percent reliable transportation in the future.

Intercontinental transportation providers will also need to develop larger and faster transportation systems for the movement of both air and ocean freight. This may mean larger cargo aircraft for dedicated high volume routes and bigger container ships that can move larger loads at faster speeds than available today. Such systems are in development, but commercialization will require significant capital investment. For instance, Fastship Atlantic, Inc., plans a 1998 introduction of a 1360 TEU container ship with a speed of 37.5 knots in up to 18 foot waves. This ship will reduce U.S. to Western Europe crossing times from 7-8 days to 3.5 days (Sayre, 1995). Such developments will help create additional demand for postponement oriented transportation services in their own right by lowering costs and increasing the competitive range of specialized production sources.

The need for reliability and consistency in postponement oriented logistics systems will also force the continued development of integrated door to door providers of transportation services that can complete seamless moves across countries. Such services could be provided by non-asset based operators such as international versions of domestic intermodal marketing companies (IMC's) which link together specialized carriers through intermodal transportation and information systems. However, it is possible that there will be an acceleration of the trend towards asset-based integrated transportation providers who offer one-stop shopping for multi-modal capacity linking all regions of the world. Carriers such as CSX and Canadian Pacific are examples of transportation providers with multiple mode services in several countries. United Parcel Service also has combined air and ground modes for international service through ownership of the assets in each mode.

The postponer's demand for integrated services is also likely to lead to development of global full-service third party logistics firms. Such firms will be capable of providing a range of services in multiple countries, including warehousing, inventory management, order processing, customs brokerage, transportation and final form light manufacturing. Many firms are moving toward such services including Exel Logistics, J.B. Hunt Logistics, Nedlloyd Districenters, TNT Contract Logistics and UPS Worldwide Logistics.

Postponement based logistics systems will also require movement toward larger global transportation companies that operate in all or most regions of the world. The operating merger of Northwest and Lufthansa, and the possible merger of Canadian Pacific and Canadian National provide recent examples. In the trucking sector, companies such as TNT have been operating internationally for years. More recently, a number of United States trucking companies have moved to increase their presence throughout North America and Europe. This trend is likely to accelerate and expand to companies with a presence on multiple continents.

Postponement based international logistics systems will also require that international transportation providers develop strategic alliances with manufacturers in order to assure the kind of reliability that is necessary in zero inventory systems. Such alliances have been an important feature of domestic logistics systems in the United States in recent years (Bowersox, 1990). Manufacturers pursuing postponement logistics are dependent on their transportation providers and typically desire a small number of closely integrated partners that provide highly customized services. This could lead to concentration in the international transportation industry and emergence of mega transportation companies.

Postponement based logistics systems will also cause an increasing demand for premium international transportation services in both small package and heavy freight markets. In the former case, shippers will be seeking integrated door to door services that rely on air movements over long distances and intermodal rail/truck movements for intra-regional international operations. In heavier freight markets, premium services in demand will consist of integrated intermodal operations involving ocean/rail and truck combinations, using new generations of high speed container ships and seamless interfaces between modes.

Finally, all international transportation services providers will be required to offer value-added services such as full real-time tracing capability, customs facilitation through in-house brokerage services, enroute diversion and processing and other services that facilitate postponement oriented logistics strategies. EDI oriented communication systems will be critical to such services.

V. CONCLUSIONS

International logistics can play a critical role in helping marketers to gain a competitive advantage in the marketplace, while at the same time helping the firm to reduce costs in the global market. The importance of international logistics has increased with rising levels of world trade. In fact, more effective and efficient international logistics and transportation have contributed to the growth in trade by facilitating sourcing of components and intermediate goods on a cost-effective global basis, and by extending the competitive reach of manufacturing plants into global markets. However, international logistics operations are more complex than domestic operations due to the long distances and time involved in international transportation, because of trade and customs barriers, and because of the often unfamiliar modes of transportation, documentation and currency issues.

Traditionally, international logistics has relied on speculative strategies in which inventories are positioned in forward warehouse locations to meet anticipated demand. Such systems typically utilize slower and more cost effective transportation modes between plants and forward warehouses. Speculative strategies have been necessary because of trade barriers, customs delays, and a lack of premium transportation services at competitive rates. However, as trade barriers have been reduced, and new communications, information processing and transportation technologies and institutions have been brought to bear, logisticians have been able to adopt postponement based logistics strategies. Such strategies postpone the final form and geographic positioning of inventories as long as possible, and then rely on fast order communications and transportation to assure customer service levels. By eliminating warehousing and excess inventory levels, overall costs can be reduced despite higher transportation costs. Such systems also result in more consumer choice and better customer service and, in fact, can give the firm a significant competitive advantage in the international marketplace.

However, postponement based strategies require a government policy environment which facilitates and encourages the removal of trade and customs barriers. Postponement based systems also require a policy environment which favors fast and reliable transportation services. Policy must support congestion free infrastructure, competition amongst transportation providers, and premium based transportation services such as small package air freight systems. Postponement based systems also require centralized corporate logistics organizational structures and/or decision making that cuts across individual country subsidiaries. Given the potential for postponement based systems, managers need to reassess their international logistics systems and consider designs that eliminate forward inventories and warehouses in favor of direct shipments to market via premium transportation services. Transportation providers need to develop sophisticated technological capabilities which will facilitate fast and reliable customized services that can be offered to manufacturers and other shippers on a partnership basis. Such carriers need to be able to offer their services across modes, and on a global basis.

ACKNOWLEDGMENT

The author wishes to thank Dr. Donald J. Bowersox of Michigan State University for his assistance in the preparation of this paper.

REFERENCES

Kearney, A.T. (1990). *International logistics: Battleground of the 90's*, A policy report.

Alderson W. (1957). *Marketing behavior and executive action*. Homewood, IL: Richard D. Irwin, Inc.

Anderson, D.L. (1985). International logistics strategies for the 1980's. *International journal of physical distribution and materials management*, 15 (4), 5-19.

Bahree, B. (1995). World exports of goods rose 9% in 1994, Outpacing the growth of production. *The Wall Street Journal*, (April 4), A2.

Bleakley, Fred R. (1995). Foreign investment in U.S. surged in 1994. *The Wall Street Journal*, (March 15), pp. A2.

Bowersox, D.J., & Sterling, J.U. (1982). Multinational logistics. *Journal of Business Logistics*, 3 (2), 15-24.

Bowersox, D.J. (1982). Some unresolved channel research opportunities and one framework for integration. In M.G. Harvey and R.F. Lusch (eds.), *Marketing channels: Domestic and international perspectives*, 5-8.

Bowersox, D.J. (1990). The strategic benefit of logistics alliances. *Harvard Business Review*, 68 (July-August), 36-45.

Bucklin, L.P. (1965). Postponement, speculation and the structure of distribution channels. *Journal of Marketing Research*, 29, 26-31.

Dunning, J.H. (1988). The eclectic paradigm of international production: A restatement and some possible extensions. *Journal of International Business Studies*, 19, 1-19.

Davies, G.J. (1987). The international logistics concept. *International Journal of Physical Distribution and Materials Management*, 17 (2), 20-27.

Fawcett, S.E., Taylor, J.C., & Smith, S.R. (1995). The realities of operating in Mexico: An exploration of manufacturing and logistics issues. *International Journal of Physical Distribution and Logistics Management*, 25 (3), 49-67.

Ferguson, A.R. (1994). Reform of maritime policy. *Regulation*, 17, (2), 28-36.

Heaver, T.D. (1992). The role of customs administration in the structure and efficiency of international logistics: An international comparison. *The International Journal of Logistics Management*, 3 (1), 63-72.

Journal of Commerce Staff. (1994). Pacific ports gear up for launch of big ships. *Journal of Commerce*, 1A.

Mongelluzzo, B. (1994). California ship interests take on clean-air plan. *Journal of Commerce*, 1A.

O'Laughlin, K.A., Cooper, J., & Cabocel, E. (1993). *Reconfiguring European logistics systems*, prepared by Andersen Consulting and the Cranfield School of Management for the Council of Logistics Management, Oakbrook, IL, 1-373.

Page, P. (1994). Shippers howl as logistics needs fall victim to aviation impasse between U.S. and Canada. *Traffic World*, (October 17), 38,42.

Picard, J. (1983). Physical distribution organization in multinationals: The position of authority. *International Journal of Physical Distribution and Materials Management*, 13 (1), 20-32.

Quinn, F.J. (1987). Union Carbide goes on the offense. *Traffic Management*, 26, 78-85.

Ryan, L. (1994). Legion of challenges confronts global transport into next century. *Journal of Commerce*, (June 21), 2B.

Sayre, C. (1995). Something new on the seas. *Distribution*, 94, 30-36.

Shapiro, R.D. (1984). Get leverage from logistics. *Harvard Business Review*, 62, 119-126.

Stalk, G., Evans P., & Schulman, L. (1992). Competing on capabilities: The new rules of corporate strategy. *Harvard Business Review*, 70, 57-69.

Taylor, J.C., & Closs, D.J. (1993). Logistics implications of an integrated U.S.-Canada market. *International Journal of Physical Distribution and Logistics Management*, 23 (1), 3-13.

Thomas, J. (1994). A healthy transportation strategy in Europe. *Distribution*, 93, 56-60.

U.S. Department of Commerce. (1994). *U.S. foreign trade highlights 1993*. Washington DC.

U.S. International Trade Commission. (1994). *The year in trade: Operation of the trade agreements program, 45th report, 1993, USITC publication 2769*, Washington D.C.

Watson, R. (1994). Postponed transport summit stalls U.S., Mexico trucking agreement. *Journal of Commerce*, (March 25), 3B.

Zarocostas, J. (1994). Swiss to vote on ban of trucks in alps. *Journal of Commerce*, (February 18), 1A.

NEGOTIATION PROCESSES AND OUTCOMES IN INTERNATIONAL TECHNOLOGY TRANSFER

Sejo Oh and Sungil Kim

ABSTRACT

This study of negotiation processes and outcomes is tested on a sample of Korean technology buying firms. The hypotheses predicts that buyer's internal and external environment richness affect seller's negotiation strategies, and that seller's negotiation strategies affect buyer's satisfaction. The results from regression models suggest that a buyer's internal technology stock and its access to the external environment are significantly related to the seller's use of a problem-solving-approach negotiation strategy. Furthermore, the seller's use of a problem-solving-approach in negotiations positively influences buyer's satisfaction.

INTRODUCTION

Negotiation is a key aspect of organizational buying (Clopton, 1984). A buyer cannot buy unless someone else sells and vice versa; each is dependent upon the other.

Advances in International Marketing, Volume 7, pages 99-110.

This situation of mutual dependency (interdependent relationships) is complex. Both parties know that each can influence the other's outcomes and their outcomes can, in turn, be influenced by the other (Goffman, 1969; Pruitt & Rubin, 1986; Raven & Rubin, 1973). Interdependent relationships are characterized by interlocking goals-both parties need each other to accomplish their goals. Interdependent goals are important aspects of negotiation. The structure of the interdependence between different negotiating parties determines the range of possible outcomes of the negotiation and suggests the appropriate strategies and tactics that negotiators should use. Understanding the nature of the interdependence between parties in a negotiation is critical to optimally concluding the negotiation. Unfortunately, negotiation situations(or environments) do not typically present themselves with neat labels describing the nature of the interdependence between parties. Rather, negotiators make judgments about the nature of the interdependence in their negotiation situations, and the negotiators' perceptions about interdependence become as important as the actual structure of the interdependence (Bazerman, Magliozzi, & Neale, 1985; Neale & Bazerman, 1985; Neale & Northcraft, 1991; Pinkley, 1992; Thompson, 1990a, 1990b).

Bonoma and Johnson (1978) indicate that marketing scholars have begun to investigate several issues pertaining to buyer-seller interdependent negotiations (dyadic bargaining behavior, Mathews, Wilson, & Monoky, 1972 ; the management of interorganizational conflict, Stern, Sternphal, & Craig, 1973; the relative power of negotiation participants, Dwyer & Walker, 1981; the importance of communication as an aspect of negotiations, Angelmar & Stern, 1978). Though the body of research described above provides insights about the effects of organizational factors on negotiation behavior, in general it has not focused on negotiation effectiveness (Clopton, 1984). The purpose of our study is to provide some implications about the negotiation effectiveness between the buyer and the seller. Specifically, this study takes a global marketing perspective by examining the effect of buyer's external and internal environmental factors on the seller's negotiation strategies as well as the effect of the seller's strategies on the buyer's satisfaction in negotiating cross-national technology transfers in Korea.

II. TECHNOLOGY AND TECHNOLOGY TRANSFER

The importance of technology as a factor in organizational structure has been extensively treated in the organization theory literatures since Woodward's work in the late 1950s (cf. Harvey, 1968; Gerwin, 1982; Glisson, 1978; Mills & Moberg, 1982; Woodward, 1958, 1965). Organization theorists have explored how organization level technology (e.g., technical complexity in Woodward 1958's work) and department level technology (e.g., technological interdependence in Thompson's 1967 work) influenced structural design. International business and marketing researchers, however, have given relatively little attention to the interorganizational exchange of technology. Interfirm behavioral phenomena in international technology exchange have not been studied together with the social arrangements that structure the activities, and support or carry out these transformations. In brief, technology is the knowledge, tools, techniques, and actions used to transform organizational inputs into outputs (Daft, 1986). To understand the effects of technology on interorganizational exchange, we need to distinguish technology as a stock of accumulated knowledge, tools, and procedures at the given time from technology as the flow or acquisition of specific skills, tools, and so on over a given period of time (cf. Kim, 1984). The distinction is sharpened in our study, thus we regard technology stock as a resource of the acquiring firm; the "flowing" technology is a resource of the supplier.

In the classical literature on technology transfer, the increment of productive capacity resulting from the import of foreign capital or machinery is regarded as technology transfer (e.g., Kohtler, Rubenstein, & Douds, 1973). For a technology transfer to be truly effective, the imported technology must be assimilated because it must be absorbed through technological mastery that its subsequent modification, improvement, and extension become possible (Mytelka, 1985). By permitting flexibility in response to changing costs and competitive conditions, technological mastery increases the long-term viability of the firm as well as its contribution to domestic economic growth and social welfare.

III. NEGOTIATION ENVIRONMENT AND NEGOTIATION STRATEGY

Zeithmal and Zeithmal (1984) indicate that marketing involves facilitating the exchange relationship that exists between an organization and its external environment. And marketing principles and processes are applicable to exchange beyond those involving the products and services of profit-oriented business. Marketing's concern with the organization-environment exchange process and the broadening of the marketing concept have been considerably emphasized. Pfeffer and Salancik (1978) developed a conceptualization of the organization-environment relationship through the resource dependence model. They argue that organizations have varied degrees of dependence on external entities, particularly for the resources they require to operate. In many instances, the external control of these resources may reduce managerial discretion, interfere with the achievement of organizational goals, and ultimately threaten the existence of the focal organization.

Lloyd and Thomas (1992) specified two perspectives on negotiation environment research. The first perspective is that the negotiators tend to emphasize competitive interaction by limiting the exchange of information between the parties (traditional adversarial environment, Stern & El-Ansary, 1988). This approach leads to a stronger position for the dominant negotiator, which may force a zero-sum game (Bacharach & Lawler, 1981). The second perspective is that the opposite environment is the cooperative environment. This negotiation environment is more likely in contractual relationships and partnerships because both parties recognize that the other party plays a necessary role in the relationship (Heide & John 1990). In this approach, because negotiators may be more likely to exchange information, each party may gain more from the relationship than they would gain in an adversarial environment (Bacharach & Lawler, 1981; Bowersox & Cooper, 1992; Noordwier, John, & Nevin, 1990; Stern & El-Ansary, 1988).

The problem-solving-approach (hereafter PSA) to marketing negotiations involves first an emphasis on posing questions and getting information from clients about their needs and preferences. Second, once the buyer's requirements and circumstances are fully understood, the seller accommodates the product/service offering to the client's need (Campbell et al., 1988). PSA can be defined concisely as a set of negotiation behaviors that are cooperative, integrative, and information-exchange-orientation. In interdependent situations, problem solving is essentially a process of specifying the element of a desired outcome, examining the components available to produce the outcome, and searching for a way to fit them together.

A person can approach problem solving in negotiation from his own perspective and attempt to solve the problem by considering only the components that affect his own desired outcome. Rubin and Brown (1975) describe negotiations as a voluntary relationship that is also one of mutual dependence, that is, interdependence. Traditional organization theory tends to view the environment as a deterministic influence to which organizations must adapt their strategies, structures, and processes (Duncan, 1972, Lawrence & Lorsch, 1967; Neghandi & Reimann, 1973). The traditional environmental determinism perspective conceptualizes the environment as a causal variable. Organizational performance is dependent upon the efficient and effective adaption of organizational characteristics to environmental contingencies.

In contrast, theory and research in management and the social sciences have conceptualized the relationship between the organization and the external environment (Aldrich, 1979; Child, 1972; Galbraith, 1977; Kotter, 1979; Miles & Snow, 1978; Pfeffer, 1978; Pfeffer & Salancik, 1978; Porter, 1979, 1980). They argue that organizations can and do implement a variety of strategies designed to modify existing environmental conditions. Therefore the following hypotheses are proposed:

Hypothesis 1.   Buyer's access to rich output markets is positively associated with seller's use of a problem-solving-approach.

Hypothesis 2.   Greater levels of buyer's technology stock are positively associated with seller's use of a problem-solving-approach.

IV. NEGOTIATION STRATEGY AND NEGOTIATION OUTCOME

Clopton (1984) reviewed competitive and coordinative negotiation behavior. A competitive strategy can be characterized as one in which the negotiator maintains high levels of aspiration and high limits for negotiation outcomes, and uses very inflexible behavior aimed at forcing concessions from the other party. Therefore coorperation is a passive component of a competitive strategy and is used primarily to avoid a deadlock or breakdown in the negotiations. Coordinative behavior is facilitated when bargainers adopt a problem-solving orientation to negotiations and show a relatively high degree of trust and cooperation. Through experimental studies, Pruitt and Lewis (1975) suggest that coordinative behavior tend to increase joint outcomes. The negotiator's evaluation of the outcome is based on their perception of how close the outcome is to their initial goals (Clopton, 1984; Neale, 1984; Neale & Bazerman, 1985). Lloyd & Thomas (1992) revealed that when the negotiators are working coorperatively, using a problem-solving orientation, their differences will be resolved through a mutually beneficial outcome (Lloyd & Thomas, 1992; Graham, 1986; Perdue, Day, & Michaels, 1986; Pruitt & Lewis, 1975). In Sawyer and Guetzkouw's (1965) discussion of international negotiation, they clearly describe the endogenous nature of the negotiation process. For more information regarding theory development in this area, readers are advised to read these excellent reviews (e.g., Rubin & Brown, 1975; Pruitt, 1981). Research into the effects of early coorperative or competitive attitudes on the course of negotiation lead to the conclusion that the early initiation of cooperative behavior tends to promote the development of trust and a mutually beneficial cooperative relationship. Such strategies tend to maximize the number of alternative solutions considered, thus allowing negotiations to optimize outcomes.

Angelmar and Stern (1978) focused on applying content analysis to negotiation communications by the use of a theoretically sound category system. They concluded that a considerable body of knowledge has been generated to determine to what extent and under what conditions various offering strategies and tactics affect negotiation outcomes (p. 100). Weitz (1981) advocates a seller's perspective to marketing negotiations, suggesting that the most appropriate measures of negotiation effectiveness are individual economic outcomes of sellers and satisfaction of their clients. He argues against the use of mutual negotiation solutions as the best measure of success, even though most studies have focused on joint outcomes as the dependent variable. Our study focuses on the relationship between sellers' PSA negotiation strategies and outcome variables. Therefore the following hypothesis is proposed:

Hypothesis 3. The more sellers use a problem-solving-approach negotiation strategy, the more buyers' satisfaction is increased.

V. METHOD

A. Sample

Our sample frame was technology buying firms in Korea that have engaged in technology transfer negotiations for contracts lasting for more than three years with foreign sellers in a recent six-month period. The list of the sample frame was obtained from the Korean Department of Science and Technology. All contractual results of technology transfer negotiations in Korean are reported to the Department of Science and Technology. Additionally, in cases where one company had engaged in more than one negotiation during the time period, we only included the most recent one. The reason for this was to eliminate any multiplying effects of organizational characteristics on the negotiation process. The size of the sampling frame was 290 cases from a total of 410 cases, because among 410 cases, 57 cases with a contract period of less than three years and 63 cases that represent multiple observations from one firm that were not appropriate for our study. Among the 290 cases, we randomly selected 235 cases and then telephoned each to: (1) verify addresses, (2) identify the negotiation manager for technology transfer, and (3) call attention to a forthcoming survey. Of these, 10 were eliminated because of incorrect addresses (3 cases), change in personnel (4 cases), and declined participation (3 cases). Thus, the questionnaires along with a gift (envelope opener) of appreciation were sent out to 225 firms. One month after mailing we had received 134 returns. The response rate was 60 percent (134/225).

Among the 134 buying firms we found 22 firms were joint-venture firms which transact the technology with their joint venture partners. They were deleted because they represent internal transactions. Thus, the sample size for our study was 112 cases. In general, the participants were presidents in cases of small firms and product development managers in cases of large firms. We promised a summary of results to interested respondents.

B. Measures

Initial items for scale development were selected from the literature and cross-checked by several businessmen highly involved in technology transfer. If follow-up discussions did not yield consensus the discrepant items were deleted. All constructs were measured with multiple items. All responses are recorded on five-point scales.

Environmental richness items were generated from the interpreted domain of the construct and related scales in the technology transfer and marketing literature (Achrol & Stern, 1988; Dwyer & Welsh, 1985; Dwyer & Oh, 1987; Etgar, 1977; Kim, 1984). It includes domestic market opportunities, purchase availability of materials and equipments, the extent of competitors' buying the same technology, the degree of competition among technology holding firms, the favor to the buyer of governmental guidelines on distribution or domestic content, governmental participation in the structuring of technology buying competition, and governmental warranty for the firms' technology purchases.

Items for technological stock included the buying firm's ability and expertise for absorbing the technology, for developing the technology itself, for getting information about technology holding firms, as well as its ability to invest, produce, and penetrate foreign markets. PSA items were included concerning the degree of mutual problem-solving, and the buyer's perceived impression of seller's negotiation strategies (accommodating, honest, unbiased and cooperative, Campbell et al., 1988).

Perceived satisfaction items as a global evaluation of fulfillment from the relationship were inspired especially by Gaski's concise instrument (Gaski & Nevin, 1985), which showed predictive sensitivity to exercised coercive and reward power. Our five-item scale included: (1) overall satisfaction with negotiations of the technology transfer; (2) perceptions of overall goodness for business on the basis of rewards and costs; (3) evaluations of constraints derived from the technology seller; (4) satisfaction with performance during the negotiation; and (5) satisfaction related to the pre-negotiation expectations.

VI. RESULTS

A. Reliability and Validity

Table 1 summarizes the reliability of the measures. The reliability of each scale was assessed by coefficient alpha. Item-to-total correlations were used to delete items impairing convergence and consistency (Table 2). All alpha reliabilities are greater than .80 except the environmental richness variable. Churchill and Peter (1984) indicate that the .5 criterion is characteristic of much of the published research in marketing. All measurement items of relevant variables were retained.

B. Model Estimation

The hypothesized relationships are tested in two separate Ordinary Least Squares regression equations. In the first equation, the seller's PSA is expressed as

Table 1. Scale Reliability

	Number of Items		Cronbach's
Scale	Inital	Final	Alpha
Environmental richness:	8	8	.53
Buyer's technology stock:	6	6	.80
Seller PSA:	5	5	.88
Buyer satisfaction:	5	5	.86

Table 2.   Correlation Matrix

Variable	1	2	3	4
1. Environmental richness:	.18[a]			
2. Buyer's technology stock:	.31[b]	.48[a]		
3. Seller PSA :	.35[b]	.08	.75[a]	
4. Buyer satisfaction:	.26	.28	.40[b]	.49[a]

Note: [a]Diagonal entries are scale variances
[b]Significant $p < .05$

Table 3.   Regression Results

Equation	Coefficient	Estimate	t-value
1. PSA = B1 +	B1	1.01	.97
B11 RICH +	B11	.36	2.45[a]
B12 TECH	B12	.02	−.12
$R^2 = .13, F = .23^b$			
2. SAT = B2 +	B2	.52	9.61[a]
B21 PSA	B21	.30	3.14[a]
$R^2 = .09, F = 9.71^a$			

Note: [a]Significant at $p < .05$
[b]Significant at $p < .10$

KEY:
RICH=Buyer's environmental richness,
TECH=Buyer's technology stock,
PSA=Seller's problem-solving-approach,
SAT=Buyer's satisfaction.

a function of the buyer's environmental richness and technology stock. The second equation is the relationship between seller's PSA and buyer's satisfaction.

In the Table 3, seller's problem solving negotiation strategy is affected by buyer side environmental richness (Eq.1: $B11 = .36$, $t = 2.45$; $p < .05$), but buyer side technology stock is not related to seller's problem solving negotiation strategy (Eq.1 : $B12 = -.02$, $t = -.12$). Therefore Hypothesis 1 is supported but hypothesis 2 is not supported. Furthermore, seller's PSA positively influenced buyer's satisfaction. Therefore Hypothesis 3 is supported (Eq.2 : $B21 = .30$, $t = 3.14$; $p < .05$).

VII.   DISCUSSION

Our results indicate that environmental richness has a significant effect on the seller's PSA in international technology transfer. More specifically, the buyer's domestic market size and the trend of demand, the buyer's competitive advantages, and favorable governmental policies to technology transfer are positively related to the seller's PSA. However, buyer's technology stock did not influence the seller's PSA. That is, external environment munificence is more important in formulating a seller's negotiation strategy than internal environmental munificence. This is because transferring technology as a total package is preferred, but absorption capacity of the buyer's firm is not a significant factor.

Our results also indicate that seller's behavior (PSA) has a significant effect on buyer's satisfaction. In other words, the buyer's satisfaction appears to be dependent on the seller's use of a reciprocating and cooperative approach. This is consistent with the results of Campbell et al. (1988) in intercultural negotiation research. Therefore, the seller's PSA (where gathering information about buyers' needs and performance is emphasized) enhances negotiation outcomes in Korea as well. As a possible explanation for these findings, Michelini (1971) advocated that the effects of anticipated future interaction on negotiation are a function of its interaction with the perception of the other. Anticipated future interaction leads to a greater cooperation when the other is cooperative, and to a greater competition when the other is seen as competitive (Rubin & Brown, 1975, p. 236). Further research on technology transfer might try to isolate the critical facets of technology stock within classes of technology exchange. Plausibly, buyer's abilities for technology absorption and extension differ from process technologies (surface mount circuitry) and product technologies (digitalized communication equipments). The former may render a portion of the buyer's technology stock obsolete (e.g., its old assembly process efficiencies) while placing higher demands on distribution and marketing know-how. Product technologies, on the other hand, may exhibit high variance in their demand for and complexity of integration with the buyer's technology stock.

The above factors may account for the significant portion of variance left unaccounted for in our regression models. Future research begs for richer measures of the firm and dyad-level governance and outcomes of technology transfer. This study lays the groundwork for subsequent research using more complex exchange models (cf. Frazier, Speckman, & O'Neal, 1988; Pfeffer & Salanck, 1978; Williamson, 1985) by supporting the generality of their principal basis to international technology exchanges.

REFERENCES

Achrol, R.S., & Stern, L.W. (1988). Environmental determinants of decision-making uncertainty in marketing channels. *Journal of Marketing Research*, 25, 36-50.

Aldrich, Howard E., (1979), *Organizations and environments*. Englewood Cliffs, NJ: Prentice-Hall, Inc., 110.

Angelmar, R., & Stern, L.W. (1978). Development of a content analytic system for analysis of bargaining communication in marketing, *Journal of Marketing Research*, 15, 93-102.

Bacharach, S., & Lawler, E. (1981). *Bargaining: power, tactics, and outcomes*, San Francisco: Jossey-Bass Inc. Publishers.

Bazerman, M.H., Magloiozzi, T., & Neale, M.A. (1985). Integrative bargaining in a competitive market. *Organizational Behavior and Human Decision Processes*, 35, 294-313.

Bonoma, T., Bagozzi, R., & Zaltman, G. (1978). The dyadic paradigm with specific application toward industrial marketing. In T. Bonoma & G. Zaltman (Eds.), *Organizational buying behavior* (pp. 49-66). Chicago: American Marketing Association.

Bowersox, D., & Cooper, M.B. (1992). *Strategic marketing channel management*. New York: McGraw-Hill Book Company.

Burgelman, R.A., & Maidique, M.A. (1988). *Strategic management of technology and innovation*. Homewood, IL, Irwin, Inc.

Campbell, N.C.G., Graham, J.L., Jolibert, A., & Meissner, H.G. (1988). Marketing negotiations in France, Germany, the United Kingdom and the United States. *Journal of Marketing*, 52, 49-62.

Child, J. (1972). Organizational structure, environment and performance: The role of strategic choice. *Sociology*, 6, 2-22.

Churchill, G.A., & Peter, J.P. (1984). Research design effects on the reliability of rating scales: A meta-analysis. *Journal of Marketing Research*, 21, 360-375.

Clopton, S.W. (1984). Seller and buying firm factors affecting industrial buyers' negotiation behavior and outcomes. *Journal of Marketing Research*, 21, 39-53.

Daft, RL. (1986). *Organization theory and design*. St. Paul, MN: West Publishing Company.

Duncan, R. (1972). Characteristics of organizational environments and perceived environmental uncertainty. *American Science Quarterly*, 20, 680-693.

Dwyer R.E., & Walker, O.C. (1981). Bargaining in an asymmetrical power structure. *Journal of Marketing*, 45, 104-115.

Dwyer R.E., & Oh, S. (1987). Output sector munificence effects on the internal political economy of marketing channels. *Journal of Marketing Research*, 24, 347-358.

Dwyer R.E., & Welsh, M.A. (1985). Environmental relationships of the internal political economy of marketing channels. *Journal of Marketing Research*, 12, 397-414.

El-Ansary, A., and Stern, L.W. (1972). Power measurement in the distribution channel. *Journal of Marketing Research*, 9, 47-52.

Etgar, M. (1977). Channel environment and channel leadership. *Journal of Marketing Research*, 15, 69-76.

Frazier, G.L., Spekman, R.E., & O'Neal, C.R. (1988). Just-in-time exchange relationships in industrial markets. *Journal of Marketing*, 52, 52-67.

Galbraith, J. (1977). *Designing complex organizations*. Reading, MA: Addison-Wesley.

Gaski, J.F., & Nevin, J.R. (1985). The differential effects of exercised and unexercised power sources in a marketing channel. *Journal of Marketing Research*, 12, 130-42.

Gerwin, D. (1982). The comparative analysis of structure and technology: A critical appraisal. *Academy of Management Journal*, 25, 532-552.

Glisson, C.A. (1978). Dependence of technological routinization on structural variables in human service organizations. *Administrative Science Quarterly*, 23, 383-95.

Goffman, E. (1969). *Strategic interaction*. Philadelphia, PA: University of Pennsylvania Press.

Graham, J.L. (1986). The problem-solving approach to negotiations in industrial marketing. *Journal of Business Research*, 14, 549-566.

Harvey, E. (1968). Technology and the structure of organizations. *American Sociological Review*, 33, 247-59.

Heide, J., & John, G. (1990). Alliances in industrial purchasing relationships. *Journal of Marketing Research*, 27, 24-36.

Kim, K.Y. (1984). American technology and Korea's technological development. In Karl Moskowitz, (Ed.), *From patron to partner* (pp. 484-505). Lexington, MA: Lexington Books.

Kohtler, B.M., Rubenstein, A.M., and Douds, C.F. (1973). A behavioral study of International technology transfer between the United States and West Germany. *Research Policy*, 21-46.

Kotter, J. (1979). *Power in management* New York: AMACOM

Kozima, K. (1978). *Japanese direct foreign investment*. Charles E. Tuttle Co.

Lawrence, P.R., & Lorsh, J.W. (1967). New management job: The integrator. *Harvard Business Review*, 45, 142-151.

Leatt, P., & Schneck, R. (1981). Nursing subunit technology: A replication. *Administrative Science Quarterly*, 26, 225-236.

Lloyd M.R., & Page, T.J. (1978). The development and test of a model of transaction negotiation. *Journal of Marketing*, Vol. 56, 18-32

Mathews, H.L., Wilson, D.T., Monoky, Jr., J.F. (1972). Bargaining behavior in a buyer-seller dyad. *Journal of Marketing Research*, 6,, 103-5.

Michelini, R.L. (1971). Effects of prior interaction, contact, strategy, and expectation of meeting on gain behavior and sentiment. *Journal of Conflict Resolution*, 15, 97-103.

Mills, P.K., & Moberg, D.J. (1982). Perspectives on the technology of service organizations. *Academy of Management Review*, 7, 467-478.

Mytelka, L.K. (1985). Stimulating effective technology transfer: The case of textiles in Africa. In N. Rosenberg & C. Frischtak, (Eds.), *International technology transfer, concepts, measures, and comparison*. New York, NY: Praeger Publishers.

Neale, M.A. (1985). The effects of negotiation and arbitration cost salience on bargainer behavior: The role of the arbitrator and constituency on negotiator judgement. *Organizational Behavior and Human Performance*, 34, 97-111.

Neale, M.A., & Razerman, M. (1985). The effects of framing and negotiator overconfidence on bargaining behavior and outcomes. *Academy of Management Journal*, 28(1), 34-49.

Neale, M.A., & Northcraft, G.B. (1991). Behavior negotiation theory: A framework for conceptualizing dyadic bargaining. In L. Cummings & B. Staw (Eds.), *Research in Organizational Behavior* (Vol. 13, pp. 147-190). Greenwich, CT: JAI Press.

Noordewier, T., John, G., Nevin, J. (1990). Performance outcomes of purchasing arrangements in industrial buyer-vendor relationships. *Journal of Marketing*, 54, 80-93.

Nunnaly, J. (1978). *Psychometric theory*. Second Edition, New York : McGraw Hill.

Perdue, B., Day, R., & Michaels, R. (1986). Negotiation styles of industrial buyers. *Journal of Marketing Research*, 15, 171-6.

Pfeffer, J., and Salancik, G.R. (1978). *The external control of organizations*. New York : Harper and Row.

Pinkley, R.L. (1992). Dimensions of conflict frame: Relation to disputant perceptions and expectations. *The International Journal of Conflict Management*, 3, 95-113.

Porter, M.E. (1979). How competitive forces shape strategy. *Harvard Business Review*, 57, 137-145.

Porter, M.E. (1980). *Competitive strategy*. New York: The Free Press.

Pruitt, D.G. (1981). *Bargaining behavior*, New York:Academic Press, Inc.

Pruitt, D.G. & Rubin, J.Z. (1986). *Social conflict: Escalation, stalemate and settlement*. New York: Random House.

Pruitt, D.G. & Lewis, S.A. (1975). Development of integrative solutions in bilateral negotiation. *Journal of Personality and Social Psychology*, 31, 621-633.

Raven, B.H., & Rubin, J.Z. (1973). *Social psychology: People in groups*. New York: John Wiley and Sons.

Rubin, J.Z., & Brown, B.R. (1975). *The social psychology of bargaining and negotiation*. New York: Academic Press, Inc.

Sawyer, J., and Guetzkow, H. (1965). Bargaining and negotiation in international relations. In H.C. Kelman (ed.), *International behavior: A social-psychological analysis* (pp. 464-520). New York: Holt, Rinehart and Winston.

Stern, L., & El-Ansary, A. (1988). *Marketing channels*. Englewood Cliffs, NJ: Prentice-Hall, Inc.

Stern, L., & Sternthal, B., & Craig, C.S. (1973). Managing conflict in distribution channels: A laboratory study. *Journal of Marketing Research*, 10, 169-79.

Thompson, J. (1967). *Organizations in action*. New York: McGraw-Hill Book Co.

Thompson, J. (1990a). An examination of naive and experienced negotiators. *Journal of Personality and Social Psychology*, 59, 82-90.

Thompson, J. (1990b). Negotiation behavior and outcomes: Empirical evidence and theoretical issues. *Psychological Bulletin*, 108, 515-32.

Weitz, B.A. (1981). Effectiveness in sales interactions: A contingency framework. *Journal of Marketing*, 45, 95-103.

Williamson, O.E. (1985). *The economic institutions of capitalism: Firms, markets, relational contracting*. New York, A Division of Macmillan, Inc.

Woodward, J. (1958). *Management and technology, problems of progress in industry*, No. 3. London: Her Majesty's Stationery Office.

Woodward, J. (1965). *Industrial organization: Theory and practice*. London: Oxford University Press.

Zeithaml, C.P. & Zeithaml, V.A. Environmental management revising the marketing perspective. *Journal of Marketing*, 48, 46-53.

EVALUATION AND MANAGEMENT OF PROFESSIONAL SERVICES IN KOREA

Mary Anne Raymond and William Rylance

ABSTRACT

While many studies have addressed the use of marketing by firms that provide professional services in Europe and the United States, very little data exists on the marketing and management of professional services in East Asian countries. Also, it is not clear how organizations select and evaluate providers of professional services in the diverse and unique markets of this dynamic region. This exploratory study focuses on foreign service firms in Korea. First, the research provides a background on the Korean culture and business practices in Seoul that may affect the way foreign service firms compete in the Korean market. Then, the factors that influence the selection and evaluation of professional service providers (accounting firms, legal firms, management consultants, advertising agencies, public relations firms) in Korea are analyzed. While the fees that firms charge may be similar, it is important to determine what level of value and service clients expect and how clients choose the provider. At the same time, it is important to determine how providers determine and satisfy the expectations of clients. In addition, the study examines organizational factors that affect the management of professional service firms and how organizations are positioned on several key service aspects. Moreover, an in-depth consider-

Advances in International Marketing, Volume 7, pages 111-125.

ation of the unique cultural context and how relationships affect decisions is highly
relevant. By conducting in-depth interviews and administering surveys with both
users and providers of professional services in Korea, the results are useful in planning and implementing service management strategies in Korea.

With the free trade movement in Europe, the privatization of businesses which
were once state-owned in many countries, the industrialization of many countries,
and the rapid growth of economies in Asia, the service industry continues to grow
worldwide. In the world's most developed service market, the United States, services account for 54 percent of the gross national product (GNP) and over 75 percent of nonfarm employment. The annual growth rate of the service industry in
Korea is over 10 percent, which is higher than the growth rate of the gross national
product in Korea. With the GNP in Korea forecast to be over $800 billion by the
year 2001, Korea will be a larger export market for services and one of the 10 largest economies in the world (Kim, 1995; Taylor, Wilson, & Miracle, 1994). Worldwide growth, especially in developed economies, is expected to accelerate
dramatically as the global economy moves from the industrial to the information
revolution, and Korea is expected to be a vital part of that growth (Kim, 1995).

While services are a key component of the GNP both in the United States and
Korea, the means of achieving a competitive advantage within the service industry
varies from market to market and company to company. While the success and sur-
vival of service firms may depend upon the delivery of superior service quality
(Parasuraman, Zeithaml, & Berry, 1988), it is not clear whether this holds true, or
is a dominant factor in all markets. Other intangible but significant drivers may be
important factors and such drivers may be rooted in complex cultural issues. Culture and tradition affect both expectations and relationships between customers
and providers in different markets. Korea is a rapidly developing market with a
diverse cultural, economic, and political environment and this diversity affects
businesses competing in that market (*The Economist,* 1994).

There have been many studies and much research on services marketing; however, most of the studies focus on the marketing of services in the United States. As
more and more service firms enter international markets, it is important to determine whether the same standards for service quality exist and how service providers are selected and evaluated. When a firm plans to compete in a foreign market,
it is important *not* to assume that one understands the culture and business practices without actually having information from or experience in that respective
culture.

Specifically, this exploratory study examines the selection, evaluation, and management of professional services in Korea, one of the world's fastest growing
economies (Kim, 1995). The study examines the impact that cultural differences
and business practices may have on the selection and evaluation of service providers, specific differences and difficulties that service firms encounter in doing busi-

ness in Korea and how client expectations and service delivery may vary in Korea. The results of the study have implications for not only service firms in Korea, but for consumer and industrial goods companies in Korea as well as firms that plan to enter the Korean market in the future.

In order to understand specific management implications as well as how professional services are selected and evaluated in Korea, it is first necessary to understand the Korean culture and its influence on business practices. Information about the Korean culture and business practices provides the background for developing the survey instruments and the information is also beneficial in understanding the results of the study.

This paper presents the results of an exploratory study designed to determine which factors influence the selection and evaluation of professional service providers in Korea. While several dimensions of SERVQUAL (Parasuraman, Ziethaml, & Berry, 1991) were included as factors, factors specific to the Korean culture and general business factors were also utilized in the study. The study addresses the differences and difficulties of foreign service firms doing business in Korea. First, an overview of the Korean culture and Korean business practices that may affect the selection, evaluation, and management of professional services is presented. Second, an overview of the service industry as it relates to the selection and evaluation of services is presented. Third, the method and results are discussed. Then, the conclusions, the managerial implications and future research directions are discussed.

I. BACKGROUND

A. The Korean Culture and Korean Business Practices

Korea is a very dynamic, rapidly developing market which has experienced an industrial, political and social revolution in the last 50 years. The gross national product has been increasing annually and much of the growth has been led by stronger investments in facilities and an increase in exports. The service industry has also shown a strong growth rate. Much of the growth and many of the changes in Korea affect Korean businesses as well as foreign businesses in Korea (Kim, 1995). However, many aspects of the Korean culture as well as Korean business practices have a tremendous impact on business operations and should be understood in order to compete in the market.

B. Relationships

Korea is a web of relationships and interrelatedness. Many business decisions are the result of relationships (*The Economist,* 1994). In terms of mutual trust and interdependence, an enormous amount of solidarity exists within certain social groupings, particularly family members and friends and such ties are carefully cultivated. The most important ties are family/blood affinities, school alumni, military alumni, and company work groups. Kinship ties are the strongest of all and many of the successful Korean conglomerates (chaebols) are built on family ties, both immediate and through "cross-chaebol marriages." School alumni are also extremely important, especially in the job-hunting arena and the exchange of favors.

Agreements, "kintracts," between two parties who are related by blood or close friendship are often much stronger than "contracts." In other words, the binding power of an agreement is only as strong as the personal relationship of the people who made the agreement. The "kintract" is the substance of the agreement and the "contract" is a formality. The "kintract" requires continuous attention and cultivation to remain viable (Setton, 1995). Thus, entertainment expenses, which are necessary to strengthen relationships, are often very high in Korea, regardless of a company's profitability. Social events are also popular to welcome new employees into the work group.

In Korea the importance of investment in human relationships reigns supreme. Koreans are much more conscientious about "human" debts than financial debts per se. The *chong* or attachment developed compels them to return the favors. Human debts can be called in when the time is right and they are much more flexible than financial debts. If they do feel indebted such friends will go out of their way to pull strings, introduce one to the right people, extend a hand in solving problems, and even stick to a written contract.

C.   Individualism versus Collectivism

In these relationships, especially in a country higher in collectivism such as Korea individual interests are often consciously subordinated to group interests—collectivism over individualism (Alden, Hoyer, & Lee, 1993). By subordinating one's personal interests to those of a group, one is overcoming individual limitations. This assumes that a person's individuality is discovered by cultivating harmony within the inner circle of relationships (family and close friends). Therefore, the goal for the service provider in Korea must be to bring the customer into that inner circle. In addition, foreign firms which focus on operational systems and procedures must not ignore the Korean employee's need for a sense of belonging or identity beyond the specific job description.

D.   Communication

Another area important for doing business in Korea involves communication with Koreans. In East Asian societies, what one says often carries much less weight than what one does. "Acting the truth" or observing the basic human relationships is very important. Again, relationships are critical. In fact, influence may not have as much to do with one's rational powers of persuasion as it does with the depth of one's relationships and the reputation one has with a circle of contacts. Therefore, the critical question is how to succeed in cultivating relationships whereby trust can flourish. Familiarization, or regular, informal contact through which *chong* or attachment to people is reinforced, followed by meaningful participation in the essential rituals through which one associates with affiliated groups, and empathy for the culture are areas on which to focus (Setton, 1995). How can a foreigner who is regarded as being on the very outer rim of the concentric circles of relationships become considered as "part of the family?" One may begin by working out the category of one's relationship to particular groups or individuals, particularly in terms of age.

The basic rituals involved in forming acquaintances, particularly in the business world, are bowing and exchanging name cards, followed by eating and drinking. The most important ritual in terms of forming ties is the drinking ritual. It is a matter of honor to consider the ties of friendship and group solidarity, symbolized by the exchange of glasses. Koreans appreciate foreigners that understand and are interested in their culture. They are very gratified if foreigners discover positive things about the Korean culture.

E. Drivers of Korean Management Strategy

In addition to the importance of personal relationships, there are three primary drivers that distinguish Korean management strategy from that of other countries. These include a strong focus on rapid, external growth of organizations as opposed to gradual development based on the cultivation of internal resources, sensitivity towards and compliance with higher authority (government policy), and a general tendency for short-term planning (Yugun, 1993). Korean managers often tend to focus on visible results in terms of rapid growth, particularly outward expansion, rather than growth strategies aimed at increasing market share through the long-term strengthening of competitiveness in strategic areas although this appears to be changing. The tendency to expand is partially derived from a desire for social status in terms of the accumulation of property and power, a highly optimistic "can do" entrepreneurial spirit, and aggressive leadership patterns.

Adaptation to government policy and the establishment and maintenance of formal and informal relationships with relevant government departments and figures, is a cornerstone of the "environmental adaptation" policy of Korean businesses. In Korea government takes on a much more authoritarian role in the guidance and control of the market economy. There is often control over key resources and capital necessary for the management of enterprises through regular five year economic development plans which identify and promote key areas of growth. To achieve policy goals, the Korean government has opted for economic inducement rather than the enforcement of restrictions, particularly through selective support. Therefore, a priority of management in Korean businesses is the cultivation and maintenance of relationships with the government bureaucracy on various levels, formally and informally. It is also important to note that domain management activities have become less of a priority recently, particularly as external financial support is less urgently needed by the larger Korean conglomerates who have secured their own financial institutions. In addition, with President Kim's current economic policy, 'globanomics,' there is a trend toward increased deregulation and less red tape (Kim, 1995).

F. Background on The Service Industry

In the last twenty years, there have been numerous papers and books written on service. While the SERVQUAL studies (Parasuraman, Ziethaml, & Berry, 1991, 1988) establish five key dimensions of service quality (assurance, reliability, responsiveness, tangibles, and empathy), it is unclear whether these same dimensions are as important in international markets. While many of these studies address the importance of service and how service can be used as a competitive advantage (Bharadwaj, Varadarajan, & Fahy, 1993; Onkvisit & Shaw, 1989; Ostrom & Iacobucci, 1995), very few studies actually address how to implement quality service. Berry (1995) presents a framework for implementing great service and discusses specific actions that firms must take to deliver superior service quality. Maister (1993) emphasizes that since professional service providers have much face-to-face interaction with clients and since clients require customized services, it is critical for firms to attract and keep highly skilled employees. Thus, the people in professional services firms become a key to competitive advantage.

Strategies in the service industry differ in many ways from those in product-based companies although many managers try to plan strategies in product-oriented terms. Customization is not only necessary in service firms, but also a source of sustainable competitive advantage. Therefore, few management decisions and tasks are routine or standardized like they may be in consumer or industrial goods companies. While some activities may be more systematic than others, each situation is different. While products develop a brand identification by offering consistent quality, services develop a reputation based on the type and quality of service provided. Reputation serves as an indicator of quality and may serve as a competitive advantage. In addition, reputation or image may serve as a barrier to entry for other competitors and may help if a provider decides to enter a foreign market.

Competitive advantage in service industries is often the result of skills, capabilities, and resources, provided that the firm offers services desired by clients (Bharadwaj, Varadarajan, & Fahy, 1993). The image of service firms, particularly people-based service firms, such as professional service providers depends on employees to build their reputations and sell their services. Client contact, face-to-face interaction, and client confidence are such critical components of professional service providers that the employees are literally the firms' "assets." Therefore, professional service firms must not only compete for clients but also for employees (Maister, 1993). Companies must manage their assets. That is, they must manage their employees and do quality control. Quality control in service companies involves an employee's attitude and performance. The employees that perform the service make or break a company. The confidence that clients buy in service companies indicates quality (Onkvisit & Shaw, 1989).

Companies that consistently provide superior service and help clients maximize their benefits can differentiate themselves and build and maintain client relationships (Berry, 1995). While superior service quality may be difficult to define, Parasuraman, Ziethaml, and Berry (1988, 1991) developed and refined the SERVQUAL model which showed that service expectations were the result of word of mouth, past experience, customer needs, and the provider's promotions. However, if customers' expectations are different from what the service firm perceives, a gap exists and may result in unsuccessful service delivery and ultimately, damage the reputation of the service firm. The relationship with the customer would also probably be weakened.

Managing expectations becomes a key activity, especially in the Korean market where many services are new and not well understood. If service delivery does not meet customer expectations or fails to reflect the service firms' communications or marketing promise, the disappointment or failure will seriously damage reputations and hinder future endeavors.

Five key determinants of service quality (Berry, 1995) do appear to be generally applicable to Korea assuming the more intangible cultural sensitivities are taken into account and managed. In order of importance, the key determinants as perceived by consumers, are: reliability (dependence and accurate performance), responsiveness (prompt and helpful service), assurance (trustworthy, instills confidence, knowledgeable and courteous), empathy (can relate to client's situation), and tangibles (physical environment, promotional materials). Not only do these factors determine service quality, but they are also criteria for the selection and evaluation of professional service firms. These service components are important in Korea, but the underlying strength of a service and its sustainability, may well be strengthened by complex culture-specific relationships influenced by the affinities or "relationship circles."

II. CURRENT STUDY

A. Purpose

The purpose of this exploratory study is to determine which factors are most influential in the selection and evaluation of professional service providers in Korea. The study seeks answers to the following research questions concerning professional service providers in Korea.

1. What factors are the most influential in the selection and evaluation of professional service providers in Korea? Specifically, given the importance of relationships, how important are different relationships in the selection and evaluation of service providers?
2. What factors in a service provider's organization are most important and how do individual organizations rate on service attributes?
3. What are the biggest differences and difficulties in doing business in the service industry in Korea versus doing business in the service industry in Western markets?

B. Sample

In order to examine the differences and difficulties of doing business in the service industry in Korea, the sample was selected from foreign service providers with offices in Seoul, Korea. The sampling frame consisted of service firms listed in the *Fall Directory 1994 for AMCHAM* (American Chamber of Commerce in Korea) and *The British Chamber of Commerce Constitution Membership Directory 1994*. The firms in the sample were both service providers and users of professional services. One hundred service firms, including financial institutions, management consultant firms, advertising agencies, research firms, and engineering service firms, were selected. In-depth interviews were conducted with a top executive at six of the firms and surveys were sent to the top executive identified at all 100 firms in the sample. Five surveys were returned because the firms did not utilize other professional services in Korea and most of their services were prearranged through contracts in the United States. Therefore, the effective sample size was 95. A total of 31 usable surveys was returned for a response rate of 33.0 percent.

C. Survey Instrument

Respondents were asked to rate 13 different factors regarding the selection of professional service providers from never influential (1) to always influential (5). The factors included culturally-based factors such as the provider's understanding of Korean culture, government influence, and family relationships, friendships, and university affiliations between the firm and the provider's employees. SERVQUAL dimensions and generic factors such as accessibility, previous experience, expertise, image, and brand name were also included. Then, respondents were asked to indicate the importance of 10 service aspects for evaluating professional service providers from not important at all (1) to always important (5). SERVQUAL dimensions such as the provider's accessibility, reliability, and responsiveness as well as market specific and generic factors such as the provider's knowledge and understanding of the customers' needs, the company, the industry, the marketplace, the courtesy of employees, and the provider's utilization of company input were used as service aspects.

Respondents were then asked to rate the importance of nine factors in their own organizations including employee attitude and commitment, low turnover, incentive programs, empowerment of employees, cultural sensitivities, and client satisfaction. Then respondents indicated their organization's position on a scale of 1 to 5 (with descriptors given) against a variety of service attributes such as service culture, customer orientation, customer understanding, employee attitude, and employee loyalty. Respondents were then asked to respond to several open-ended questions which had been used in the in-depth interviews. The open-ended questions provided respondents an opportunity to expand on differences and difficulties of doing business in Korea, differences in customer expectations, and how they adapted their services for Korea.

III. RESULTS OF THE STUDY

A.   Selection of Professional Service Providers

While relationships are particularly important in the Korean culture and respondents commented on the importance of those relationships in the discussion section, most companies in this study do not select providers based on relationships. As shown in Table 1, only three (10.0%) of the respondents said that friendships between the firm and the provider's employees were always influential in selecting professional service providers. The average score was 2.93 meaning that these relationships were only sometimes influential. The same held true for university affiliations between the firm and the provider's employees with only three (10.0%) stating that these relationships were always influential. The average score was 2.21 meaning that university affiliations were rarely influential in selecting providers. Family relationships were even less influential with an average score of 1.97 and only one (3.0%) stating always influential. However, one of the biggest differences in doing business in Korea that respondents discussed in the open-ended questions concerned the importance of relationships. While relationships were not identified as a key criterion for the selection of service providers, the importance of relationships in doing business in Korea was considered very important. Respondents also mentioned an increase in entertainment expenses necessary in building relationships. It is important to note that the influence of factors may differ in Korean businesses and at different levels in the organization.

Twenty-two (71.0%) of the respondents said expertise is always influential in the selection of service providers, with an average score of 4.71. Other factors with average scores indicating that they were always influential in the selection of professional service providers were accessibility (4.3), previous experience (4.3), provider's understanding of business (4.3), service guarantee (4.2), and image of

Table 1. Influence of Factors in Selection of Professional Service Firms

Factors	Mean Scores
Expertise	4.7
Previous Experience	4.3
Provider's Accessibility	4.3
Provider's Understanding of Business	4.3
Image of Provider	4.1
Provider's Understanding of Korean Culture	3.9
Brand Name of Firm	3.6
Worldwide Network or Alliances	3.3
Friendships Between Employees	2.9
Government Influences/Relationships	2.6
University Alumni Affiliations	2.2
Family Relationships	2.0

provider (4.1). For a complete summary of the average ratings for all the factors influential in the selection of providers, see Table 1.

B.   Evaluation of Professional Service Providers

When asked how important various service aspects were when evaluating professional service providers, the quality and the responsiveness of the provider were each mentioned by 19 (61.0%) of the respondents as always important and the average scores for each of these variables were 4.65 and 4.58, respectively. The provider's reliability was always important to 18 (58.0%) of the respondents and the provider's understanding of the marketplace was always important to 17 (55.0%) of the respondents. An interesting result considering the face-to-face contact required in the service industry was that only one (3.0%) said that courtesy of provider's employees was always important and the average score was only 3.65. For a complete summary of the importance of various service aspects used in the evaluation of professional service providers, see Table 2.

C.   Importance of Service Aspects in Organizations

Respondents also rated the importance of different factors in their organizations. As shown in Table 3, twenty five (81.0%) said client satisfaction was always important with an average score of 4.94. However, when asked to rate how their respective organizations were positioned with respect to listening to the customer, only six (19.0%) utilized both formal and informal means, such as surveys and direct contact and feedback to identify expectations. The average score (position) was 3.37 indicating that most providers relied on informal means and complaints

Table 2. Importance of Service Aspects in the Evaluation of Professional Service Firms

Service Aspect	Mean Score
Quality of Firm's Performance	4.6
Responsive of Firm	4.6
Firm's Reliability	4.5
Firm's Understanding of the Marketplace	4.5
Firm's Understanding of Customers' Needs	4.4
Firm's Handling of Problems and Complaints	4.3
Firm's Accessibility	4.1
Firm's Utilization of Client's Input in Service	4.1
Firm's Knowledge of Client's Company and Industry	3.6

Table 3. Importance of Factors in Organization

Factor	Mean Score
Client Satisfaction	4.9
Employees' Attitude and Commitment to Service	4.6
Employees' Identification with Firm's Goals	4.4
Cultural Sensitivities	4.4
Low Employee Turnover (Loyalty/Satisfaction)	4.1
Employee Empowerment To Make Decisions	3.8
Incentive/Motivation Programs	3.6
Physical Environment (Offices, Tangibles)	3.5

to identify customer needs. When providers were specifically asked how they determined and satisfied expectations of clients, many mentioned staff feedback and perceptions while others stated that the finished results, or the fact that business continues indicated that clients were satisfied.

Another service aspect that was always important to 20 (65.0%) of the respondents and had an average score of 4.65 was the employee's attitude and commitment to customer service. However, as noted above, the courtesy of the provider's employees was not always influential in evaluating providers. Sixteen (52.0%) of the respondents indicated that an understanding of Korean business practices was always important. For a complete summary of the importance of service aspects in organizations, see Table 3.

D. Differences and Difficulties of Doing Business in Korea

When asked to discuss the biggest difficulties and differences in doing business in Korea versus in Western markets, the amount of government intervention and regulation was a major problem for most respondents. For example, five respondents mentioned that the vague and pervasive censorship laws in Korea present complex challenges for the creativity of a foreign advertising firm, especially as the rationale for certain decisions and approvals appear to lack consistency. The financial community also suffers badly from an over-regulated environment and restricted capital markets making the provision of internationally standard services complex. However, the respondents stated that their clients often viewed this as a problem of the service firm rather than the regulatory environment in which it operates. In addition, the government may assign a provider of financial services in some situations, which affects the provider's ability to compete for clients. Tight regulations on work visas affect the staffing of offices as foreign service firms struggle to recruit high caliber local employees. Since most professional service industries are relatively new in Korea, there is not a reservoir of experienced talent. Recruiting and retaining quality Korean employees is a major problem for many firms in most sectors. The major chaebols recruit on campuses and through complex and highly influential family and academic alumni relationships and it is difficult for foreign firms to do that.

Another major difficulty is that many Koreans do not understand the values and benefits of service providers. Many large Korean firms are reluctant to source "outside" services and have their own financial institutions, advertising agencies, transportation companies, and hotels. Since Korean companies are not accustomed to paying for service, much time must be spent on establishing and then managing expectations.

Because Korea is a country higher on collectivism, more things are done in groups. Many decisions involve groups and take much longer. More work is done in teams. Group members often discuss wages and other motivational aspects which may cause problems. While many workers say they want more money for good performance, the "group" may not be happy if one individual gets a reward and another one does not get a reward. Therefore, it may be difficult to implement compensation bonuses as a differentiator. It is also difficult for clients to admit mistakes at lower levels in their organizations. There is often miscommunication and a higher turnover of clients. Finding the right person to work with and contact in Korean firms is also very difficult for foreign firms.

E.   Differences in Customer Expectations in Korea

Customer expectations in Korea are typically lower than in Western markets. Many Koreans do not expect service nor do they expect to pay for it. While most of the respondents mentioned the importance of being a leader in customer service and a leader in quality, they must convince Korean businesses and Korean staffs of the benefits and values of service quality.

Respondents stated that there was very little difference in the way they measured client satisfaction and expectations in Korea. Very few companies had a formal method for measuring or evaluating client satisfaction and expectations. Instead, they depend on the perceptions of their Korean staffs, informal discussions and research, and limited surveys. Many respondents felt that the fact that their business continued indicated client satisfaction.

F. How Foreign Service Firms Adjust/Adapt Their Service System for Korea

In order to compete in Korea, foreign service firms have to adjust their services and their marketing strategies. All of the service firms utilize Korean staffs to learn and adjust to sensitivities in the Korean market. The Korean staff provides client feedback and input for service systems.

One of the most important adjustments that foreign service firms make is the emphasis on and necessity of cultivating and maintaining personal relationships. More time and money are spent on socializing and entertainment expenses. While not always influential in the selection of professional service providers, school affiliations and family relationships are important for recruiting employees and serve as an means of entry to meet potential clients. One respondent said that they lost a major client when an employee from the same university as a client's employee left the company.

Other major differences involve the longer length and details of meetings and documents. Discussions do not just involve marketing strategies, but they also involve the exchange of ideas, cultural, social, and political issues. Strategies and plans must constantly be adjusted to meet changing time lines. There is a sense of "urgency" of every project.

IV. CONCLUSIONS AND IMPLICATIONS

From the results of the study, it appears that Korean businesses are becoming more aware of the importance of service, but change is slow and service providers must be patient. In order to be a global competitor, Korean firms realize that they must become more service-oriented. As foreign firms enter the Korean market and Korean firms enter international markets, customer satisfaction and service will be critical for achieving a competitive advantage. With "globanomics" and increased deregulation, Korea will become a more important market and there will be more opportunity for professional service firms. At the same time, foreign service firms must understand the rules of doing business in Korea, respect the hierarchies, and try to build personal relationships. In many cases the relationships are the only means of entry for meeting potential clients. It may not be only a single-contact customer which needs to be considered. It can also be important for a service firm to develop relationships with its customer's customers, its employees, suppliers, distributors, retailers, relevant government offices, the media, the financial community, consumer groups, and others relevant to each unique customer situation. The time and money spent on building and maintaining relationships help Korean management understand the benefits of professional service firms. It is also important to be very diplomatic and respectful and courteous in building relationships.

As Koreans become more service conscious, they will also become aware of the profit potential of service providers. Therefore, the image and reputation that professional service providers establish will be very important. Positive word-of-mouth among Koreans, especially given the importance of relationships is a powerful marketing tool. An understanding of business practices and the culture, relationships, government regulations, reputation, and word-of-mouth affect foreign firms selling products and services in Korea.

In analyzing the results of the study, a number of contradictions are apparent. While the majority of firms rate client satisfaction and quality performance as the most important factors in evaluating service, only one respondent had a formal system of getting client feedback. Many firms also recognized the importance and scarcity of skilled employees, but few, if any, have dedicated training systems aimed at tailoring service to the unique needs of the Korean customer. This contradicts the high score given to the importance of the employee's attitude and commitment and its impact on service quality.

Foreign service providers must create a sense of "belonging" among both employees and clients. They must try to create *chong* between people, customers, and the firm. The firms must develop customer presentations aimed at establishing and managing expectations of service delivery, cost, value, and realistic benefits to the customer. While these adjustments will not guarantee success, they will certainly improve the competitive position of the providers.

This study was limited to foreign service firms doing business in Korea. If Korean businesses had been included in the study, the results may have been different. Also, the results may have been different if staff members had completed the surveys versus the top executives. Future research should examine whether these same findings apply to Korean businesses and other Asian markets. Finally, as the service industry continues to grow in the Korean market, a longitudinal study can be done to see how the factors influencing the selection and evaluation of service providers may change over time.

REFERENCES

Alden, D.L., Hoyer, W.D., & Lee, C. (1993). Identifying global and culture-specific dimensions of humor in advertising: A multinational analysis. *Journal of Marketing,* 57, 64-75.

Berry, L. (1995). *On great service.* New York, NY: The Free Press.

Bharadwaj, S,G., Varadarajan,P.R., & Fahy, J. (1993). Sustainable competitive advantage in service industries: A conceptual model and research propositions. *Journal of Marketing*, 57, 83-99.

Kim, K. (1995). Kim Young Sam's 'globanomics': How it has evolved and what it means for the U. S. *The Washington Post*, (August 25), A20.

Maister, D.H. (1993). *Managing the professional service firm.* New York, NY: The Free Press.

Onkvisit, S., & Shaw, J.J. (1989). Service marketing: Image, branding, and competition. *Business Horizons*, 13-18.

Ostrom, A., & Iacobucci, D. (1995). Consumer trade-offs and the evaluation of services. *Journal of Marketing*, 59, 17-18.

Parasuraman, A., Zeithaml, V.A., & Berry, L.L. (1988). SERVQUAL: A multiple-item scale for measuring consumer perceptions of service quality. *Journal of Retailing*, 64, 12-40.

Parasuraman, A., Berry, L.L., & Zeithaml, V.A. (1991). Refinement and reassessment of the SERVQUAL scale. *Journal of Retailing*, 67, 420-450.

Setton, M. (1995). Characteristics of Korean management. Working Paper.

Taylor, C.R., Wilson, R.D., & Miracle, G.E. (1994). The impact of brand differentiating messages on the effectiveness of Korean advertising. *Journal of International Marketing*, 2 (4), 31-52.

The Economist. (1994). Seoul's big splash. (November 5), 69-70.

Yugun, S. (1993). *Hangukui kyongyong*. Seoul, Korea: Pakyongsa.

PART III

INTERNATIONAL ADVERTISING

THE CHANGING INFORMATION CONTENT OF ADVERTISING:
A LONGITUDINAL ANALYSIS OF KOREAN MAGAZINE ADS

Young Sook Moon and George R. Franke

ABSTRACT

The late 1980s saw Korean advertising agencies become more open to affiliations and joint ventures with foreign agencies. To examine whether the changing Korean advertising industry was accompanied by changing levels of advertising information content, this study replicates Moon and Franke's (1987) analysis of Korean magazine ads for domestic and international brands. The results show that information levels remained stable in ads for international brands from 1985 to 1994, but dropped in domestic ads. The specific types of information used in advertising also varied over time. Several factors that may have contributed to the observed changes are identified.

I. INTRODUCTION

The Korean advertising market has experienced tremendous growth in the past several decades and is now the second largest in Asia, behind only Japan in total

Advances in International Marketing, Volume 7, pages 129-144.
Copyright © 1996 by JAI Press Inc.
All rights of reproduction in any form reserved.
ISBN: 1-55938-839-0

expenditures. With increasing liberalization of Korean investment and trade regulations, the role of international products has substantially increased in the Korean market. The 1995 opening of Korea's retail market is expected to further boost the presence of foreign advertisers (*Advertising Age*, 1995). Thus, improved understanding of Korean advertising practices may prove helpful to international marketers.

One important characteristic of advertising is the information it provides consumers that helps them make more knowledgeable purchase decisions. The information content of advertising has attracted considerable research attention following pioneering conceptual work by Nelson (1974) and an influential empirical study by Resnik and Stern (1977). Resnik and Stern established a classification system for advertising information based on fourteen criteria, or cues, representing categories of information useful to the consumer. Since 1977, this procedure has been used in more than fifty studies to measure advertising information content in different media, countries, and time periods (Abernethy & Franke, 1996).

A study by Moon and Franke (1987) used the Resnik-Stern procedure to examine Korean magazine advertisements for domestic and international brands appearing in 1985. At that time, the Korean advertising industry was dominated by a few major conglomerates' in-house agencies, and foreign agencies were excluded from the Korean market. According to one critic, the prevailing Confucian ethic, with its emphasis on respect and subordination to superiors and elders, put a damper on advertising creativity. Advertising was traditionally seen as a necessary evil, rather than a useful marketing tool, and younger employees who may have had a more sophisticated understanding of the role of advertising had difficulty in proposing ads that might displease their elders (*Far Eastern Economic Review*, 1984, p. 53). Since then, there have been important changes in the Korean advertising industry, including numerous joint ventures between Korean and foreign advertising agencies and a greater presence of agency personnel assigned from abroad (*Korea Annual*, 1992). These international ties, along with greater experience with advertising in foreign markets and increased competition from foreign advertisers in domestic markets, were expected to boost the quality of Korean advertising (*Business Korea*, 1986, 1992; *Far Eastern Economic Review*, 1984).

The purpose of this study is to replicate Moon and Franke's (1987) research to determine whether changes in the information content of Korean magazine advertising have accompanied these changes in the Korean advertising industry. The following section gives a brief overview of the literature on the information content of advertising and discusses the Korean advertising industry. Then, the methods used by Moon and Franke (1987) are described and applied to a sample of 1994 magazine ads. The 1994 results are presented and compared with the findings for 1985. Finally, implications of the findings are discussed and conclusions are offered.

II. BACKGROUND

A. Information Content in Advertising

Resnik and Stern (1977) developed a method for the systematic investigation of the information content of TV commercials. Rather than attempting to measure what people get from an ad or how useful they perceive the information in the ad to be, Resnik and Stern's content analysis procedure is designed to reveal objectively the types of information contained in the ad. The procedure involves determining which, if any, of the fourteen information cues shown in Table 1 are present. Resnik and Stern (1977), and many subsequent researchers, considered an ad to be informative if it contained at least one of the cues.

In a meta-analysis of the information content literature, Abernethy and Franke (1996) found that magazine advertising contains an average of 2.38 cues per ad.

Table 1.   Resnik-Stern (1977) Advertising Information Cues

1	Price—What does the product cost? What is its value-retention capability? What is the need-satisfaction capability/dollars?
2	Quality—What are the product's characteristics that distinguish it from competing products based on an objective evaluation of workmanship, engineering, durability, excellence of materials, structural superiority, superiority of personnel, attention to detail, or special services?
3	Performance—What does the product do and how well does it do what it is designed to do in comparison to alternative purchases?
4	Components—What is the product comprised of? What ingredients does it contain? What ancillary items are included with the product?
5	Availability—Where can the product be purchased? When will the product be available for purchase?
6	Special Offers—What limited-time nonprice deals are available with a particular purchase?
7	Taste—Is evidence presented that the taste of a particular product is perceived as superior in taste by a sample of potential customers? (Advertiser opinion is inadequate).
8	Nutrition—Are specific data given concerning the nutritional content of a particular product, or is a direct specific comparison made with other products?
9	Packaging—What package is the product available in which makes it more desirable than alternatives? What special shapes is the product available in?
10	Warranties—What post-purchase assurances accompany the product?
11	Safety—What features are available on a particular product compared to alternatives?
12	Independent Research—Are results of research gathered by an independent research firm presented?
13	Company Research—Are data gathered by a company to compare its product with a competitor's presented?
14	New Ideas—Is a totally new concept introduced during the commercial? Are its advantages presented?

Source: Resnik and Stern (1977) and Stern, Krugman and Resnik (1981).

Significant variation was observed across countries in terms of the presence and number of information cues after controlling for several study characteristics, including sample size, coder training, assessment of intercoder reliability, and omission of small ads and duplicate ads. The only previous investigation of Korean magazine advertising, besides Moon and Franke's (1987), reports 3.23 cues per ad in 1988 (Keown et al., 1992). This finding is based on a sample of only 30 ads from a single magazine, though, so its generalizability may be limited.

Relatively few studies on advertising information content have had an explicit longitudinal focus, and only one has looked at information trends in non-U.S. advertising. Two replications of the Resnik and Stern (1977) study found that the proportion of TV commercials containing information had not changed over time (Stern & Resnik, 1991; Tom et al., 1984), though the average number of cues per ad increased from .67 in 1975 to .85 in 1986 (Stern & Resnik, 1991). Pollay, Zaichkowsky and Fryer (1980) examined United States and Canadian TV commercials and found no change in information content from 1971-1973 to 1977. Healey, Fisher, and Healey (1986-1987) found stable information levels in commercials from 1981 to 1985 for light-advertising product categories, but reported a significant decrease for heavy-advertising products. Using a modified set of information cues, Pollay (1984) found evidence of a decline in information content in U.S. magazine ads from the 1900s through the 1970s. Chou, Franke, and Wilcox (1987) used Resnik and Stern's cues without modification and found no change in the information content of U.S. magazine advertising between 1970, 1975, and 1985. Healey and Kassarjian (1983) found increasing information levels in magazine ads for two product categories from 1970 to 1976, versus nonsignificant declines in two other categories. Kassarjian and Kassarjian (1988) extended the Healey and Kassarjian findings to 1984 with mixed results, though no significance tests were reported for the changes from 1976 to 1984. Overall, the evidence available suggests that U.S. information levels were relatively stable in the 1970s and 1980s, though there were fluctuations within specific product categories.

The literature reports greater variations in information levels across product categories than across time, but the lack of a standard product classification scheme hampers precise comparisons and conclusions. In general, Abernethy and Franke (1996) show that reported information levels are significantly higher for durable goods than for nondurables. For comparability with the 1985 findings, this study uses the same product classification scheme as Moon and Franke (1987).

B.   The Korean Advertising Industry

Advertising expenditures in Korea during 1994 exceeded 4 trillion won, or approximately 5 billion U.S. dollars (Chang et al., 1995). Korea's population is about 44 million, so spending per capita is low by Western standards. Nevertheless, this amount reflects tremendous growth from earlier levels. From 1979 to

1993, Korea's GNP grew at an annual rate of 8 percent, but this rate was far outpaced by the 23 percent annual growth in Korean advertising expenditures (*Business Korea*, 1994). The growth in spending was accompanied by a tremendous expansion in the number of advertising agencies. The first Korean advertising agency opened in 1976. Until 1982 there were only four agencies with full recognition by the Korean Broadcasting Advertising Corporation, or KOBACO. The number grew to 12 in 1988 and 121 in 1994.

KOBACO is a government regulatory agency that acts as the exclusive sales arm for every television and radio station in Korea. Though not directly involved with the print media, KOBACO influences magazine and newspaper advertising indirectly. Some advertisers must use print because broadcast ads are not allowed in their product categories. Little television commercial time is available each day, and 95 percent of it is controlled by fewer than ten Korean companies, so that few commercial breaks are available for other Korean or foreign advertisers (Chai, 1994). Finally, KOBACO pays a commission only to agencies meeting its standards for recognition. Therefore, unaccredited agencies may recommend that clients advertise in the print media, which have fewer restrictions on who is paid a commission (*Business Korea*, 1986). Of course, this incentive for using print has declined as more agencies have received recognition. Korea's growing cable TV industry, overseen by the Korean Cable Communications Commission rather than KOBACO, will also expand the media alternatives available to advertisers (Chai, 1994).

Non-equity affiliations existed between Korean and foreign agencies in the early 1980s, but it was not until 1987 that foreign agencies were allowed to invest in or form joint ventures with Korean advertising agencies. Foreign ownership was restricted to minority stakes until 1991, when the Korean advertising market was completely liberalized. Affiliations between domestic and foreign agencies proliferated, so that by 1994 twelve of the top fifteen agencies in Korea had some foreign connection. As many as 40 percent of the employees in joint agencies were assigned from abroad (*Korea Annual*, 1992).

The right to know is held to be a basic consumer right in Korea, and the Consumer Protection Board reports the results of periodic inspections of consumer goods to help consumers make informed purchase decisions (*Handbook of Korea*, 1993). The Fair Trade Commission controls false and unfair advertising practices, and several industry associations regulate their own activities (Boddewyn, 1992). However, no laws prescribe the types or amounts of information that advertising in Korea should contain. Interestingly, Keown et al. (1992) reported *lower* information levels in Korean advertising than in three other countries in three of the four media studied, though the small sample sizes and narrow selection of media outlets in each country limit the generalizability of findings from this study. A larger sample and broader mix of publications are necessary for reliable conclusions about the use of information in Korean magazine advertising.

III. METHOD

As in Moon and Franke (1987), ads for the study were sampled from selected issues of five major nationally-distributed consumer magazines. Two general interest and three women's magazines were used. These five magazines have high advertising rates and represent the largest publications in their classes. Ads in the March, June, September, and December 1994 issues of each magazine were selected to avoid potential bias from seasonal advertising practices. All one-page and larger ads were coded, with duplicate ads omitted from the analysis. The ads sampled were predominantly in Korean, though the use of foreign languages for brand names and even slogans was often found in international ads. Foreign words were usually though not always accompanied by Korean translations.

All ads were coded on two major dimensions, information content and brand origin. Information content was measured by recording which of the fourteen Resnik-Stern cues were present in the ad. Brand origin was coded as domestic (strictly Korean) or international. International brands included both strictly non-Korean products (e.g., Pepsi, Seiko) and joint Korean-foreign products (e.g., a vitamin from Roche Korea Co.), which were too few in number to treat as a separate category.

Magazine advertising has shared in the overall growth in Korean advertising expenditures: The sampling plan that obtained 573 unduplicated ads in 1985 magazines produced a sample of 1,380 unduplicated ads in 1994 magazines. Domestic and international advertising grew at the same rates over time, so that their relative occurrence was unchanged. Domestic ads comprised 71 percent of the samples in both time periods and international ads made up the remaining 29 percent.

One other category, product type, was also coded for each ad. Products were classified into six categories: durables and household goods, apparel and personal care items, foods and beverages, drugs, services, and other. These categories are fairly common in information content research (Abernethy & Franke, 1996), but the major justification for choosing them is to be consistent with Moon and Franke (1987).

One experienced judge fluent in Korean and English coded all the ads. To assess intercoder reliability, a second trained judge coded fifteen percent of the sample. While the use of multiple judges for every ad is desirable (Franke, 1992), this was precluded by resource constraints and the large sample size. Fortunately, the intercoder agreement was high for both the information content codings (92.9%) and the brand origin codings (93.0%), suggesting little potential error from the use of a single judge.

The raw data analyzed by Moon and Franke (1987) were unavailable. In most cases, though, comparisons of the 1985 and 1994 results involved straightforward analyses of tabulated values using loglinear procedures and analysis of variance. Except for information content within product categories, the analyses gave the same results as if the raw data had in fact been used. A simultaneous analysis of the

Table 2. Information Content by Year and Brand Origin[a]

Number of Cues	1985						1994					
	Domestic		International		Total		Domestic		International		Total	
0	69	17.0%	43	25.7%	112	19.5%	160	16.3%	71	17.7%	231	16.7%
1	111	27.3%	55	32.9%	166	29.0%	407	41.6%	182	45.4%	589	42.7%
2	88	21.7%	32	19.2%	120	20.9%	266	27.2%	94	23.4%	360	26.1%
3	77	19.0%	29	17.4%	106	18.5%	115	11.7%	46	11.5%	161	11.7%
4	48	11.8%	7	4.2%	55	9.6%	22	2.2%	6	1.5%	28	2.0%
5+	13	3.2%	1	0.6%	14	2.4%	8	0.9%	2	0.5%	11	0.8%
Total[b]	406	70.9%	167	29.1%	573	100%	979	70.9%	401	29.1%	1380	100%
Mean[c]	1.92		1.43		1.77		1.45		1.36		1.42	

Notes: [a]ANOVA results:

Year: $F=19.4$; $d.f.=1,1949$; $p<.001$.
Origin: $F=21.9$; $d.f.=1,1949$; $p<.001$.
Year × Origin: $F=10.2$; $d.f.=1,1949$; $p<.001$.
[b]This row is now percentages within years; all other percentages are column percentages.
[c]T-test results:
1985, Domestic versus International $t=3.93$; $d.f.=571$; $p<.001$.
1994, Domestic versus International: $t=1.51$; $d.f.=1378$; $p<.131$.
Domestic, 1985 versus 1994: $t=6.89$; $d.f.=1383$; $p<.001$.
International, 1985 versus 1994: $t=0.76$; $d.f.=556$; $p<.448$.

effects of year, brand origin, and product category was not possible; instead, product type and brand origin were analyzed within years, and specific comparisons were made using t-tests.

IV. RESULTS

A. Use of Information

Moon and Franke (1987) report that 80.5 percent of Korean magazine ads contained one or more information cues in 1985, with an average of 1.8 cues per ad. In 1994, 83.3 percent of Korean magazine ads contained one or more cues, but the average number of cues had dropped to 1.4 (Table 2). The increase in the proportion of informative ads is nonsignificant, whereas the decline in the amount of information presented is significant at $p < .01$.

The decline in information levels is due almost entirely to the domestic ads in the samples. A factorial ANOVA shows a significant interaction ($p < .001$) between year and origin. Comparisons of means via t-tests show that the decline in the mean number of cues in domestic ads from 1.92 to 1.45 is significant ($p < .001$), whereas the drop from 1.43 to 1.36 cues per international ad does not approach significance ($p > .44$).

Table 3. Specific Cues by Year and Origin[a]

Information Category	Year	Origin			z-statistics from Logit Analysis		
		Domestic	International	Total	Year	Origin	Year × Origin
1. Price/Value	1985	116 28.6%	56 33.5%	172 30.0%			
	1994	282 28.8%	68 17.0%	350 25.4%	3.60*	1.82	−3.69*
2. Quality	1985	82 20.2%	13 7.8%	95 16.6%			
	1994	40 4.1%	14 3.5%	54 3.9%	5.90*	2.83*	2.10*
3. Performance	1985	144 35.5%	47 28.1%	191 33.3%			
	1994	136 13.9%	47 11.7%	183 13.3%	8.54*	1.97*	0.53
4. Components/ Contents	1985	163 40.1%	37 22.2%	200 34.9%			
	1994	298 30.4%	77 19.2%	375 27.2%	2.37*	5.72*	0.96
5. Availability	1985	150 36.9%	48 28.7%	198 34.6%			
	1994	364 37.2%	234 58.4%	598 43.3%	−5.38*	−2.09*	5.29*
6. Special Offers	1985	9 2.2%	4 2.4%	13 2.3%			
	1994	44 4.5%	28 7.0%	72 5.2%	−2.81*	−0.83	0.59
7. Taste	1985	5 1.2%	2 1.2%	7 1.2%			
	1994	14 1.4%	2 0.5%	16 1.2%	0.65	0.96	−0.91
8. Nutrition	1985	10 2.5%	2 1.2%	12 2.1%			
	1994	15 1.5%	3 0.7%	18 1.3%	0.95	1.45	0.01
9. Packaging or Shape	1985	43 10.6%	16 9.6%	59 10.3%			
	1994	157 16.0%	43 10.7%	200 14.5%	−1.68	1.60	−0.98
10. Guarantees/ Warranties	1985	8 2.0%	4 2.4%	12 2.1%			
	1994	28 2.9%	20 5.0%	48 3.5%	−1.66	−1.13	0.55

11.	Safety	1985	10	2.5%	3	1.8%	13	2.3%	2.68*	0.96	−0.46
		1994	6	0.6%	1	0.2%	7	0.5%			
12.	Independent Research	1985	26	6.4%	4	2.4%	30	5.2%	3.36*	2.24*	−0.04
		1994	14	1.4%	2	0.5%	16	1.2%			
13.	Company Research[b]	1985	1	0.2%	0	0.0%	1	0.2%	1.20	0.45	n.a.
		1994	6	0.6%	2	0.5%	8	0.6%			
14.	New Idea	1985	11	2.7%	3	1.8%	14	2.4%	1.68	1.17	−0.26
		1994	14	1.4%	3	0.7%	17	1.2%			

Notes: *$p < .05$ (critical value is $z > 1.96$ in absolute value)
[a]Percents are relative to n's within years and origins.
[b]Logit analysis is not feasible; z-statistics for year and origin are from pairwise tests.

137

B.   Type of Information

Table 3 shows the use of specific cues by brand origin in the two time periods studied. The major cues in 1985 were price/value, performance, components/contents, and availability. In 1994, availability was the most common form of advertising information, followed by components/contents and price/value. Packaging/shape information was found in at least ten percent of magazine ads in both 1985 and 1994. Quality information was fairly common in 1985, being found in 17 percent of the ads, but dropped to under 4 percent in 1994.

To test for differences in the use of cues by brand origin and time period simultaneously, a logit analysis was performed using the SPSS loglinear procedure (Norusis, 1990). (This procedure could not be used with the company-research cue due to the empty cell for international brands in 1985. For this cue, year and origin effects were analyzed independently). The procedure produces z-statistics that can be treated as standard normal deviates, so that the critical value for significance at the .05 level is plus or minus 1.96. Positive z-statistics in Table 3 indicate greater use of the information cue in 1985 in domestic ads, or in either domestic 1985 ads or international 1994 ads, for the time main effect, origin main effect, and interaction, respectively. Reflecting the overall pattern shown in Table 2, the time effects and origin effects are generally positive; that is, more cues were used in 1985 and in domestic ads than in 1994 and international ads. Specifically, quality, performance, components/contents, and independent research cues were significantly more common in 1985 and in domestic ads. Price/value and safety cues were more common in 1985 than in 1994, but did not vary over brand origin. Information on product availability and special offers reversed this trend, increasing from 1985 to 1994. Availability was also featured more often in international ads than in domestic ads.

The main effects must be interpreted in light of three significant interactions. Though quality information was more common overall in 1985 than 1994, the difference was much greater for domestic ads than for international ads. The price/value cue was also more common overall in 1985, though in this case the declining use was found entirely in the international ads. The availability cue followed a reversed pattern, with international ads responsible for the increased use of the cue.

C. Information Cues within Product Categories

As in previous research (cf. Abernethy & Franke, 1996), there is a strong relationship between product type and the amount of information provided (Table 4). Overall, ads for drugs and durable/household goods were most informative, though there were significant interactions between product type and brand origin in both 1985 and 1994. (Because the raw data for 1985 were unavailable, separate two-way ANOVAs were performed for 1985 and 1994 rather than a combined three-way ANOVA.)

T-tests within each product category show that in 1985, domestic advertising used significantly more cues than international advertising in all product categories except apparel/personal care and other. The pattern was more varied in 1994. Domestic advertising had significantly more cues for foods and beverages (and marginally more in apparel/personal care ads), whereas international advertising had significantly more cues for durables/household goods (and marginally more for services).

The amount of information in domestic advertising declined in all product categories from 1985 to 1994, though in the case of apparel/personal care and other products the decline was nonsignificant. Information in international advertising increased for services and durable/household goods, declined in advertising for drugs and other products, and was relatively stable in the remaining product categories. Given the small n's used in most of the international comparisons, none of the differences were significant at the .05 level. Also, as shown in Table 2, the increases and decreases balanced out so that there were only slight changes in international advertising overall.

V. DISCUSSION

This study has identified several differences in the amount and type of information included in Korean magazine advertising over the past decade. Though there was a slight and nonsignificant increase in the proportion of ads considered to be informative, since they contained at least one of Resnik and Stern's fourteen cues, the average number of cues presented declined almost twenty percent from 1985 to 1994. This decline was concentrated in the ads for domestic products, which went from an average of 1.92 cues per ad in 1985 to 1.45 cues in 1994.

A potential explanation for the lower information levels in international ads in 1985 is that, historically, Koreans deemed anything foreign to be automatically good (Trucco, 1983, p. M-22). This attitude might have led to ads for international brands that relied on a foreign image rather than on specific product information. Over time, as the Korean government liberalized restrictions on foreign investments and international marketers, foreign branded goods became more common in Korea. Increasing familiarity with both foreign and domestic brands might have allowed consumers to rely on their own experiences more than on an assumed quality level for foreign brands. However, this logic suggests that foreign marketers would now need more informative advertising to give consumers specific reasons to buy. Instead, the change observed was a decline in information for domestic brands, not an increase in information levels for foreign brands. Furthermore, international ads reduced their use of information on price/value and quality over time and increased their focus on product availability—the most common cue

Table 4. Information Use Within Product Categories[a]

Product Category	Year	Total[b] n	Total[b] mean	Domestic[c] n	Domestic[c] mean	International n	International mean	Origin t	Origin p
Durables/Household	1985	154	2.33	116	2.50	38	1.82	2.64	.009
	1994	348	1.94	267	1.85	81	2.23	-2.72	.007
		$t=3.38\ p<.001$		$t=4.89\ p<.001$		$t=-1.72\ p<.089$			
Apparel/Personal care	1985	206	1.18	138	1.22	68	1.10	0.66	.509
	1994	568	1.14	362	1.19	206	1.06	1.74	.082
		$t=0.51\ p<.612$		$t=0.30\ p<.764$		$t=0.31\ p<.756$			
Food/Beverage	1985	75	1.61	53	1.92	22	0.86	3.26	.002
	1994	173	1.30	139	1.42	34	0.79	3.23	.001
		$t=2.03\ p<.044$		$t=2.77\ p<.006$		$t=0.24\ p<.089$			
Drugs	1985	61	2.80	39	3.05	22	2.36	2.58	.012
	1994	51	2.39	37	2.51	14	2.07	1.52	.135
		$t=2.23\ p<.023$		$t=2.43\ p<.018$		$t=0.87\ p<.388$			
Services	1985	38	1.79	30	2.00	8	1.00	2.96	.005
	1994	108	1.24	73	1.15	35	1.43	-1.90	.061
		$t=3.87\ p<.001$		$t=5.16\ p<.001$		$t=-1.51\ p<.138$			
Others	1985	39	1.41	30	1.30	9	1.78	-1.15	.256
	1994	132	1.17	101	1.16	31	1.22	-0.37	.713
		$t=1.52\ p<.131$		$t=0.71\ p<.480$		$t=1.64\ p<.110$			

Notes: [a]Standard deviations are not available for 1985. Comparisons with 1994 are based on pooled standard deviations reconstructed from the t-statistics.
[b]One-way ANOVA on information content by product type:
    1985: $F=25.2$; $d.f.=5,567$; $p<.001$.
    1994: $F=43.9$; $d.f.=5,1374$; $p<.001$.
[c]Two-way ANOVA on information content by product type and origin:
    1985: $F=14.8$; $d.f.=11,561$; $p<.001$.
    1994: $F=20.1$; $d.f.=11,1368$; $p<.001$.

in international ads in 1994. Thus, attitudes toward foreign products do not explain the declining information levels for domestic products after 1985.

An alternative explanation is that the growing homogeneity of information levels may reflect increased parity in the Korean market among both domestic and international brands. Advertisers may have fewer copy points for differentiation, and thus may be trying to create an impression or image rather than attempting to communicate concrete information (cf. Stern & Resnik, 1991). In fact, observation of the Korean advertising industry indicates that brand image is emerging as a key factor in advertising strategy, so that reliance on product claims is reduced. As shown by the content analysis, there is also greater competition through sales promotion and other special offers.

The homogenization of information levels can also be attributed to the growing foreign presence in Korean advertising agencies. In 1985, all Korean advertising was prepared by domestic agencies that had few affiliations with international agencies. With growing numbers of domestic and international agency affiliations, joint ventures, and transfers of foreign personnel to Korea, the Korean agency business became less distinctively Korean and reflected a more global perspective. This dilution of Korean agencies would tend to make domestic ads more like international ads, as found in this study.

Analyses within product categories show that the only domestic goods to avoid large declines in information levels had little information to start with. Even categories where consumers might demand useful information, such as drugs and durable goods, showed a drop of more than one-half cue per ad on average. It is not clear why domestic and international ads should show such divergent strategies for two product categories, durables/household items and services. These categories show the greatest *decreases* in information levels for domestic goods and the greatest *increases* for international goods. Non-Korean marketers may feel a greater need to convey detailed product information for high-involvement products such as durables or to indicate product availability and special offers for services (cf. Abernethy & Butler, 1992). It is interesting to note that imports are taking an increasing share of the market in these categories relative to domestic brands, though this trend is not necessarily connected to the disparities in advertising information levels.

Though the focus of this study is on changes in information content over time, the findings are also useful for comparing information levels in Korean magazine advertising with advertising in other countries. Abernethy and Franke (1996) report that across studies, 88.6 percent of magazine ads are found to contain at least one information cue. This is higher than the 83.3 percent found for 1994 Korean advertising and the 80.5 percent found for 1985, but the differences are not large. Korean advertising falls shorter in terms of the amount of information presented. The average of 2.38 cues per ad reported by Abernethy and Franke is almost 1 cue, or 68 percent, higher than the 1.42 cues found in this study. For 1985, the difference is .61 cues, or 34 percent higher than the mean of 1.77 reported by

Moon and Franke (1987). These lower levels may be explained by two aspects of Korean culture (Miracle, Chang, & Taylor, 1992; Moon & Franke, 1987). Korea has a high context culture in which messages may need little explicit verbal content because much information is implicit in the situation or is already internalized in the recipient (Hall, 1976). The context established by a Korean ad may communicate information in ways not assessed by the systematic, objective Resnik-Stern coding system. Also, traditional values in Korea discourage direct confrontations, stressing instead decorum in business rivalry as well as gentle moods in advertising (Boddewyn & Marton, 1978, p. 39). Thus, emotional appeals may be more popular than rational, informative messages.

VI. CONCLUSION

This study presents a longitudinal analysis of Korean magazine advertising over the past decade. The results show changes in the amount and type of information featured in advertising for domestic and international brands. A key finding is that advertising information levels were equal across brand origins in 1994, whereas advertising for domestic brands contained significantly higher information levels than advertising for international brands in 1985 (Moon & Franke, 1987).

This conclusion is limited to the types of information studied. Resnik and Stern's classification system provides an objective means of evaluating each ad against a uniform set of criteria. However, some relevant information cues may be omitted from this classification scheme (cf. Moon & Franke, 1987). Thus, this study gives a useful but possibly incomplete picture of the information in Korean magazine advertising; different results might be obtained if a broader set of cues were used.

With the opening-up of the Korean agency business, large multinational agencies have brought new techniques and new incentives for the Korean advertising industry to grow and develop. Industry members predicted that increased international influence would raise standards for Korean advertising (*Business Korea*, 1992). This study suggests that the changing Korean advertising industry resulted in lower information levels for consumers. However, there is a crucial difference between information provision and information utilization (e.g., Jacoby, 1974, 1977). Utilization depends on the quality and usefulness of the information and the consumer's situation and motivation to obtain information. Fewer information cues, presented in a more relevant and interesting way, may be more useful to the consumer than a mass of dry facts. Of course, examining trends in the quality of Korean advertising is beyond the scope of this study.

Korea is one of the fastest growing markets in the world and presents tremendous opportunities to international marketers. Multinational companies are becoming more aggressive in their pursuits of international markets, presenting domestic marketers with strong new competition. Both domestic and international marketers must be sensitive not only to determining what products and services they can sell but also to communicating relevant information to consumers (Belch & Belch, 1995). Also, despite the internationalization of Korean advertising, differences are still found between domestic and international ads in certain product categories. Therefore, as indicated by Miracle, Chang and Taylor (1992), foreigners working in the Korean advertising environment are likely to encounter unexpected attitudes toward certain advertising practices.

Advertising is often the most effective method of communicating with potential buyers in mass markets. However, advertising in the consumer interest should begin with the communication of product features and competitive advantages that the consumer can use in making intelligent buying decisions. Thus, cross-cultural research on information content in advertising as well as regulatory concerns and consumer demands are critical issues to global marketing practices in developing countries.

REFERENCES

Abernethy, A.M., & Butler, D.D. (1992). Advertising information: Services versus products. *Journal of Retailing*, 68, 398-419.

Abernethy, A.M., & Franke, G.R. (1996). The information content of advertising: A meta-analysis. *Journal of Advertising*, in press.

Advertising Age. (1995). Emerging markets: A mixed bag of promise and pitfalls, (May 15), I-12-I-14.

Business Korea. (1986). The reach for maturity, 4 (July), 59-65.

Business Korea. (1992). The name game: Korean firms want to be known abroad, 9 (February), 35.

Business Korea. (1994). Ad spending surges on strong consumer demand, 12 (July), 41-42.

Belch, G.E., & Belch, M.A. (1995). *Introduction to advertising and promotion*, 3rd ed. Chicago: Richard D. Irwin, Inc.

Boddewyn, J.J. (1992). *Global perspectives on advertising self-regulation*. Westport, CT: Quorum Books.

Boddewyn, J.J., & Marton, K. (1978). *Comparison advertising: A worldwide study*. New York: Hastings House.

Chai, D. (1994). Cable opens new horizons for So. Korean advertisers. *Advertising Age*, (March 21), I-6.

Chang, W.H., Palasthira, T.S., & Kim, H.K. (1995). *The rise of Asian advertising*. Seoul: Nanam.

Chou, L., Franke, G.R., & Wilcox, G.B. (1987). The information content of comparative magazine advertisements: A longitudinal analysis. *Journalism Quarterly*, 64 (1), 119-24, 250.

Far Eastern Economic Review. (1984). Necessary evil rather than useful marketing tool, 125 (July 19), 53-54.

Franke, G.R. (1992). Reliability and generalizability in coding the information content of advertising. *Asian Journal of Marketing*, 1, 7-25.

Hall, E.T. (1976). *Beyond culture*. Garden City, NY: Anchor Press/Doubleday & Company, Inc.

Handbook of Korea. (1993). Seoul, Korea: Korean Overseas Information Service.

Healey, J.S., Fisher, M.E., & Healey, G.F. (1986/1987). Advertising screamers versus hummers. *Journal of Advertising Research*, 26, 43-49.

Healey, J.S., & Kassarjian, H.H. (1983). Advertising substantiation and advertiser response: A content analysis of magazine advertisements. *Journal of Marketing*, 47, 107-117.

Jacoby, J. (1974). Brand choice behavior as a function of information load: Replication and extension. *Journal of Consumer Research*, 1, 33-42.

Jacoby, J. (1977). Consumer use and comprehension of nutrition information. *Journal of Consumer Research*, 4, 119-129.

Kassarjian, H.H., & Kassarjian, W.M. (1988). The impact of regulation on advertising: A content analysis. *Journal of Consumer Policy*, 11 (3), 269-285.

Keown, C.F., Jacobs, L.W., Schmidt, R.W., & Ghymn, K.-I. (1992). Information content of advertising in the United States, Japan, South Korea, and the People's Republic of China. *International Journal of Advertising*, 11 (3), 257-267.

Korea Annual. (1992). Seoul, Korea: Yonhap News Agency.

Miracle, G.E., Chang, K.Y., & Taylor, C.R. (1992). Culture and advertising executions: A comparison of selected characteristics of Korean and U.S. television commercials. *International Marketing Review*, 9 (4), 5-16.

Moon, Y.S., & Franke, G.R. (1987). The information content of domestic and international advertising: An analysis of Korean magazine ads. In S. Douglas (Ed.), *AMA Summer Educators' Conference Proceedings* (p. 98). Chicago: American Marketing Association.

Nelson, P. (1974). Advertising as information. *Journal of Political Economy*, 82, 729-745.

Norusis, M.J. (1990). *SPSS advanced statistics student guide*. Chicago: SPSS Inc.

Pollay, R.W. (1984). Twentieth-century magazine advertising. *Written Communication*, 1 (1), 56-77.

Pollay, R.W., Zaichkowsky, J., & Fryer, C. (1980). Regulation hasn't changed ads much! *Journalism Quarterly*, 57 (3), 438-446.

Resnik, A., Stern, B.L. (1977). An analysis of information content in television advertising. *Journal of Marketing*, 41, 50-53.

Stern, B.L., Krugman, D.M., & Resnik, A. (1981). Magazine advertising: An analysis of its information content. *Journal of Advertising Research*, 21, 39-44.

Stern, B.L. & Resnik, A.J. (1991). Information content in television advertising: A replication and extension. *Journal of Advertising Research*, 31, 36-46.

Tom, G., Calvert, S., Goolkatsian, R., & Zumsteg, A. (1984). An analysis of information content in television advertising: An update. In J. Leigh & C.R. Martin (Eds.), *Current Issues and Research in Advertising* (pp. 159-165). Ann Arbor: University of Michigan.

Trucco, T. (1983). International profile is key to agency growth. *Advertising Age*, 54, (October 24), M20-M23.

ENVIRONMENTAL INFLUENCES ON U.S. MULTINATIONAL ADVERTISING AGENCIES:
A MARKET DEVELOPMENT PERSPECTIVE

Alan T. Shao

ABSTRACT

Environmental factors in all market types pose problems for multinational advertising agencies. However, the extent of these problems has been ambiguous. This study of 344 affiliates in developed, newly-industrializing and less-developed markets demonstrates that there is strong agreement regarding the degree to which restrictions pose problems in each market type and that media restrictions are vehicle-specific. It was also found that legal and economic factors were cited most often by affiliates to pose major problems to their operations. For those looking to avoid heavy competition in advertising, developing countries offered the most relief but market size was considerably greater in developed nations.

Advances in International Marketing, Volume 7, pages 145-158.
Copyright © 1996 by JAI Press Inc.
All rights of reproduction in any form reserved.
ISBN: 1-55938-839-0

I. INTRODUCTION

Advertising is an art and globally the picture is constantly changing. In Asia, for example, satellite and cable systems (e.g., STAR and TVB) are dramatically increasing the number of promotional choices available to advertisers. Throughout Eastern Europe, similar mechanisms are making it more convenient for advertisers to promote their wares and build brand recognition and customer loyalty. As the European Union, North American Free Trade Agreement, ASEAN, and other regional associations continue to advance in their cooperative efforts, undoubtedly there will be even greater opportunities for advertisers to promote their products and services to larger groups.

While only a few of the major world changes have been noted, it is apparent that business opportunities are no longer concentrated in economically sophisticated markets; the unlimited possibilities in newly-industrializing countries (NIC) and developing nations [or "less developed countries" (LDC)] are becoming increasingly obvious. Enticements from these less heralded countries include growing GNP per capita, more sophisticated infrastructures (especially in newly-industrializing nations), inexpensive labor costs, and governmental support of foreign businesses. The advertising industry has taken note of these world changes and is re-shaping market structures to take full advantage of these opportunities.

The problem is that advertising agencies must oftentimes work around certain uncontrollable environmental elements in foreign markets. But there is little empirical information available to advertisers about what to expect regarding environmental forces that may interfere with their operations in markets other than developed nations. How different are newly-industrializing and developing markets from developed countries according to advertising practitioners? Economically there are huge deviations. But to advertising agencies seeking to set up global networks or looking to simply open affiliates in promising markets, what should they expect? Should ad agencies be concerned about market development or should they proceed in markets as if, as Levitt (1983) stated, "Different cultural preferences, national tastes and standards, and business institutions are vestiges of the past?" It is the objective of this exploratory study to contrast various environmental forces by market development level to determine whether significant differences exist in the advertising industry. If differences are detected, inquiries will be made into the extent of these deviations. The findings were drawn from a 344 agency affiliate survey of advertising activities in 51 countries.

II. BACKGROUND

Despite its obvious importance to advertising practitioners, commentaries addressing environmental forces in developed, newly-industrializing and developing markets have been rare and those that have been available tended to be rather myopic in nature. Some authors have examined some situational factors abroad. For example, Shao and Hill (1992) looked at the availability of qualified advertising personnel worldwide and unsurprisingly concluded that there were more advertising talent shortfalls in developing than developed countries, although the gap was less than they expected. Kanso (1992) studied the effect of culture on advertising standardization. In his study of 96 international advertising managers of U.S. consumer durable manufacturers, he found that most firms were guided by the localized approach. Toyne and Walters (1993) provided ten recommendations for advertising in Third-world countries and stated, without surprise, that "Promotional activities in developing countries often require significantly different approaches from those used in more advanced or industrialized countries" (p. 568). Other authors have looked narrowly at environmental factors from individual or regional perspectives (e.g., Benedetto, Tamate, & Chandran, 1992; looked solely at the Japanese market; Mueller, 1992 and Ramaprasad & Hasegawa, 1992 looked only at Japanese and American commercials; and Zandpour, Chang & Catalano, 1992 looked specifically at French, Taiwanese and U.S. commercials). Some studies that also looked too narrowly at the advertising environment are too dated to be useful in such a changing industry worldwide (e.g., Dunn & Lorimor, 1979; Elinder, 1965; Weinstein, 1970; Lo & Yung 1988). While country-specific and regional studies have contributed quite a bit of knowledge to our understanding of advertising abroad, there is an absence of empirical studies from *global* perspectives comparing how environmental forces influence advertising in different market types.

The few studies that looked at the market environment from the perspective of market development had apparent shortcomings. Hill and Boya (1987) examined only one side of the spectrum. They looked at how consumer goods were promoted in developing markets and concluded that there were few differences in media usage. Boddewyn (1981) studied the global spread of advertising regulation. He concluded that while regulations will continue to expand, they will do so in different ways (e.g., Scandinavian countries have their Consumer Ombudsman, Anglo-Saxon nations have their heavy reliance on self-regulation, and developing markets strongly protect their cultural identities).

Considering that there are numerous examples of business blunders in the advertising arena (Ricks, 1983), advertisers—especially multinationals—must do a better job in understanding their environments worldwide since so many large agencies are global players. But before we empirically examine the impact of environmental factors in various market types on advertising operations, it is necessary to clarify the differences among these types of markets.

III. RESEARCH ISSUES

As previously noted, those advertising agencies who are either presently, or are planning to operate in multiple foreign markets must have a firm grasp on the realities of the environment in different market development types. Therefore, a series of research questions (RQ) are offered. First, since each media vehicle foreign firms consider using for promotional purposes possesses its own set of restrictions, it is necessary for advertising agencies to understand the restrictiveness of each media type. Therefore:

RQ1: How restrictive is television, radio, newspaper, poster, magazine, and direct mailing when advertising in each market type?

There are market conditions that cause varying degrees of problems for agencies in different market types. The diversity of cultures, economies, laws and the like necessitate that businesses recognize where differences occur and may threaten their performance. Therefore:

RQ2: To what extent do particular market conditions (i.e., cultural, economic, social, political, and legal factors) create problems for advertising agencies' operations?

Competitive intensity in each type of market should be known by all players since competition heavily influences companies' strategies (Porter, 1980). The degree of competition may play an important role into whether an agency enters a particular market. Therefore:

RQ3: What is the level of competition in developing, newly industrializing, and developed markets?

Finally, a look at total billings in each type of market development will indicate how markets have performed relative to other potential arenas where competition exists. This is important for future planning. Therefore:

RQ4: What is the market size, as measured by total billings, in each of the market development types?

IV. METHODOLOGY

A. Data

The population surveyed consisted of all foreign affiliates of U.S.-based advertising agencies. Sampling procedures were two-fold. The aim of the first part was to identify agencies with six or more active overseas affiliates so that they could qualify as "multinational" according to the terms laid out by Aharoni (1971). Twenty-one international agencies met this criterion and were contacted by telephone. Out of the 21 agencies, 15 agreed to allow their foreign affiliates to participate in the study. Four of the six agencies that would not agree to participate in the study stated that their operations were presently being acquired by large competitors. It was later revealed that the acquiring agencies were among the fifteen that had originally agreed to participate in the study. Therefore, in essence 19 of the 21 agencies originally contacted participated in the study, increasing the representativeness of the target market.

The second part of the sampling procedure involved contacting affiliate agencies. Surveys were mailed to managing directors at 755 different foreign affiliates of multinational ad agencies. Twenty five were returned as undeliverable since the business was either no longer in operation or the agency was no longer affiliated with the parent company. Of the remaining 730 questionnaires, however, 344 useable questionnaires were returned, a 47 percent response rate. This extent of response is high considering surveys were mailed worldwide and used only one language. Similar surveys of this magnitude tend to have response rates ranging from 23 percent to 52 percent (Carpano, Chrisman, & Roth, 1994; Katz & Lancaster, 1989). Lack of participation from over half of the sampling group may be attributed to laziness, length of the questionnaire (8 pages), poor mailing systems in the home country (perhaps some of them were lost in the mail), and misplacement of surveys once they arrived at the agencies.

To examine whether geographic biases were present in the sample, chi-square analysis was used to compare whether the proportion of respondents in each region (Africa, Europe, North America, etc.) were consistent with actual regional profiles for U.S. agencies operating abroad. Results indicated that regional responses did not differ from actual distribution since the critical value (12.592) exceeded the computed value (4.76).

B.   Questionnaire Design

The measuring instrument was heavily influenced by advertising practitioners. Executives from two leading agencies (a Vice President at Bozell, Jacobs, Kenyon & Eckhardt and an Account Manager at Young & Rubicam) assisted in the questionnaire design. After several reviews and amendments, the instrument was further examined by advertising executives at two other agencies (Senior Vice Presidents of International Operations at BBDO and Grey Advertising). Their suggestions were minor, indicating that the instrument was ready for use.

The questionnaire was designed to elicit information about media restrictions, general environmental forces, competition intensity, and market size. First, six different types of media vehicles were listed and respondents were asked to indicate the extent they perceived each vehicle to be restricted in their countries. Choices ranged from "no restrictions" to "certain products cannot be legally advertised on this medium." Second, respondents were asked to indicate, from a list of eleven factors agreed upon by the two advertising executives, the degree each market condition affected their ability to advertise products. Respondents could choose from the following list: multiple languages/dialects, religious factions/groups, different ethnic groups/races, inflation, limits on importing ad materials, restrictions on hiring foreigners, legal restrictions on ad claims, consumer groups, literacy problems, foreign exchange limits, and government bias toward advertising. Choices ranged from "not a factor" to "definite problem." Third, firms were asked about the number of agencies they considered to be major competitors in their markets. Choices ranged from "no major competitors" to "over 8." The final category was eventually collapsed to represent the "7 to 8" group.

V. RESULTS

A. Media Restrictions

The results offer some interesting insights into the advertising industry throughout the world. Table 1 shows the media restriction intensities detected in each of the market development types. Surprisingly, most of the respondents in each market type agreed on the degree of restrictions in their markets. Regarding television, the majority of respondents in each market type stated that certain products could not be advertised in their markets. The only considerable stray from this agreement was found in NICs where one-third of the respondents noted that there were no restrictions in their markets. But as an overall group, 79 percent of all respondents stated that certain products could not be advertised. This may be attributed to the reality that certain "sensitive" products such as cigarettes, alcohol and condoms are often severely limited regarding when and where they may be advertised.

There was also considerable agreement regarding the degree of restrictiveness for products advertised on the radio. While there was strong agreement between respondents in developing and less-developed countries that certain products cannot be advertised on the radio, it appears that there are far fewer limitations in newly-industrializing nations. This finding may be attributed to the likelihood that business development in these nations is growing at a much faster pace than are certain regulatory groups. It must be noted that in NICs many (38%) of the respondents believed that certain products could not be advertised on the radio. Also, in LDCs a substantial proportion of respondents (44%) believed that their markets were relatively free of restrictions. These findings may be explained by realizing that the sample covered many types of product and service categories and that each respondent likely perceived the restriction intensity independently of other products they did not offer. Therefore, although the overall business environment may be restrictive, it is reasonable to expect exceptions since the respondents usually offered different types of items—which would probably have different promotional restrictions.

Table 1.   Media Restrictions By Market Development

TELEVISION RESTRICTIONS	DC	NIC	LDC	Total
No restrictions	26	12	20	58
	(12%)	(34%)	(26%)	(17%)
Limited market coverage	11	0	1	12
	(5%)	(0%)	(1%)	(4%)
Cannot advertise	185	23	56	264
certain products	(83%)	(66%)	(73%)	(79%)
Total	222	35	77	334
	(67%)	(11%)	(23%)	
Chi-Square = 18.36688	df=4			p < .01
RADIO RESTRICTIONS	DC	NIC	LDC	Total
No restrictions	51	20	33	104
	(24%)	(59%)	(44%)	(32%)
Limited market coverage	12	1	2	15
	(5%)	(3%)	(3%)	(5%)
Cannot advertise	152	13	40	205
certain products	(71%)	(38%)	(53%)	(63%)
Total	215	34	75	324
	(66%)	(11%)	(23%)	
Chi-Square = 23.24313	df=4			p < .001
DIRECT MAIL RESTRICTIONS	DC	NIC	LDC	Total
No restrictions	151	25	44	220
	(76%)	(81%)	(62%)	(73%)
Limited market coverage	3	2	17	22
	(2%)	(6%)	(24%)	(7%)
Cannot advertise	44	4	10	58
certain products	(22%)	(13%)	(14%)	(19%)
Total	198	31	71	300
	(66%)	(10%)	(24%)	
Chi-Square = 40.12201	df=4			p < .001

Note: No significant differences were found regarding newspaper, poster and magazine restrictions.

There was strong agreement regarding the restrictiveness of advertising through direct mail. Unlike the restrictions on television and radio, an overwhelming majority of respondents in each market type stated that they perceived no limitations to exist in their markets. This is good news to many direct-mail marketers in Eastern Europe and China who are looking to take advantage of new market opportunities by soliciting business through mail-order catalogues, samples and coupons (*The Economist*, 1991; *Marketing News*, 1991). It is common knowledge that recipients of mail in LDCs tend to pay close attention to the message inside since they are not accustomed to getting information and/or "gifts" at no cost. A stronger sense of obligation motivates this target to carefully read the promotional contents. Once again, however, there were some respondents indicating that they felt at least some limitations were present. But again this finding may be attributed to the sampling of various types of businesses offering different products. Different products typically will encounter different restrictions.

No significant differences were detected from the respondents in each of the market types in terms of the remaining media vehicles (newspapers, posters and magazines). This is surprising since the availability and sophistication of each vehicle tends to vary considerably.

B.   Environmental Factors

Regarding market development, to what degree do environmental conditions pose problems to advertising agencies? Table 2 shows the percentages of agencies reporting that market conditions created significant problems to their operations. It appears that the market conditions causing problems for agencies differed among market types. That is, there was little agreement among the respondents in each market type regarding which market conditions caused definite problems to their operations. In developed markets, legal restrictions on ad claims, multiple languages, restrictions on hiring foreigners and limits on the importation of ad materials were the most often cited problems. It is not surprising to find legal restrictions encompassing three of the top four spots since regulatory agencies are generally well-established in developed markets. In particular, legal restrictions on advertising claims emanating from those agencies with the highest billings was expected since false and misleading advertising has been a well-debated issue in most industrialized nations (Boddewyn, 1982; Burton, 1984; Turner, 1991; Zanot, 1985). For example, a law like The Consent Order of the Federal Trade Commission (which encourages advertisers to refrain from certain advertising practices and claims) has caused unrest among advertisers in developed nations.

In NICs, inflation, limits on the importation of advertising materials, foreign exchange limitations and legal restrictions on advertising claims were the most often cited severe problems. It is interesting to note that two of the top four involve economic concerns (inflation and foreign exchange limits) and the other two are legal restrictions (importing of ad materials and advertising claims). NICs are known to rely heavily on their exports, making them vulnerable to changes in interest rates and foreign exchange. Since much advertising is currently being conducted in all NICs, these markets have had ample opportunity to create guidelines

Table 2. Percentages Of Agencies Reporting Specific Problems
By Market Development

Market Condition	DC	NIC	LDC
Multiple languages/dialects*	11.5	2.9	13.8
Religious factions/groups	1.8	2.9	11.4
Different ethnic groups/races	5.7	2.9	12.7
Inflation	6.3	31.4	21.5
Limits on importing ad materials	9.3	20.0	35.0
Restrictions on hiring foreigners	10.6	8.6	27.8
Legal restrictions on ad claims*	18.1	14.3	11.3
Consumer groups*	7.1	0.0	4.0
Literacy problems	2.8	8.8	17.9
Foreign exchange limits	5.9	17.6	26.3
Government bias of advertising	1.4	5.9	6.4

Note: *denotes non-significant differences

Table 3. Competitive Intensity By Market Development

COMPETITION INTENSITY	DC	NIC	LDC	Total
no major competitors	3	1	2	6
	(1%)	(3%)	(3%)	(2%)
1 - 4	63	9	37	109
	(28%)	(27%)	(47%)	(32%)
5 - 8	88	15	26	129
	(38%)	(44%)	(33%)	(38%)
more than 8 competitors	74	9	14	97
	(32%)	(26%)	(18%)	(28%)
Chi-Square= 13.34407		df=6		p < .05

regarding when, how, who and what can and cannot be said through all of the available advertising vehicles.

In LDCs, limitations on importing ad materials, restrictions on hiring foreigners, foreign exchange limits and inflation were cited most often by respondents as creating problems for their advertising operations. Economic concerns were not surprising, since many developing nations are experiencing high rates of inflation and considerable foreign exchange fluctuations. The other top restrictions were also expected since developing nations typically encourage foreign companies to train their unskilled people. Because agencies cannot import all of their advertising materials, they must develop some of it in their markets. This development process would likely benefit the nationals hired by the agency since they can learn from the experience.

C. Competitive Intensity

As stated by Porter (1980), competition intensity tends to increase as the number of competitors expand. Results indicate that in all market types, respondents perceived competition to be somewhat intense (see Table 3). While few in each market type stated that there were no major competitors, there seems to be the most competition in NICs, followed by developed and then developing markets. Seventy percent of the NIC respondents felt that they had at least five major competitors, whereas only 60 percent in DCs and 51 percent in LDCs claimed to have this same level of competition intensity. In general, it seems that the world has lost its innocence since it is getting more difficult to find an unmined, uncluttered market.

It was not unexpected to find competition to be so fierce in NICs since these are markets typically characterized by rapid per capita GNP growth. It was obviously not unusual to find developed nations to be highly competitive. What was surprising was the considerable competition intensity in developing markets. Oftentimes companies will operate in developing regions simply to avoid heavy competition and skim the market for what it's worth—hoping that it will continue to improve and provide additional opportunities. However, it seems that from an advertising standpoint, promotional opportunities have already been realized to some degree.

D. Market Size

Table 4 shows the total amount of money spent on advertising in each market type. As expected, developed countries had the most expenditures with 72 percent (45 + 27) of the respondents indicating that they competed in markets with ad expenditures exceeding $1 billion. NICs had the second most ad expenditures with 78 percent (63 + 14) of the respondents competing in markets between $100 million and $1 billion. Finally, developing countries had 83 percent (19 + 64) of the respondents competing in markets with ad expenditures less than $500 million. While these findings are not earth-shattering, they do demonstrate the wide variance between those competing in each market type. The fact that over 70 percent of the respondents in developed markets were competing in markets with ad expenditures exceeding $1 billion while less than one-quarter of those in either NICs or LDCs competed in this size of market clearly demonstrates that there is a much smaller "pie" to divide among competitors in the latter two market types. Therefore, perhaps future empirical studies need to examine the motivations behind competing in markets where there is substantially less to gain in the short-run. Certainly there are other motivations besides lesser competition intensity and the market's long-term promise.

VI.   SUMMARY AND CONCLUSIONS

This study examined the perception of market restrictions in the advertising industries of developed, newly-industrializing and developing nations. First, it was

Table 4.   Market Size By Market Development

MARKET SIZE	DC	NIC	LDC	Total
less than $100 million	1	0	15	16
	(1%)	(0%)	(19%)	(5%)
$100 million - $500 million	11	22	51	84
	(5%)	(63%)	(14%)	(24%)
$500.01 million - $1 billion	51	5	10	66
	(22%)	(14%)	(12%)	(19%)
$1.01 billion - $5 billion	103	8	4	115
	(45%)	(23%)	(5%)	(33%)
over 5 billion	63	0	0	63
	(27%)	(0%)	(0%)	(19%)
Chi-Square = 217.22723		$df=8$		$p < .001$

revealed that specific products could not be advertised on television and radio (except in NICs regarding the latter), but that no restrictions were perceived to exist when using direct mail—regardless of the type of market. This highlights an important promotional opportunity for ad agencies entering into NICs or developing countries. Since consumers have not been inundated with direct mail in the past (particularly in LDCs), they tend to be much more tolerant of it and in fact will oftentimes pay close attention to its contents. The reality that no advertising restrictions were perceived to exist by respondents demonstrates tremendous opportunities for practitioners in NICs and LDCs. No significant differences were detected when promoting products in other print forms (i.e., newspaper, poster and magazines).

Second, it was found that legal and economic restrictions posed definitive problems to advertisers in each market type, although the order differed by market development level. These impediments are unavoidable and oftentimes uncontrollable but must be paid attention to by ad agencies since they can greatly impede the effectiveness of their operations. Cultural and social considerations were not named as often probably because most U.S. multinational advertising agencies hire local people to run their overseas affiliates.

Third, it was revealed that NICs were the most competitive in the advertising industry, although most people would probably believe competitive intensity is more fierce in developed nations. But considering the rapid economic growth of NICs, ad agencies are rushing to the four "little dragons" in Asia (Hong Kong, Singapore, South Korea and Taiwan) and the Latin American countries of Brazil and Mexico to promote their clients' wares. Considering that the individual markets are comparably small to industrialized nations, competition is indeed intense for a relatively small "piece of the pie," but could pay big dividends in the long run. Take, for example, those setting up shops in Hong Kong and Taiwan, anticipating the formation of "Greater China" in the not-so-distant future. Since these two nations are often viewed as potential gateways into China, many businesses see setting up an operation in either Hong Kong or Taiwan as a prerequisite to gaining access to the some 1.3 billion Chinese (future) consumers.

Finally, not surprisingly, it was found that the market size in the advertising industry was greatest in developed nations, followed by NICs and developing countries. In fact, developed nations had advertising expenditures in many cases billions of dollars greater than those in either of the other market types. Therefore, it seems that the combination of reduced competitive intensity along with perceived future market potential offers powerful motivation for agencies to set up shops in currently less lucrative markets, when compared to developed nations. But marketers must not underestimate the potential of developing nations. In fact, a closer look at those currently in developing markets reveals that over 60 percent of respondents were operating in markets ranging from $100 million to $500 million. With markets opening up and GDP per capita rising, the economic future of many growing nations is promising.

Although it is obvious that some significant environmental differences among market types occur, these deviations should not necessarily be construed as overwhelming obstacles for foreign businesses. Newly-industrializing and developing countries offer marketing opportunities that developed countries do not offer. Since some products are not permitted to be promoted in many developed countries (e.g., tobacco-related goods), regardless of media vehicle, companies may seek less restrictive markets to penetrate. Also, since competition is less intense in developing nations, those unable to "battle the big guys" may prefer to establish themselves in less competitive areas, especially when those markets are viewed as having a strong potential for becoming newly-industrializing or more fully developed. Foreign businesses must remember that at one time or another, every country had developing market characteristics. In conclusion, progressive multinationals can ill afford to put their heads in the sand when it comes to overseas expansion. The status quo simply will not do. Therefore, when taking a global perspective, neither NICs nor developing markets should be ignored.

REFERENCES

Advertising Age. (1989). Foreign agency income report, pp. 72-77.

Aharoni, Y. (1971). On the definition of a multinational corporation. *The Quarterly Review of Economics and Business,* 11 (3), 27-37.

Ball, G., & McCulloch, D. (1993). *International business,* 5th ed. New York: BPI/Irwin.

Belobaba, E. (1989). Perestroika under pressure. *Canadian Business Review,* 16, 39-41.

Benedetto, C., Tamate, M., & Chandran, R. (1992). Developing creative advertising strategy for the japanese marketplace. *Journal of Advertising Research,* 32 (1), 39-48.

Boddewyn, J. (1981). The global spread of advertising regulation. *MSU Business Topics,* 29 (2), 5-13.

Boddewyn, J. (1982). Advertising regulation in the 1980s: The underlying Global forces. *Journal of Marketing,* 46, 27-35.

Brener, H. (1979). Brazil. In S.W. Dunn & E.S. Lorimor (Eds.), *International advertising and marketing*. Columbus, OH: Grid Publishing.

Burton, J. (1984). Malaysia clamps down on tv advertising. *Advertising Age*, 26-27.

Carpano, C., Chrisman, J., & Roth, K. (1994). International strategy and environment: An assessment of the performance relationship. *Journal of International Business Studies*, 25 (3), 639-656.

Dunn, S., & Lorimor, E. (1979). *International advertising and marketing*. Columbus, OH: Grid Publishing.

Elinder, E. (1965). How international can European advertising be? *Journal of Marketing*, 29 (April), 7-11.

Hill, J. and Boya, U. (1987). Consumer goods promotions in developing countries. *International Journal of Advertising*, 6, 249-264.

Keegan, W. (1989). *Global marketing management*, 4th ed. Englewood Cliffs, NJ: Prentice-Hall, Inc.

Kanso, A. (1992). International advertising strategies: Global commitment to local vision. *Journal of Advertising Research*, 32 (1), 10-14.

Katz, H., & Lancaster, K. (1989). How leading advertisers and agencies use cable television. *Journal of Advertising Research*, 29 (1), 30-38.

Levitt, T. (1983). The globalization of markets. *Harvard Business Review*, (May-June 1993), 6.

Lo, T., & Yung, A. (1988). Multinational service firms in centrally planned economies: Foreign advertising agencies in the PRC. *Management International Review*, 28 (1), 26-33.

Lorimor, E. (1979). Mexico. In S.W. Dunn & E.S. Lorimor (Eds.), *International advertising and marketing* (pp. 478-486). Columbus, OH: Grid Publishing.

Marketing News. (1991). Global coupon use up; U.K., Belgium tops in Europe, 25 (16), 5.

Mueller, B. (1992). Standardization vs. specialization: An examination of westernization in Japanese advertising. *Journal of Advertising Research*, 32 (1), 15-24.

Onunkwo, C. (1979). Nigeria. In S.W. Dunn & E.S. Lorimor (Eds.), *International advertising and marketing* (pp. 441-448). Columbus, OH: Grid Publishing.

Pope, D. (1973). *The making of modern advertising*. New York: Irwin.

Porter, M. (1980). *Competitive strategy: Techniques for analyzing industries and competitors*. New York: New York Press.

Preston, I. (1987). A review of the literature on advertising regulation, 1983-87. In J. Leigh & C. Martin (Eds.), *Current issues & research in advertising 1987* 10, 297-321.

Ramaprasad, J., & Hasegawa, R. (1992). Creative strategies in American and Japanese TV commercials: A comparison. *Journal of Advertising Research*, 32 (1), 59-70.

Ricks, D. (1983). *Big business blunders: Mistakes in multinational marketing*. Homewood: Dow Jones-Irwin.

Shao, A., & Hill, J. (1992). Executing transnational advertising campaigns: Do U.S. agencies have the overseas talent? *Journal of Advertising Research*, 32 (1), 49-58.

Survey of Current Business. (1993). The international investment position of the United States.

The Economist. (1991, April 13). Partial to parcels, 64.

The Europa World Year Book. 1990 (1990), Europa publications limited, 1.

Toyne, B., & Walters, P. (1993). *Global marketing management*. Second Edition. Boston: Allyn and Bacon.

Turner, R. (1991). Coke pops Brazilian comparative ad. *Advertising Age*, (September 9), 28.

United Nations Industrial Development Organization. (1989). *Industry and development global report*. Vienna: United Nations.

Weinstein, A. (1989). Development of an advertising industry in Asia. *MSU Business Topics* (Spring), 28-36.

World Tables. (1984). *Economic data, World bank*. Baltimore: John Hopkins University Press.

World Economic Outlook. (1990). *A survey of the staff of the IMF*. Washington, DC: IMF.

Yu-huang, Y., & Cheng, C. (1979). Taiwan. In S.W. Dunn & E.S. Lorimor (Eds.), *International advertising and marketing* (pp. 441-448). Columbus, OH: Grid Publishing.

Zandpour F., Chang, C., & Catalano, J. (1992). Stories, symbols, and straight talk: A comparative analysis of French, Taiwanese, and U.S. TV commercials. *Journal of Advertising Research*, 32 (1), 25-38.

Zanot, E. (1985). Unseen but effective advertising regulation: The clearance process. *Journal of Advertising*, 14 (4), 44-59.

ADVERTISING PRESENTATIONS OF THE INDEPENDENT VERSUS INTERDEPENDENT SELF TO KOREAN AND U. S. COLLEGE STUDENTS

Julie Scott Wilcox, Gyungtai Ko, James W. Gentry, Michael Stricklin and Sunkyu Jun

ABSTRACT

Multiple "selves" exist for all people, as we demonstrate at times an "independent self" which emphasizes one's own best interests and at other times an "interdependent self" which considers the interests of one's in-group as well (or possibly before) one's own interest. The relative likelihood of the independent versus the interdependent self varies across cultures. Advertisements targeted to the independent and interdependent selves were presented to college students in the United States and in Korea. The vast literature on individualism/ collectivism creates strong expectations for an interaction: Koreans would prefer the interdependent appeal while U.S. respondents would prefer the independent appeal. No such interaction was found. Numerous explanations are offered.

Advances in International Marketing, Volume 7, pages 159-174.
Copyright © 1996 by JAI Press Inc.
All rights of reproduction in any form reserved.
ISBN: 1-55938-839-0

As marketers in the United States learn to practice in a global economy, many adjustments are necessitated by the extremely individualistic culture in which they were socialized. The classic Hofstede (1980) study provides the inference that approximately 70 percent of the world is collective, while the U.S. is at an extreme in terms of individualism. Related to the individualism/collectivism continuum are the differing definitions of "self"—the "independent self" prevalent in individualistic cultures versus the "interdependent self" more likely to be found in collective cultures. The premise upon which this study is based is that advertising in the U.S. has focused on the independent self, and that adjustments will be needed in collective cultures to target the interdependent self. The study will investigate the use of interdependent versus independent appeals to position a headache remedy to Koreans and Americans.

I. THE VARYING DEFINITIONS OF SELF

Triandis (1989a) suggests that an individual's self concept has implications for the way the individual samples information (more frequently sampling information that is self-relevant than information that is not), processes information (more quickly processing information that is self-relevant than information that is not), and assesses information (assessing more positively information that supports the individual's current self-structure rather than information that challenges it). Therefore, it may follow that in order to achieve maximum sampling, processing, and assessment of advertising information, ad copy should be relevant to the audience based upon the individual's self concept. Thus, advertisers must understand that there are different self concepts which will respond quite differently to appeals.

A. Independent Self Construal

Independent cultures stress separateness, independence, and uniqueness (Miller 1988; Shweder and Bourne 1984). In order to be independent, one must see oneself as an individual whose internal thoughts make one's behavior relevant. Those with an independent view of the self are generally thought of as coming from individualistic cultures, such as that of the United States, where attending to the self, the appreciation of one's differences from others, and the importance of self assertion are stressed. Markus and Kitayama (1991) stress that the independent self is responsive to the social environment; however, this is because others, or the social situation, can verify and affirm the individual's view of self.

Triandis (1989a) contends that in individualistic cultures social behavior is determined by personal goals that overlap only slightly with the goals of collectives, such as family, work group, tribe, or political allies. If there is a conflict between personal goals and the group's goals, it is acceptable to place the goals of the self ahead of the goals of the group. The identity of the independent self is defined by what one has. Independent cultures are characterized by self-reliance, competition, personal values, emphasis on feeling different (and better than others), and distance from the ingroup, with socialization coming largely from peers. Triandis (1989a) suggests the more complex and affluent the culture, the more likely that culture is to be individualistic. This is the case because complexity (found in cultures where the economy is based on specialization) creates separation, distinction, and different lifestyles. Thus, affluence allows people to become independent. If these traits are indeed descriptive of individuals within individualistic cultures, it follows that advertising copy would be more effective if it stressed the traits which are thought to be most important to them.

B.   Interdependent Self Construal

Interdependent cultures, by contrast, insist on connection of human beings to one another. In a study of the Japanese, Sampson (1988) found that people who are interdependent see themselves as part of a social relationship and realize that one's behavior is determined by the perception of the thoughts, feelings, and actions of others in the relationship. Fulfilling the needs, desires, and goals of the group will in turn fulfill the individual's own needs, desires, and goals. Those with an interdependent view of self generally come from collectivistic cultures such as Japan, where an emphasis is placed on fitting in with others. This view of self and others features the person as connected to, and less differentiated from, others. People are motivated to find a way to fit in.

Triandis (1989b) suggests that, in collectivistic cultures, social behavior is determined by goals shared with a collective, and identity is defined by the relationship to the group. The goals of the collective are placed ahead of personal goals. Collective cultures are characterized by an emphasis on family, fitting in, and harmony. The interdependent self will not claim to be better than others, and will not express pleasure over being superior to others. Thus, advertising appeals directed to an independent self may be offensive to those who are interdependent.

C.   The Varying Self in an Advertising Context

Several components of culture have been studied in order to compare and contrast the receptivity to marketing communication across cultures. Hall (1976) sees culture as a "highly selective screen" which allows some stimuli through, while rejecting others. Hall (1976) contends that cultural context influences the encoding and decoding of messages, and the meaning of messages is influenced by context, the importance of which varies dramatically cross-culturally.

In high-context cultures, non-verbal cues combine with verbal communication, and the understanding of the message depends on the context in which it is presented. Interpersonal relationships and the good of the group guide the interaction in high-context societies at the expense of task orientation or individual ambition (Riddle 1986). The interdependent self is likely to be a part of a high-context culture.

In low-context cultures, communication relies on the verbal message, and depends less on non-verbal cues and shared assumptions. The independent self is likely to be part of a low-context culture, which places more value on task completion and individual ambitions (Riddle 1986).

A recent study by Han and Shavitt (1994) found context differences in a study of the advertising content of two popular magazines in the United States and in Korea. They found that the ads in the magazines published in the U. S. were rated significantly more individualistic in theme for both personal and shared products, and the ads featured in the Korean magazines were rated significantly more collectivistic for both product types.

II. HYPOTHESES

The preceding discussion leads to our hypotheses:

Hypothesis 1.   Those in a collective culture will prefer advertisements using the portrayal of an interdependent self to one using an independent self.

Hypothesis 2.   Those in an individualistic culture will prefer advertisements using the portrayal of an independent self to one using an interdependent self.

III. METHODOLOGY

An experiment was conducted by manipulating the copy of an advertisement so that one version represented what is traditionally thought of as an independent point of view, and another version represented the interdependent orientation. Each version of the ad was tested among subjects from a culture representative of an individualistic society and also from a culture representative of a collectivistic society. The experiment measured each subject's attitude toward the advertisement, attitude toward the product, and intention to buy.

The questionnaire was developed in English and then translated into Korean by a bilingual Korean Ph.D. student; it was then back translated into English by a second bilingual Korean Ph.D. student. The two versions were compared, and any discrepancies were corrected. Data were collected during the time period of June to September 1993. The data from the United States were collected from undergraduate marketing and journalism classes at the University of Nebraska-Lincoln. The Korean data were collected from undergraduate marketing classes at the Chonbuk National University in Chonju, Korea. Both universities are located in areas with agriculture-based economies, and both universities are located in state capitals. We acknowledge that neither sample is representative of the population as a whole; thus, the study should be considered as an exploratory convenience study.

The surveys consisted of either the individualistic or collectivistic ad, the advertising effectiveness scale (Baker & Churchill, 1977), the INDCOL (Triandis et al., 1986) scale, and demographic items in that order. Respondents included 182 students in the United States and 150 Korean students. Among the students in the United States were 47 international students, who were eliminated from the analyses in order to get a more accurate picture of what differences may exist by virtue of culture, leaving a sample of 135 students from the United States.

A.   Independent Variables

In order to measure individual differences in independence and interdependence within each culture, the Individualism/ Collectivism scale (INDCOL) reported by Triandis et al. (1986) was used. This scale was designed to measure four dimensions: Self Reliance with Hedonism, Separation from Ingroups, Family Integrity, and Interdependence and Sociability (see the Appendix for specific items).

Triandis (1992) argued strongly that one should investigate the underlying cultural differences between cultures rather than to assume that strong differences exist. He even stated that there are greater variations within cultures than across cultures.

The following demographic variables were also obtained about the respondents: sex, age, education, whether they are from urban or rural areas, whether they grew up in a nuclear or extended family, and family size.

B.   Treatments

A series of advertisements were developed, each with an individualistic/independent version as well as a collectivistic/ interdependent version. The ads were shown to several Korean graduate students in an effort to select the ad set with subject matter most representative of the Korean culture. There was unanimous support for one set of ads, which were the ads used for the survey. The ads are for the same product; however, the copy is different. Stick figures were used to represent the people in the ad and to bring objectivity to the evaluation process, because attitudes toward advertising are often a result of a combination of elements including attractiveness of the layout, typeface used, attractiveness of models, appropriateness of the situation portrayed, and the copy. By using rough mock ups of the ads, it was hoped that the resulting attitude would be a consequence of the copy and the representation of the number of people shown in the ad.

The version directed toward the independent audience features copy discussing individual achievement ("You cannot afford to let a headache keep you from being your very best") with one stick figure shown to represent the individual. The second ad was interdependent in nature, and the copy emphasized benefits for the group ("You cannot afford to let a headache keep you from spending quality time with those you care about"), showing four stick figures to represent the group. The same ads were translated into Korean, and back translated by two bilingual Korean Ph. D. students.

C.   Dependent Variables

The Baker and Churchill (1977) Advertising Attitude Measurement scale was used to measure the respondent's attitude toward the ad and product, and the intention to buy. The attitude toward the ad items are Interesting, Appealing, Believable, Impressive, Attractive, Informative, Clear, and Eye Catching.

Table 1. Sample Profile

	United States	Korea
Sample Size	135	150
Ad Type		
Individualistic	66	75
Collectivistic	69	75
Sex		
Male	65	137
Female	70	13
Mean Age	22	23
Major		
Business	69	149
Journalism	41	0
Other	25	1
Home Town		
Urban	95	55
Rural	40	95
Family Type		
Nuclear	110	48
Extended	25	102
Family Size		
2 or fewer	4	3
3 to 4	66	27
5 or 6	51	76
7 or more	14	44

IV. RESULTS

The sample profile is shown in Table 1. Far more male students (91%) than female students answered the survey in Korea. The Korean students were from larger families, were more likely to have grown up in an extended environment, and were more likely to have grown up in a rural home town.

A. Individualism/Collectivism

Even though directly measuring the degree of individualism/ collectivism between the two samples is not necessary to test the hypotheses, a *t*-test was performed to determine if there was a difference in the means between the respondents in the United States and Korea on the measurement of individualism and collectivism. The available literature has clearly established that this difference exists between cultures. The United States has been found to be representative of an individualistic culture, and Korea has been found to be representative of a collectivistic culture (Hofstede, 1980). It was expected that the research would find that the Korean respondents would be significantly more collectivistic, and the American students would be significantly more individualistic. The t-test found that there was not a significant difference between the two samples (Korean I/C = 70.5; U.S. I/C = 71.0) in the degree of individualism/collectivism. We suggest that the failure to find differences may reflect a homogeneity of youth globally, as has been noted by Mueller (1990). Korea's rapid economic growth, the urbanization process, and the increasing exposure to Western communication may have resulted in college-aged individuals developing strong independent selves.

B. Attitude Measures

Analysis of Covariance was used to compare the attitude toward the ad and product and the intention to buy, across cultures and across ad types. The individual's score on the individualism/ collectivism scale was used as the covariate. The cell means are shown in Table 2. When comparing the means by country, Korean respondents found both the independent and interdependent ads to be more interesting [$F(1,279)=47.8$, $p<.001$], impressive [$F(1,279)= 15.8$, $p<.001$], and eye catching [$F(1,277)=44.2$, $p<.001$] than the U. S. respondents. The U. S. respondents found the ads to be more believable [$F(1,277)=55.9$, $p<.001$], informative [$F(1,279)=13.2$, $p<.03$], and clear [$F(1,279)=45.9$, $p<.001$]. There was no difference in response between the two samples toward the ratings of the appeal and attractiveness of the ads; apparently neither group found the stick figures to be aesthetic. The Korean respondents felt the ads were more distinctive [$F(1,279)=11.8$, $p<.001$], were more likely to intend to buy the product [$F(1,279)=3.3$, $p<.04$], and more likely to seek the product actively in the store [$F(1,279)=25.3$, $p<.001$]. The pattern of results indicates that Koreans found the stick-figure ads more unusual,

Table 2. Attitude Means By Ad Type And Country

	UNITED STATES		KOREA	
	Independent	Interdependent	Independent	Interdependent
Interesting	2.9	3.0	3.8	3.7
Appealing	3.1	3.3	3.6	3.3
Believable	4.5	4.6	3.3	3.1
Impressive	2.6	3.0	3.3	3.8
Attractive	2.6	2.8	2.9	2.1
Informative	3.5	3.6	3.2	3.1
Clear	4.8	4.9	3.6	3.2
Eye Catching	2.4	2.7	4.0	3.6
Overall	3.3	3.5	3.5	3.2
Compares with				
Similar Products	2.1	2.3	2.8	2.7
Try Product	3.6	3.6	3.8	3.7
Buy Product	3.4	3.6	3.7	3.9
Seek Product				
in Store	2.2	2.5	3.2	3.2

that U. S. respondents found them more credible, and that neither group found them appealing.

A comparison of the means by ad type found that there was very little difference in terms of finding one type of ad more interesting, believable, attractive, informative, clear, appealing, or eye catching. The overall reaction toward the ads was also very similar. Respondents found the interdependent ad to be more impressive [$F(1,279)=4.6$, $p<.04$]. There was also very little difference in attitude toward the product.

It was expected that the U. S. sample would have a more positive attitude toward the independent ad in terms of attitude toward the ad and the product, and would be more likely to buy the product. It was also expected the reverse would be true for the Korean sample. It was not expected that either sample would find either ad attractive or eye catching, since the graphic consisted of stick figures.

There was very little difference in attitude toward the ad or attitude toward the product, when looking at the responses for the independent ad versus the interdependent ad. Further, none of the expected interactions (Koreans like interdependent ads more while U. S. respondents like independent ads more) were found.

Even though the U. S. attitude means are very similar toward the independent versus interdependent ad, the attitude toward the interdependent ad is higher (and significantly so [$p<.05$] for impressive and eye catching) in each case. The means for the Korean sample again are very similar when comparing the attitude toward the independent versus interdependent ad. However, the independent ad scored higher for seven of the eight dimensions and significantly so ($p<.05$) for appealing, attractive, clear, and eye catching. When the attitude toward the ad measures were summed and used as the dependent variable, the interaction was marginally significant [$F(1,277)=2.8$, $p<.10$]. Note, however, that the interaction was just the opposite of that expected a priori. However, even though the Korean respondents found the independent ad more interesting, they were still slightly more likely to buy and seek the product depicted in the interdependent ad as was expected.

C.   Investigation of the Scales

One strength of our study was the incorporation of scales which have received a great deal of use in North America. To investigate whether they were used similarly in both cultures, we performed factor analyses on the INDCOL and attitude scales across the two cultures. The Attitude toward the ad factors are shown in Table 3. Baker and Churchill (1977) expected the eight items to break into two components: Cognitive (believable, informative, and clear) and Affective (interesting, appealing, impressive, attractive, and eye catching). This structure was found in the U. S. data, but not in the Korean data in which believable loaded with

Table 3.   Attitude Toward the Ad Factors

UNITED STATES Variable	Factors	
	Affective	Cognitive
Interesting	.79	.14
Appealing	.67	.37
Impressive	.83	.06
Attractive	.82	.03
Eye Catching	.64	.21
Believable	.21	.69
Informative	.22	.64
Clear	−.04	.72

KOREA Variable	Factors		
	Aesthetics	First Impression	Communication
Appealing	.84	.01	.19
Believable	.67	−.07	.33
Attractive	.62	.43	.26
Interesting	.45	.48	.23
Impressive	.03	.84	−.06
Eye Catching	.00	.74	.26
Informative	.13	.04	.84
Clear	.17	.15	.74

two Affective items and three other Affective items loaded separately. It would appear that Korea's high context culture does not yield advertising components having a more simplistic affect/cognition dichotomy; in particular, believability may be more associated with aesthetic elements than with information presentation. A high context culture may equate effort in presentation with the earnestness of its designer.

The INDCOL items are shown in the Appendix, and the U. S. and Korean factors are shown in Tables 4 and 5. Triandis et al. (1986) found that the items loaded into four factors: Self-Reliance with Hedonism, Separation from In-groups, Family Integrity, and Interdependence and Sociability. Subsequently, Triandis et al. (1988) found that Family Integrity was the factor with the greatest difference across cultures. Ko (1991), using student samples from the same two universities included in this study, found the overall reliability of the INDCOL scale to be low; however, he also found the Family Integrity factor to vary the most across cultures. As can be noted in Tables 4 and 5, the Family Integrity items did not factor together in either culture. Thus, even the use of a frequently selected scale developed by some of the best people in cross-cultural psychology does not insure the valid measurement of a critical dimension. Both sets of factors in Tables 4 and 5 have five common labels (Self Reliance, Performance Orientation, Separate from

Table 4.   Individualism/collectivism Factors in the United States

Item*	Self Reliance	Performance Orientation	Separation from Ingroups	Me Orientation	Family Orientation	Independence
IC3	.76	−.03	−.16	.14	.01	.15
IC4	.58	.32	.05	−.24	−.06	.14
IC5	.57	.20	.05	.08	.10	.26
IC11	.65	.08	.26	.24	−.04	−.09
IC7	.29	.73	−.01	−.28	−.06	−.06
IC10	.07	.68	−.01	.29	.11	.06
IC12	.02	.65	.20	.37	−.02	−.02
IC8	−.27	.16	.73	.03	−.02	.22
IC9	.09	.10	.68	.04	.19	−.02
IC14	−.36	.14	.60	.09	.09	.09
IC2	.20	.18	.08	.78	−.12	−.01
IC13	.01	.07	−.37	.49	.33	.05
IC15	−.14	.16	−.06	.07	.71	.09
IC16	.19	−.17	.18	−.11	.75	−.08
IC1	.02	.02	.07	−.12	.17	.76
IC6	.28	−.05	.07	.06	−.08	.61
IC17	.09	.05	−.06	.38	−.37	.51

Note: *Items are listed in the Appendix.

Table 5. Individualism/Collectivism Factors in Korea

Item*	Self Reliance	Family Orientation	Separation from Ingroups	Performance Orientation	Independence
IC1	.70	.01	−.09	−.03	.14
IC3	.48	−.32	−.01	.19˙	−.36
IC5	.64	−.03	.03	−.06	.44
IC6	.57	−.28	−.01	.36	−.13
IC11	.53	.18	−.08	.28	.19
IC14	.48	.02	.36	−.31	.22
IC13	−.05	.62	.43	−.11	−.05
IC15	−.01	.75	.06	.01	−.12
IC16	−.01	.71	.01	.00	.14
IC8	−.08	.03	.82	.13	.14
IC9	.00	.15	.82	−.12	.13
IC2	.15	.08	−.09	.60	.08
IC12	.03	−.32	.07	.64	.02
IC17	−.04	.04	−.09	.68	.25
IC4	.13	.07	.17	.24	.49
IC7	−.01	−.08	−.04	.09	.64
IC10	.11	.03	.16	−.08	.66

Note: *Items are listed in the Appendix.

Ingroup, Family Orientation, and Independence), but the items constituting the factors vary across cultures. In addition, the U. S. findings include a unique "Me Orientation" factor.

We also used the Leung-Bond approach (Leung & Bond, 1989) in an attempt to "deculturalize" the data. Each scale was standardized within subject and then across items before conducting factor analyses. As per Triandis et al. (1993), the eigenvalue of one rule was used to determine the number of factors rather than the screen in technique. The resulting factors from the two cultures were less similar than the standard factor analyses, as well as being less interpretable.

Our evaluations of the scale usage in the two cultures suggest that great care must be taken in using U. S.-developed scales in other cultures.

V. CONCLUSIONS AND IMPLICATIONS

The goal of this study was to understand better how differences in culture, and its influence on the individual's sense of self, may affect attitude toward advertising. This was an exploratory study and, therefore, the findings should not be generalized to the Korean and United States populations as a whole. However, the findings may reveal possible trends in each country, and may provide some guidance for further cross-cultural research.

Existing literature suggests strongly that the independent/ individualistic members of society are more likely to view themselves as unique, experience a stronger achievement drive, and pursue personal goals. The literature also suggests that the collectivistic/interdependent members of society are more likely to see themselves as part of a group and are motivated to fit in and share a common goal. Based on the existing research, it was hypothesized that the members of a known individualistic society (United States) would have a more positive attitude toward an advertisement reflecting the individualistic/independent characteristics as opposed to one with a collectivistic/ interdependent theme. It was also hypothesized that the opposite would be true for members of a known collectivistic society (Korea).

The data did not confirm that respondents from the United States were more individualistic, nor were the Korean respondents found to be more collectivistic. The available literature clearly demonstrates that the United States is an individualistic society, while Korea is known to be a collectivistic society. The fact that these data found no significant difference between the cultures is puzzling. Many of our categorizations of cultures on cultural dimensions are still based on the Hofstede study of work attitudes conducted nearly 20 years ago. Given the great amount of change since then, especially in the last six years, more current assessments of cultures are needed to provide an updated view.

Our findings indicate that both cultures may be undergoing a shift. This shift may be more evident, and possibly more extreme, among college students than the general population. There appears to be serious question whether student samples are representative of the cultures as a whole. The literature suggests that Korea has been undergoing a shift toward industrialization and democracy for several years, and the findings may be an indication that the youth in Korea are very non-traditional. It may be that youth, regardless of cultural origin, are more homogeneous than the culture as a whole (Mueller, 1990), or perhaps the two cultures are becoming more similar, with each shifting toward the center of the scale, with individualism/collectivism on either end. This study certainly demonstrates that more cross-cultural research needs to be conducted to determine if individualism/collectivism exists as it has been traditionally viewed, and if characteristics of youth in any culture are reflective of the culture as a whole.

Another explanation for the unexpected results may have been a tendency to overgeneralize the work of Edward Hall and others to think in terms of Asian and Western differences. Clearly Asian cultures differ and it has been noted frequently (Alston, 1989; Dubinsky, et al., 1991; West, 1989) that Asian countries should not be viewed as a single homogeneous culture. For example, in studies contrasting Asian and U. S. differences in context as observed in advertising, Miracle, Taylor, and Chang (1992) found the expected patterns of results in Japan, but Miracle, Chang, and Taylor (1992) and Taylor, Wilson, and Miracle (1995) found discrepancies from the expected patterns when investigating Korean television advertising.

The data also did not confirm that the Koreans preferred the interdependent ad, nor did the sample from the United States prefer the independent ad—in fact the reverse was found to be true. The Baker and Churchill Attitude toward Advertising scale did not seem to work as well when measuring the ad/product effectiveness for the Korean sample, because the items did not factor together as they typically do when measuring attitude among respondents in the United States. Overall, Koreans found each ad to be more interesting, appealing, and impressive than did the U.S. sample. Possibly this research method was more novel to Koreans, and therefore they found the ads to more intriguing. Apparently Koreans are not as accustomed to participating in survey research as are Americans. Koreans found the ads to be less believable, informative, and clear than the respondents in the United States. It may be that it was more difficult for the Koreans to imagine that the "rough" ad could in fact be a "real" ad. The U. S. respondents, in contrast, may be more accustomed to looking at crude advertising for research purposes, and so were better able to understand what was being done in the experiment.

Further, the Koreans preferred the independent ad over the interdependent ad, except for the impressive, overall reaction, and likelihood to buy and seek the product measures. Of additional interest, the sample in the United States preferred the interdependent ad in each measure. This was the opposite of what was expected. Novelty may again explain why the interdependent approach was preferred by the sample in the U.S. Perhaps because the Koreans are accustomed to exposure to advertising with the interdependent approach, and vice versa for the respondents in the United States, each found the opposite approach more appealing. Taylor et al. (1995) found brand differentiation to be as effective among Korean students as among American students; they also found that only 3 percent of Korean commercials had a brand-differentiation focus.

Another potential explanation for the findings relates to the subject matter of the ad. The ad promoted a headache remedy, which is a personal product. Shavitt (1990) found that for different types of products, promotional appeals stressing different types of benefits are effective. Han and Shavitt (1994) contend that the type of product may restrict the degree to which the differences in individualism and collectivism are likely to be evident in advertising. They suggest that personal products, as opposed to shared products, are used by the individual and offer benefits mainly to the individual, and are not likely to be convincingly promoted by interdependent appeals.

It may be that, since a headache remedy is a personal product, Koreans preferred the ad with the independent theme. This line of reasoning would suggest that the respondents from the U.S. should have also preferred the independent ad; however, novelty may help to explain why they preferred the collectivistic ad.

It is possible that the use of rough ads was not the best methodology to use to determine differences in attitude toward the ads. The stick figure approach in the advertising was used to control issues such as dress and nationality of the models, and other cultural differences that may have affected preference for the ad. Thus the ads were a bit crude. It would be interesting to conduct the same study utilizing a real ad and compare the results.

The independent/interdependent differences in the ads are not so strong that they drove the results here. The theory base laid appears to be strong and we still believe that interdependent presentations may work better in collectivistic cultures; however, more research needs to be done to determine if this is true. The existing literature leads one to believe that cultural differences should be readily identifiable. If other studies support the finding that there are no significant differences between people in individualistic and collectivistic cultures, that would be good news for advertisers in the United States who have much experience and knowledge concerning advertising effectively to people living in individualistic cultures.

APPENDIX

Individualism/Collectivism Scale*

Factor 1:   Self Reliance with Hedonism

1. I would rather struggle with a personal problem by myself than discuss them with my friends.
2. The most important thing in my life is to make myself happy.
3. I tend to do my own thing, and others in my family do the same.
4. One does better work working alone than in a group.
5. When faced with a difficult personal problem, it is better to decide what to do yourself, rather than follow the advice of others.
6. What happens to me is my own doing.
7. If the group is slowing me down, it is better to leave it and work alone.

Factor II: Separation from Ingroups

8. If the child won the Nobel Prize, the parents should not feel honored in any way.
9. Children should not feel honored even if the father were highly praised and given an award by a government official for his contributions and services to the community.
10. In most cases, to cooperate with someone whose ability is lower than yours is not as desirable as doing the thing on your own.

Factor III: Family Integrity

11. One should live one's life independently of others as much as possible.

12. It is important to me that I perform better than others on a task.
13. Aging parents should live at home with their children.
14. Children should live at home with their parents until they get married.

Factor IV: Interdependence and Sociability

15. I would help within my means, if a relative told me that s(he) is in financial difficulty.
16. I like to live close to my good friends.
17. Individuals should be judged on their own merits, not on the company they keep.

Note: *Apparently the INDCOL scale has been updated, as some items used here are different from those reported in Triandis et al. (1993).

Source: Triandis et al. (1986).

ACKNOWLEDGMENT

The authors would like to thank Ju Yong Park for his help in the development of the instrument.

REFERENCES

Alston, J.P. (1989). 'Wa,' 'ganxi,' and 'inwha': Managerial principles in Japan, China, and Korea. *Business Horizons*, 32, 26-31.

Baker, M.J., & Churchill, G., Jr. (1977). The impact of physically attractive models on advertising evaluations. *Journal of Marketing Research*, 14, 538-555.

Dubinsky, A.J., Jolson, M.A., Kotabe, M., & Lim, C.U. (1991). A cross-national investigation of industrial salespeople: Ethical perceptions. *Journal of International Business Studies*, 22, 651-670.

Hall, E.T. (1976). *Beyond culture*. Garden City, NY: Anchor Press/Doubleday.

Han, S.P., & Shavitt, S. (1994). Persuasion and culture: Advertising appeals in individualistic and collectivistic societies. *Journal of Experimental Social Psychology*, 30, 326-350.

Hofstede, G. (1980). *Culture's consequences*. Beverly Hills, CA: Sage.

Ko, G. (1991). *A cross-cultural study of the use of subcontracting in consumer choice*. Unpublished Ph.D. Dissertation, University of Nebraska-Lincoln.

Leung, K., & Bond, M.H. (1989). On the empirical identification of dimensions for cross-cultural comparison. *Journal of Cross-Cultural Psychology*, 20, 133-151.

Markus, H.R., & Kitayama, S. (1991). Culture and the self: Implications for cognition, emotion, and motivation. *Psychological Review*, 98, 224-253.

Miller, J.G. (1988). Bridging the content-structure dichotomy: Culture and the self. In M. H. Bond (Ed.), *The cross-cultural challenge to social psychology* (pp. 266-281). Beverly Hills, CA: Sage.

Miracle, G.E., Chang, K.Y., & Taylor, C.R. (1992), Culture and advertising executions: A comparison of selected characteristics of Korean and U.S. television commercials. *International Marketing Review*, 9, 5-17.

Miracle, G.E., Taylor, C.R., & Chang, K.Y. (1992). Culture and advertising executions: A comparison of selected characteristics of Japanese and U.S. television commercials. *Journal of International Consumer Marketing*, 4, 89-113.

Mueller, B. (1990). Degrees of globalization: An analysis of the standardization of message elements in multinational advertising. In J.H. Leigh & C.R. Martin (Eds.), *Current Issues and Research in Advertising*, (Vol. 12, pp. 119-133). Ann Arbor: University of Michigan, Division of Research.

Riddle, D.I. (1986). *Service-led growth: The role of the service sector in world development*. New York: Praeger.

Sampson, E.E. (1988). The debate on individualism: Indigenous psychologies of the individual and their role in personal and societal functioning. *American Psychologist*, 43, 15-22.

Shavitt, S. (1990). The role of attitude objects in attitude functions. *Journal of Experimental Social Psychology*, 26,. 124-148.

Shweder, R.A., & Bourne, E.J. (1984). Does the concept of the person vary cross-culturally. In R.A. Shweder & R.A. LeVine (Eds.), *Culture theory: Essays on mind, self, and emotion* (pp. 238-254). Cambridge: Cambridge University Press

Taylor, C.R., Wilson, R.D., & Miracle, G.E. (1995). The impact of brand differentiating messages on effectiveness in Korean advertising. *Journal of International Marketing*, 3, 31-52.

Triandis, H.C. (1989a). The self and social behavior in differing cultural contexts. *Psychological Review*, 96, 506-520.

Triandis, H.C. (1989b). Cross-cultural studies of individualism and collectivism. In John Berman (Ed.), *Nebraska symposium on motivation* (pp. 41-121). Lincoln, NE: University of Nebraska Press.

Triandis, H.C. (1992). Individualism and collectivism as cultural syndromes. *Proceedings*, Society for Cross-Cultural Research, Santa Fe.

Triandis, H.C., Bontempo, R., Betancourt, H., Bond, M., Leung, K., Brenes, A., Georgus, J., Hui, C.H., Marlin, G., Setiadi,B., Sinha, J.B.P., Verma, J., Spangenberg, J., Touzard, H., & Montmollin, G. (1986). The measurement of the etic aspects of individualism and collectivism across cultures. *Australian Journal of Psychology*, 38, 257-267.

Triandis, H.C., Bontempo, R., Villareal, M.J., Asai, M., & Lucca, N. (1988). Individualism/collectivism: Cross-cultural perspective of self-ingroup relationships. *Journal of Personal and Social Psychology*, 54, 323-338.

Triandis, H.C., McCusker, C., Betancourt, H., Iwao, S., Leung, K., Salazar, J.M., Sefiadi, B., Sinha, J.B.P., Touzard, H., & Zaleski, Z. (1993). An etic-emic analysis of individualism and collectivism. *Journal of Cross-Cultural Psychology*, 24, 366-383.

West, P. (1989). Cross-cultural literacy and the Pacific Rim. *Business Horizons*, 32, 3-17.

FOREIGN ELEMENTS IN KOREAN AND U.S. TELEVISION ADVERTISING

Charles R. Taylor and Gordon E. Miracle

ABSTRACT

This paper examines the presence of foreign elements in South Korean and U.S. television advertising. A content analysis of 876 Korean and 1228 U.S. commercials was conducted to measure the frequency of the use of foreign settings, foreign models as speaker characters, and foreign symbol systems as part of the message. Results indicate that relatively few foreign elements are present in U.S. advertising, while the inclusion of foreign elements in Korean advertising appears to be associated with a complex combination of factors, including features of the country's culture, history, and economic development. Implications for global advertisers are discussed.

I. INTRODUCTION

In conjunction with increased world trade in the global economy, the marketing and advertising literature has devoted much attention to whether advertising can be standardized or transferred across countries, Some have argued that standard-

Advances in International Marketing, Volume 7, pages 175-195.
Copyright © 1996 by JAI Press Inc.
All rights of reproduction in any form reserved.
ISBN: 1-55938-839-0

ization is generally not feasible (e.g., Weissman, 1967; Ricks, Arpan, & Fu, 1974; Hornik, 1980). Others saw standardization as being desirable in many instances (e.g., Elinder, 1965; Buzzell, 1968; Levitt, 1983). Still others have tended to focus on the circumstances under which standardized advertising approaches are likely to be effective. For example, Miracle (1968), Quelch and Hoff (1986), and Jain (1989) have all suggested contingencies for determining whether to standardize advertising or other marketing mix variables.

In spite of the focus on transferring strategy to international markets, little research has been done in the United States on the presence of foreign elements in advertising in specific countries. This lack of research may be due in part to the relative lack of foreign elements in U.S. advertising. However, the use of foreign settings, actors/characters, and written language is common in many countries. Haarman and Waseda (1985), for example, demonstrated the widespread use of a variety of foreign elements in Japanese advertising. While Haarman and Waseda did not suggest implications for businesses, it is apparent that the feasibility of using foreign elements in advertising in a country may have direct implications for whether (or at least to what extent), a campaign can be standardized across two or more countries. Perhaps more importantly, an understanding of why foreign elements are or are not prevalent in certain countries can lead to a deeper understanding of what types of advertisements are likely to appeal to consumers.

The purpose of this paper is to examine the types of foreign elements present in the Republic of Korea (South Korea) and the United States in order to provide a better understanding of advertising in the two countries, and to suggest implications for the transferability of advertising messages and campaigns between these two countries. In particular, data on the following types of foreign influences from a content analysis of a sample of 876 Korean and 1228 U.S. commercials will be compared:

1. Country of Setting of Advertisement
2. Nationality of Speaking Characters
3. Use of Foreign Symbol System to Identify Brand Name
4. Use of Foreign Symbol System to Identify Company Name
5. Use of Foreign Symbol System in Written Components of Message

As an emerging market, the study of advertising strategy in the ROK is particularly timely. In recent years, the ROK has become a major export market for the United States and other industrialized nations. As of 1991, the ROK ranked as the sixth leading export market for U.S. goods, placing it ahead of countries such as France, Italy, and Brazil (Jain, 1993, p. 708).

Forecasts suggest that the ROK will become an even larger export market for industrialized nations in the future. By the year 2001, forecasts call for the ROK to reach a GNP level of over 800 billion dollars, making it one of the 10 largest economies in the world (Hong, 1993). Further, the country's per capita income is expected to continue its rapid growth, rising from $2,505 in 1986 to $6,685 in 1992 and to $13,000 by the year 2000. This rapid expansion of income, a byproduct of over three decades of sustained GNP growth, will give Korean consumers increased purchasing power.

In conjunction with its economic development, the ROK has experienced a boom in its advertising industry over the past decade. The ROK now ranks as the second largest advertising market in Asia (behind Japan) with advertising expenditures in 1992 totalling more than $3.5 billion per year (Chai, 1993), up from just $418 million in 1980. As advertising expenditures have grown, opportunities for foreign firms to advertise in the ROK have increased due to the greater availability of media and the opening of advertising agencies to foreign investment (KOBACO, 1989). In order for exporters to tap the potential of the Korean market, it is important that they attempt to understand Korean culture and business practices. More generally, it is important for researchers to examine how cultural differences impact business practices, including advertising.

The remainder of the paper will begin with a review of the literature relevant to the discussion of foreign components in Korean and US advertising. First, Korea's pride in its culture, especially with regard to its language and alphabet, will be discussed. Next, the specific influence of three major foreign players in the ROK's history (China, the United States, and Japan) will be discussed. Hypotheses regarding specific elements of foreign influence in Korean advertising will be developed as part of this review. The hypotheses will then be tested against the results of a large scale content analysis of ROK and US television commercials, and conclusions will be drawn.

II. LITERATURE REVIEW

The topic of foreign elements in Korea is a particularly interesting one. Long surrounded by powerful neighbors, Korea has a history which is marked by both welcome and unwelcome interaction with other nations. Steinberg (1988, p. 29) observes:

> Korea has been surrounded by major powers since the second century B.C., and external factors have always played a role in internal policy decisions, even in periods when the state has attempted to isolate itself from the world.

The current century has been no exception, with nearly a half century of Japanese rule, followed by internal turmoil exacerbated by the Cold War, and subsequent socioeconomic changes in which foreign countries have played an important role (Kim, 1985). One feature that has been constant over time, however, is the deep respect the Korean people have for their culture (McCune, 1966; Whang, 1987).

Although Koreans take great pride in their culture, there is little doubt that the high level of contact with outsiders has left some impressions on everyday life. This has been especially true in recent years as the country's economy has made rapid advances. Often, eastern values and traditions now stand side by side with western innovation (Hoare & Pares, 1988). This feature of Korean culture led one writer to describe the ROK as "in transition, yet unchanging" (Kim, 1985).

A.   The Hangul and Pride in Korean Culture

Having existed as a distinct people for over 2000 years, Koreans are very proud of their heritage. A physically, ethnically, and culturally homogeneous group, even the recent division into North and South has not dulled the notion that the Korean peninsula is primarily populated by people of one nationality (Kang, 1988). Given the level of turmoil the land has seen, it is remarkable that the Korean culture has remained intact. Kim (1985, p. 15) observed:

> Although traditions are beginning to give way to modern ways, there is still an essence that is the heart of Korea—a national character, a philosophy of life, that is uniquely Korean.

South Koreans are not oblivious to the struggle involved in maintaining their cultural identity. Since the 1960's, there has been an increasing awareness of the country's national assets. In fact, preserving the culture has become a national priority. One manifestation of this policy is the government, "Living Treasures of Korea" program which supports people who are skilled in traditional Korean arts and crafts (e.g., ornamental knot makers, temple painters, dancers) that have been handed down from age to age. Additionally, the Ministry of Culture seeks out intangible assets and gives them official recognition and protection.

Another manifestation of the desire to preserve traditional culture has been some degree of government control over the press, the cinema, performing arts, and publishing. The desire for cultural preservation is also apparent in government regulation of advertising. KOBACO, the government regulatory body set up to oversee Korean advertising practices in the ROK was established in part to, "...promote the cultural life and welfare of the people and the media..." (KOBACO, 1989) KOBACO not only previews commercials to meet the social and ethical responsibilities of advertising, but also actively supports and promotes the arts and social welfare with its income from commissions. Thus, we can see that even within advertising practices, there is some concern that the culture must be protected from potentially damaging outside infringements.

For business related activities, preserving elements of Korean culture can be a complex task. Most economic development experts attribute much of Korea's economic development to the success of an outward looking strategy started by President Park Chung Hee in 1962 and sustained by subsequent administrations

(Park, 1987; Steinberg, 1988; Cook, 1989). South Koreans are very proud of the "economic miracle" which has taken place in the country. Yet, they realize that in addition to their own hard work, contact with outsiders has been an important component of their economic development (initially, aid from foreign sources was important; more recently, access to foreign markets and technology have become important). This realization has led to a feeling on the part of some that indigenous Korean culture and traditions must somehow be harmonized with the values imposed by industrialization in order to sustain development. Thus, the process of attempting to regulate foreign influence can be very difficult.

One element of their culture of which Koreans are particularly proud is their language—both spoken and written. Developed in the mid-fifteenth century, the Hangul (Korea's alphabet) is hailed as the world's most scientifically organized alphabet due to its phonetic efficiency, a fact which is widely known and discussed among Koreans (Suh & Park, 1974; Lee, 1987). Koreans also savor their native tongue, which they were forbidden to speak during the period of Japanese colonialization. Chinese characters have long been taught to Koreans. But periodically, there have been attempts to make the Hangul the only written language system taught in compulsory education. There is even a national holiday devoted to celebrating the development of the Hangul. Thus, we would expect the Hangul to be an important component of many Korean advertisements.

B.   U.S./Western Influence

Korea was long known as the Hermit Kingdom due to its resistance to contact with the West throughout the Yi dynasty (1392-1910). During the late 1800s, largely through missionary activities, some Koreans were exposed to Christian thought, democratic principles, and other Western ideas. To Koreans at this time, the West symbolized, "wealthy nation with strong military," and there was some feeling that the "Western instrument" (material technology) could be complemented by the "Eastern spirit" (values and culture). The reluctance to study and understand Western philosophy while wanting to adopt its instrument is, however, regarded by some as a contributing factor to Korea's misfortune in the first half of the twentieth century. It has been argued that Japan's success early in the twentieth century was due to the realization that Western function is based on Western spirit, leading them to study the philosophy underlying capitalism and Western culture. Some feel that continued Korean resistance to some aspects of Western spirit has hindered the development of indigenous technology in the ROK (Kim, K. 1988). Regardless of whether this is true, it is clear that there has always been a high level of resistance among Koreans to changing the underlying values of their culture.

There is little question that the United States has been highly influential in Korean life since World War II. To what extent this influence has been welcome is another question. On the positive side, the USA was an important military ally during the Korean War and provided substantial foreign aid which helped to build the foundation for economic take-off (Soon, 1986; Koo, 1986). More recently, the USA and the ROK have become important trading partners as well as political allies.

However, many Koreans have mixed feelings about the extent of U.S. influence in their country. In addition to a history of resistance to outside influences and the desire to preserve indigenous values, some feel that the United States has acted primarily out of self-interest in handling Korean affairs. The presence of U.S. troops, many in the capital city, Seoul, has also been a source of tension. In recent years, U.S. pressure on Korea to open its domestic market to a variety of imports has been a point of contention. For these reasons, some anti-American sentiment is likely to persist in the ROK in the foreseeable future.

In spite of the above mentioned factors, it is probably safe to assert that average South Koreans do not hold hostile attitudes towards the United States. It has probably been helpful that the United States has not tried to dictate Korean economic policy. Steinberg (1988) and others (e.g., Cook, 1989) have noted that the degree of leverage exerted by the United States and other foreign powers on ROK development policy has been "remarkably limited."

United States influence in the ROK is not likely to disappear anytime soon. The USA remains an important military ally and trade partner of the ROK. In recent years, capital and technology transfer have been particularly important (Ahn, 1985). Korea's relatively open trade policy and rising standard of living have served to increase exposure of its citizens to U.S. made goods and services, perhaps leading to greater familiarity with the culture. For quite some time now, many Korean scholars have been U.S. educated, exposing them directly to U.S. values and economic ideas. Additionally, Christianity has grown rapidly in the country, with over 8 million Koreans currently considering themselves to be Christian. The impact of such exposure as well as the adoption of "Western instrument" should not be underestimated. As Kang (1988, p. 351) observed:

> For the past four decades, American influence has been significant. At present, the Western influences on the Korean peninsula are pervasive. Indeed, to a great extent, the entire city of Seoul has been Westernized.

At the same time, Kang refers to the continued and marked separation of traditional and Western worlds within the ROK, and refers to the need to merge the two.

The close economic links between the ROK and the United States are likely to have some influence on advertising in the ROK. While Western settings and actors may infringe on the desire to preserve Korean culture to some extent, it seems likely that the there would be some level of Western influence. Specific predictions for the extent of this influence will be outlined in the hypothesis section.

C.   Chinese Influence

Chinese influence on Korean culture has been present for the entire length of Korea's known history. During the "Era of Three Kingdoms" (37 BC-668 AD) in Korean history, the Confucian model of government and social behavior had a profound effect on Korean thinking (Yum, 1987). Buddhism was also introduced via China and has played an influential role in Korean philosophy. Traditional ideas and values rooted in Confucianism and Buddhism remain a central part of Korean culture.

The depth of Chinese influence is apparent when considering the history of the Korean written language. Before the development of the Hangul in the fifteenth century, the Korean language was expressed in Chinese characters. Even after the development of the Hangul, Chinese characters have remained popular among many Korean intellectuals and at times have become a major political issue. In fact, there have been periodic attempts to ban the use of Chinese characters. One such attempt was made by the Ministry of Education in 1970 (Yang, 1983). After much debate among scholars, professors, writers, and journalists, the pro-Chinese character group won out. Yang (1983, p. 115) summarized the argument of those favoring Chinese characters as follows:

> They...pointed out that the history of Chinese characters is much longer than our Hangul, that more than 50 percent of our language derives from Chinese letters and that we can never do without them in many a field of writing.

In spite of this decision, the Korean government has tended to discourage the use of Chinese characters in recent years. At the same time, the close relationship between the Hangul and Chinese written characters demonstrates how intertwined the languages are.

Some have postulated that there has been a trend toward increased Chinese influence in the ROK in recent years. Kang (1988) observes that prior to Japanese colonialism, Koreans looked to their Chinese "big brothers" for guidance, since they did not fully understand the newly emerging (and highly Western influenced) world order. With the onset of the colonial period, however, Chinese influence declined markedly. After liberation, Chinese support of Northern forces and its position in world politics made the country an enemy of the ROK. During the 1980s and 1990s, however, some contacts have been restored, and perhaps owing to the PRC's status in the international community as well as its long-term potential as a trading partner, many Koreans seem to desire more interaction.

In terms of direct influence on the content of Korean advertising, one would expect to see few Chinese settings and actors. The close relationship of the Hangul and the Chinese language suggests that the Chinese alphabet may be visible in Korean advertising. However, efforts to curb the use of the Chinese written language make this question interesting.

D. Japanese Influence

The history of relations between Japan and Korea is one of many wars and much antagonism. Even today in the ROK, there is substantial anti-Japanese sentiment (Kim, C. 1988). Much of the resentment stems from the colonial period, when the Japanese took over and overtly attempted to suppress Korean culture in favor of their own (Yang, 1983; Kil, 1984; Kim, 1985). Manifestations of Japanese attempts to eliminate Korean culture included policies banning the teaching and public use of the Korean language as well as requiring Koreans to register with the Japanese government using Japanese names. Many Koreans also blame Japan and the colonial period for Korea being split into two halves.

These factors resulted in anti-Japanese thought being viewed as a sign of Korean patriotism during the early post-colonial days. While formal interaction between the ROK and Japan has increased recently, some tensions remain. In spite of these tensions, substantial Japanese influence is present in the life and work of the ROK today. Hoare and Pares (1988, p. 57) observe:

> South Korea's Japanese legacy is obvious, at least to outsiders, whether it is in the conduct of railway officials or the style of business leaders, but it is not an easy thing for some Koreans to accept.

While Japanese influence is, indeed, a touchy subject with many Koreans, several writers have acknowledged "latent" Japanese influences. Yang (1983), for instance, noted that Japanese styles and fashions are rapidly transported to Korea. He also noted that Japanese newspapers, magazines, television and radio are influential in determining what movies, books, and songs are transported to the ROK from the West. In general, it seems that many Koreans are influenced by Japanese popular culture, in spite of government efforts to the contrary. There has been a determined effort by the ROK government to exclude Japanese influence, including a ban on Japanese songs on TV and radio, and a prohibition (which was lifted in the early 1990s) on mentioning the names of Japanese firms (Hoare & Pares, 1988). Nevertheless, Japanese styles remain influential in Korean movies, television, and other forms of entertainment.

Though there would appear to be a substantial degree of latent influence in the lives of South Koreans, overt expressions of such influence are likely to be rare. In the next section, more specific predictions about the level of Japanese influence will be put forward.

III. HYPOTHESES

Hypotheses for five variables are put forward. They are: (1) Country of Setting of Advertisement, (2) Nationality of Speaking Characters, (3) Use of Foreign Symbol System to Identify Brand Name, (4) Use of Foreign Symbol System to Identify Company Name, and (5) Use of Foreign Symbol System in Written Components of Message. As a point of comparison, the hypotheses will be expressed for the level of use expected to be found in the content analysis of Korean advertisements relative to that found in the United States.

A. Country of Setting

Due to pride in and strong desire to preserve traditional Korean values and culture by the Korean government and people, it is likely that Korean television advertisements frequently make use of settings that are clearly Korean. Worries about explicit depiction of foreign settings infringing on Korean culture are likely to make the use of such settings (including U.S., Chinese, and Japanese settings) uncommon. Since the depiction of foreign settings is also relatively uncommon in the United States, the following hypotheses are put forward:

Hypothesis 1a.   In both the ROK and the USA, a high proportion of commercials depict recognizably local settings (i.e, set in Korea in ROK commercials or set in the United States for U.S. commercials).

Hypothesis 1b.   In both the ROK and the USA, few commercials depict recognizably foreign settings.

B. Nationality of Speaking Characters

Again, due to pride in the Korean culture and the desire to sustain and preserve it, it seems likely that most Korean advertisements contain primarily Korean actors. Since it is also the case that the foreign actors or models is relatively rare in the United States, the following predictions are made:

Hypothesis 2a.   In both the ROK and the United States, a high proportion of commercials use native speaker characters (i.e, Korean actors in ROK commercials or U.S. actors in the United States.

Hypothesis 2b.   In both the ROK and the United States, few commercials use foreign actors of models as speaking characters.

C. Symbol Systems for Written Name of Brand

Because of the pride Korean people have in their alphabet, as well as Korean being the only language spoken by everyone in the country, the use of the Hangul to indicate a product's brand name is likely to occur in the vast majority of commercials. In the United States, it is also likely that most commercials use "native" characters (i.e., the Roman alphabet) due to the traditional "melting pot" ideal and the lack of familiarity of the majority of U.S. citizens with any particular foreign language.

Because of Western, and especially U.S. influence in the recent history of the ROK, it is also probable that the Roman alphabet is used in commercials for many imported products (perhaps along with a Korean translation of the foreign brand name). In fact, it seems likely that Koreans would tend to describe products invented in the West (or exported from the west) by their Western name and describe it to some degree in Western terms. This type of foreign element would be consistent with the phenomenon of traditional and Western features standing separately, but side by side, in Korea, and is not likely to be viewed by Koreans (many of who have some familiarity the English language) as infringing upon their culture.

Some Chinese language symbols are also likely to appear due to the long history of these symbols in Korea, their popularity among intellectuals, and the familiarity of many ROK residents with some Chinese characters. However, the proportion of commercials with Chinese brand names is likely to be low due to government efforts to discourage their use and the paucity of Chinese-made products advertised on Korean television. Due to the volatile nature of historical relations with Japan, Japanese characters are likely to be virtually non-existent in Korean advertising, even for products manufactured in Japan. Other foreign symbols are also likely to be rare based on the desire for cultural preservation. Thus:

Hypothesis 3a.   In both the ROK and the United States, a high proportion of commercials use native language symbols to describe the brand name.

Hypothesis 3b.   More commercials in the ROK use foreign alphabets of symbol systems to describe a product's brand name than is the case in the United States.

D.   Symbol System: Written Name of Company

The hypotheses here are based on similar logic to those directly above, with a few modifications. Miracle, Taylor and Chang (1992) found that the name of the company producing an advertised product is shown more frequently in Korean advertising than in U.S. advertising. They suggested that Korean firms need to develop a personal relationship with customers due to the high value Korean culture places on collectivism and collectivistic behaviors. Indeed, the **chaebol** (large conglomerates), which dominate Korean business generally have good reputations with consumers. The attempt to build goodwill toward the company (rather than just the brand) leads to the company name being shown in a higher proportion of commercials than is the case in the United States. In the ROK, if a Korean company is the advertiser, the company name is likely to be shown using the Korean alphabet. It is also likely that the English alphabet will sometimes be seen to indicate the company name in Korean advertising because of the presence of U.S. imports and western developed products, but this is probably less common for company names than it is for brand names. United States advertisers generally seem to be less disposed to mentioning the company name than do Korean advertisers.

Again, some Chinese influence is probably present in the ROK with regard to company name, but it is likely to be limited. Mention of Japanese companies using Japanese symbol systems is probably virtually nonexistent. United States commercials using foreign symbols to describe the company name are generally predicted to be rare. Thus:

Hypothesis 4a. A higher proportion of ROK commercials use native language symbols to indicate the company name than is the case in U.S. advertising.

Hypothesis 4b. A higher proportion of commercials in the ROK use foreign alphabets of symbol systems to indicate the company name than is the case in the United States.

E.   Symbol System: Written Components of Message on Screen

Foreign alphabets or symbol systems are more likely to be used in the written components of the message in ROK advertising when compared to U.S. advertising. For reasons previously discussed, Roman and Chinese symbols are likely to have some presence in Korean advertising. Of course, the Korean alphabet is likely to be present in most ROK commercials. Perhaps owing in part to its earlier stage of economic development as well as the cultural and historical factors which have been previously described, the ROK is probably more open to foreign influence in general than is the United States. Thus:

Hypothesis 5. A higher proportion of ROK commercials use foreign language symbols in written elements of the message than is the case in U.S. advertising.

IV.   RESEARCH METHODOLOGY

A.   Samples

The above hypotheses are tested by using the results of a content analysis of television commercials taped off-the-air in the ROK and the United States. In order to obtain a representative sample, carefully designed specifications were followed in each country. All major dayparts were included, covering prime time, daytime, and fringe times. Taping periods were selected to avoid holidays and special events. The taping was done on consecutive days until a sufficient number of commercials was obtained. Duplicate commercials in each sample were deleted. 876 Korean and 1228 U.S. commercials were available for analysis.

The samples comprised a comprehensive range of product categories normally advertised on national television (see Exhibit 1). The samples excluded local advertising, political advocacy, government, and generic demand advertisements. As Exhibit 1 shows, representation by major product categories was generally similar for the two samples. Therefore, differences in results cannot be attributed to differences in the types of products advertised.

Commercials of all lengths were included in the samples. The proportion of 15-second commercials was 32 percent in Korea and 30 percent in the United States. However, the proportion of 30-second commercials in the ROK was only 26 percent, while it was 62 percent in the United States. The remaining 42 percent of Korean commercials were mostly 20 or 25 seconds, lengths which are a rarity in the United States. The remaining 8 percent of U.S. commercials were of various lengths. The samples are in accordance with generally accepted estimates of the proportions of these lengths in each country. Commercials of different lengths are not analyzed separately, since there is no reason to believe that the use of the foreign elements studies here is correlated with commercial length.

B.   Coding Instrument and Coding

The Korean and U.S. coders were students at major universities in Korea and the United States. They had studied advertising, and therefore were generally knowledgeable about advertising. After the coding instruments were developed and put through a translation and back-translation process to ensure equivalence of constructs, coders attended training sessions on the coding process. In each country, training was conducted in the native language, and the coding process was super-

Exhibit 1.   Product Categories in the Samples

	Korea	USA
Food, beverages, alcoholic beverages, and tobacco products	30%	29%
Over the counter drugs	13	10
Automobiles, bicycles, and related	2	9
Cosmetics, personal care	10	12
Detergent, cleaner, air freshener	6	7
Clothing and shoes, textiles and	12	2
Furniture, floor and wall coverings	3	1
Household electric appliances	2	1
Electronic products and equipment	3	1
Toys, games, and sporting goods	2	3
Other products	11	8
Retailing and services	6	17
	100%	100%

vised by a native speaker who had been trained while serving as part of the research team.

The coders were instructed to watch each commercial as many times as was necessary to determine the presence of foreign elements. For each commercial, coders indicated whether the following elements were present: domestic and foreign settings; domestic and foreign speaker characters; written name of the brand using domestic and foreign symbol systems; written name of the company using domestic and foreign symbol systems; and written components of the message which employ domestic and foreign symbol systems. For both setting and presence of speaker characters,coders were first asked to indicate whether any nation (setting) or nationality (speakers) was clearly present in the commercial. If it was, the country or nationality was then indicated. For the setting and speaker variables, coders were also given the option of "created foreign-like" if they believed that the advertiser intended to include a foreign element which could not be easily identified with one country. For the remaining variables, coders were instructed to indicate all symbol systems which appeared to describe the variable.

The content analysis process followed the guidelines of Kassarjian (1977) and Kolbe and Burnett (1991) relating to objectivity and reliability. Objectivity was enhanced through independent coding of commercials as well as the provision of coding rules and training. Inter-coder reliability was measured on a large sub-sample of the commercials in each country. Average percentage agreement for the coded variables was 86.1 percent in the United States and 85.6 percent in the ROK.

Table 1. Setting/Location of Commercials in the ROK and the United States

Location/Setting		ROK		USA	
		Frequency	(%)	Frequency	(%)
ROK		772	89.2	1	0.1
USA		0	0.0	533	43.4
Created foreign-like		16	1.7	10	0.8
Japan		0	0.0	2	0.2
Other/uncertain of country		11**	1.3	10*	0.8
Total # of commercials with recognizable setting		799	99.2%	550	44.8
Hypothesis tests	ROK	USA	chi-square	d.f.	sig.
Local setting	89.2	43.4	448.7	1	<.001
Foreign setting	3.0	1.4	9.3	1	.003

Notes: *(Canada 2; France, China, Thailand 1 each; uncertain of country 6)
**(Italy 3;, France, Mexico, Puerto Rico, Switzerland, Russia 1 each; uncertain of country 2)

V. RESULTS AND DISCUSSION

A.   Country of Setting

Table 1 shows the frequency distribution for commercial settings in each country. A striking feature is that in the vast majority (92.2%) of Korean commercials, the setting of the commercial was clearly recognizable. Moreover, the setting was recognizably Korean in just 44.8 percent of U.S. commercials, and clearly recognizable as a U.S. setting in 43.4 percent of the commercials.

Table 1 also indicates that Hypothesis 1a is supported at the .05 level of significance (which is used as a baseline in this study). Hypothesis 1a predicted that the setting of Korean commercials would be clearly identifiable as domestic when compared to U.S. commercials. In fact, the use of local settings was more than twice as common in the ROK. Koreans' pride in their culture and desire to preserve it in the face of foreign influences probably explains this finding.

Hypothesis 1b predicted that there would be no difference in the frequency of foreign settings in the two countries. Though the use of recognizably foreign settings was slightly more common in the ROK (3.0% vs. 1.4% in the United States), the difference was not statistically significant. It is clear that the use of foreign settings is uncommon in both countries. Interestingly, there were no U.S. settings in the entire Korean sample. Further, no individual foreign country was the setting of more than 0.25 percent of the commercials in either sample.

If it is assumed that today's Korean advertisers are responding to public tastes and pressures, attempts to transfer commercials from other countries that do not adjust the setting are not likely to be popular in the ROK. These results suggest that those advertising in the ROK would be well advised to use commercials which have recognizably local settings.

B.   Nationality of Speaking Characters

Table 2 indicates that there were few foreign speaker characters in either the Korean or U.S. samples. Less than 1 percent of the Korean commercials (0.8%) and just 1.6 percent of the U.S. commercials used foreign speaker characters. The U.S. commercials were more likely to use native speaker characters (75.6%) than were the Korean commercials (54.8%). Thus, as shown in Table 3, Hypothesis 2a, which predicted a higher frequency of native speaker characters in the ROK cannot be accepted. However, it should be stressed that this finding is accounted for by the fact that fewer Korean commercials had speaker characters. Of those commercials that had speaker characters, 98.5 percent of the Korean commercials had native speaker characters compared to 97.7 percent in the United States. Thus, there is actually very little difference in the frequency of native speaker characters when speaker characters are used.

Table 2. Nationality of Speaking Characters in Commercials in the ROK and the United States

		ROK		USA	
Nationality of Speaking Characters		Frequency	(%)	Frequency	(%)
ROK		475	54.8	0	0.0
USA		0	0.0	928	75.6
Created foreign-like		1	0.4	5	0.4
Japan		0	0.0	2	0.2
Other/uncertain ofcountry		6*	0.7	15**	1.2
Total # of commercials with recognizable setting		482	55.6%	950	77.4
Hypothesis tests	ROK	USA	chi-square	d.f.	sig.
Local speaker characters	54.8	75.6	98.3	1	<.001
Foreign speaker characters	0.8	1.6	2.2	1	.137

Notes: *(China 1; uncertain of country 5)
**(France 4; Italy 3; Great Britain 2; Germany, Puerto Rico, Russia 1 each; uncertain of country 5)

Hypothesis 2a, which suggested no difference in the level of foreign speaker characters is supported. Foreign speaker characters were uncommon in both countries, and no single foreign country accounted for more than 0.4 percent of speaker characters in either country.

These findings imply that there are very few instances when utilizing recognizably foreign speaker characters is considered effective by advertisers in either country. Interestingly, the Haarman and Waseda (1985) study found somewhat higher levels of foreign speakers to be present in Japanese commercials (5.9%). Yet, they suggested that it was only natural that both Japanese settings and characters were dominant in Japanese television commercials. Thus, the findings for Korean and U.S. settings and characters are not particularly surprising. It would appear that, generally, international advertisers are best advised to use foreign settings and speaker characters cautiously. The finding of the importance of using recognizably Korean settings in Korean advertising suggests a need to understand features of a country's history and culture rather than relying on general rules in considering the use of foreign elements in advertising.

C.   Use of Foreign Symbol System to Identify Brand Name

As shown in Table 3, commercials in both countries contained the written name of the brand in the native symbol system in the vast majority of cases (95.5% in the ROK vs. 95.0% in the United States). Thus, Hypothesis 3a is supported. Hypothesis 3b, which projected a higher incidence of depiction of the brand name in a for-

Table 3. Symbol System: Written Name of Brand
in the ROK and the United States

	ROK		USA	
Brand Name Appears in	*Frequency*	*(%)*	*Frequency*	*(%)*
Korean	828	95.5	0	0.0
English (Roman alphabet)	326	37.6	1167	95.0
Chinese	45	5.2	3	0.2
Japanese	3	0.3	0	0.0
(Hiragana or Katakana)				
Other/uncertain of country	8*	0.9	2**	0.2

Hypothesis tests	*ROK*	*USA*	*chi-square*	*d.f.*	*sig.*
Brand name shown in native sysmbol system	95.5	95.0	0.7	1	.695
Brand name shown in foreign sysmbol system	44.1	0.4	626.8	1	<.001

Notes: numbers do not sum to 100 due to commercials in which brand name appears in more than one language, or does not appear at all in the commercial.
　　　*(French 3; German 2; Arabian 1; uncertain of country 2)
　　　**(French, Russian 1 each)

eign language in the ROK is also supported. Over 44 percent of the Korean commercials contained this foreign element compared to less than one-half of one percent in the United States. English was used most frequently (in 37.6% of the commercials), followed by Chinese (5.2%). Just 3 Korean commercials used Japanese symbols to identify the brand name, and no United States ads did.

These results suggest that the use of foreign symbol systems to describe a brand name may be of some strategic value. The fact that English is the language of international business may give brands expressed in English a cosmopolitan appeal. Haarman and Waseda (1985) noticed that the use of foreign symbols was popular among young Japanese in particular since they are considered to be exotic. Additionally, it is likely that Koreans associate the West with style and quality in some product categories. Obviously, the use of English to describe the brand should be considered on a case by case basis, but it appears to be a viable strategy in many instances. However, the high frequency of the brand name being expressed in Korean suggests that advertisers who use a foreign language also translate the brand name into Korean, even if it is a foreign brand.

Given Korea's recent history and consumption patterns, the level of Western influence is not surprising. That there would be some Chinese symbols present is also not surprising given the longstanding respect Koreans have for Chinese culture and language. The lack of brand names expressed in Japanese, while understandable in the context of Korea's history, is interesting, since Japan exports more to the ROK than any other country. This fact again points up the need for advertisers to understand the culture, background, and environments of the countries in which they operate.

The presence of foreign symbols to describe brand names in U.S. advertising is rare. Advertisers from other nations are well advised to translate the brand name into English and to avoid the use of a foreign symbol system for most products.

D.   Use of Foreign Symbol System to Identify Company Name

Hypothesis 4a predicted that the company name would be shown in native symbols in a higher percentage of the Korean commercials than in the U.S. commercials. As Table 4 shows, support is provided for this hypothesis. 90.4 percent of the Korean commercials showed the company name using the Hangul, while 54.3 percent of the U.S. commercials displayed the company name in English. Clearly, the majority of Korean commercials make a point of including the company name. While slightly over half of the commercials include the company name, it is apparent that there are many instances when advertisers choose to focus on the brand name rather than the company name.

Table 4 shows that the use of foreign symbols to describe the company name is not uncommon in the ROK, but is very rare in the United States. Thus, hypothesis

Table 4. Symbol System: Written Name of Company in the ROK and the United States

Company Name Appears in	ROK		USA	
	Frequency	(%)	Frequency	(%)
Korean	784	90.4	0	0.0
English (Roman alphabet)	108	12.5	667	54.3
Chinese	59	6.8	2	0.2
Japanese (Hiragana or Katakana)	2	0.2	1	0.1
Other/uncertain of country	2*	0.2	1**	0.2

Hypothesis tests	ROK	USA	chi-square	d.f.	sig.
Company name shown in native sysmbol system	90.4	54.3	309.5	1	<.001
Company name shown in foreign symbol system	19.7	0.5	626.4	1	<.001

Notes: numbers do not sum to 100 due to the presence of commercials where the company name appears in more than one language, and the presence of commercials where the company is not named.
   *(Swiss1; uncertain of country 1)
   **(Russian 1)

4b, which predicted a greater frequency of this foreign element is supported. Nearly 20 percent of the Korean commercials contained a symbol system other than the Hangul to describe the company name. English had the highest total, at 12.5 percent, followed by Chinese at 6.5 percent. Only 0.4 percent of the U.S. commercials contained this type of foreign element. The use of Japanese symbols to describe the company name was rare in both countries. There was only 1 such commercial in the U.S. sample and just 2 (0.2%) in the Korean sample.

These results suggest that using the company name in Korean advertising is highly desirable. While U.S. advertisements often focus primarily on the brand, it is apparent that attempts to transfer an advertising message to the Korean market without including the company name may be ill advised. Further, these results suggest that if it is decided that the company name is to be shown in foreign symbols, the advertiser should also translate it into the Korean language and include this translation in the commercials. Advertisers of Japanese products in the ROK should probably not express the company name in Japanese symbols in most instances.

E. Use of Foreign Symbol System in Written Components of Message

Hypothesis 5 predicted that the use of foreign symbols in written components of the advertising message would be more common in the ROK than in the United

Table 5.   Symbol System: Written Name of Brand
in the ROK and the United States

		ROK		USA	
Written Components *Appear in*		*Frequency*	*(%)*	*Frequency*	*(%)*
Korean		727	83.9	0	0.0
English (Roman alphabet)		121	14.0	1131	92.1
Chinese		66	7.6	3	0.2
Japanese (Hiragana or Katakana)		3	0.3	0	0.0
Other/uncertain of country		6*	0.7	2**	0.2
Hypothesis tests	*ROK*	*USA*	*chi-square*	*d.f.*	*sig.*
Written components in native symbol system	83.9	92.1	33.6	1	<.001
Written components in foreign symbol system	22.5	0.4	329.4	1	<.001

Notes: numbers do not sum to 100 due to the presence of commercials where components of the message
appears in more than one language, and the presence of commercials where no written symbol system
is used.
   *(German 2, French 1 each; uncertain of country 4)
   **(Spanish, Russian 1 each)

States. Table 5 shows that the inclusion of foreign symbols in the written components of the message was frequent in the ROK, but infrequent in the United States.
Hence, as is also indicated by Table 5, this hypothesis is __cepted. While 22.5 percent of the commercials contained this type of influence, just 0.4 percent of the
U.S. commercials did. As with brand and company names, English was the most
common foreign language in the Korean sample, at 14.0 percent. Chinese symbols
also appeared in 66 commercials, accounting for 7.6 percent of the Korean sample.
The Japanese language was not present in the written components of any of the
U.S. commercials, and it was very rare in the U.S. sample.

It is interesting to note that, somewhat contrary to expectations, a higher percentage of U.S. commercials (92.1%) contained native symbols in written components of the message than was the case in the ROK (83.9%). This fact was due to
the somewhat more frequent usage of commercials which do not have any written
components in the message on screen in the Korean commercials rather than a reliance on the exclusive use of foreign symbols in Korean messages.

These results indicate that foreign symbols are used in the ROK in a way that
they are not used in the United States. Apparently, Korean advertisers, even of
domestically made products, frequently find that foreign symbol systems to
express the brand, company or the written components of the message are useful
from a strategic standpoint. This type of strategy is rarely found in the USA. Those
attempting to transfer elements of advertising strategy to the Korean market may
be able to include symbols foreign to the Korean market in many instances. However, as would be expected, it would appear that the use of this strategy should be
supplemented by the use of the Hangul.

V. CONCLUSION

The inclusion of foreign elements in Korean advertising is associated with a complex combination of factors, including features of a country's culture, history, and
economic development. For example, in spite of Japan's status as the leading
exporter of goods to the ROK, Japanese settings, speaker characters, and symbol
systems are virtually nonexistent. In contrast, the written Chinese language to
describe the brand name or articulate the message is not uncommon in Korean
advertising. Western influence is common in terms of the use of English to express
the brand and company or the written components of the message. However, Western settings and speaker characters are very rare in Korean advertising. Those
advertising in the ROK or in any other country must consider features of the country's culture and history in order to understand the potential for using foreign elements as a strategic tool in advertising.

The results of this study would suggest that those advertising in the Korean market avoid the use of foreign settings and speaker characters. It seems unlikely that
an attempt to transfer an advertising campaign from another country to the ROK

could be successful if it was not given a Korean setting and Korean speaking characters. Clearly, many advertisers in Korea make use of foreign symbol systems in the written components of their message, or to describe the brand or company. It would appear that the inclusion of foreign symbols can be an effective strategy in some cases, especially if done in conjunction with the use of Korean symbols. The decision whether to use foreign symbols alone or in combination is probably best made on a case by case basis, considering factors such as the company's image and the product category. It also seems that it is good advice for most firms to show the company name in all advertisements in Korea, and for foreign firms to consider the use of the Hangul to do so.

The presence of foreign elements in U.S. advertising is relatively rare. However, it was found that U.S. advertising has fewer recognizably domestic settings and does not focus as much on the company name as do Korean commercials. These types of findings should also be considered by those advertising both in the ROK and the USA. In general, the results suggest that there are clear differences in the types of foreign elements that can be used effectively in the two countries, and that advertisers must consider these differences and the reasons for them in order to effectively develop strategy.

ACKNOWLEDGMENT

This research was supported by the Hoso Bunka Foundation (Tokyo), the Korea Broadcast Advertising Corporation (Seoul), ASI Marketing Research, Inc. (Tokyo), the Yoshida Hideo Memorial Foundation (Tokyo), and Youngshin Academy (Seoul).

REFERENCES

Ahn, C.Y. (1986). Economic development of South Korea: 1945-1985. *Korea and World Affairs*, 10, 91-116.
Buzzell, R.D. (1986). Can you standardize multinational marketing? *Harvard Business Review*, 46,69-75.
Cook, C. (1989). Poor man's burden: A survey of the third world. *The Economist*, 314, 3-58.
Chai, D. (1993). Koreans audit at last: Newspapers bow to pressure from government. *Advertising Age*. 64, I3-I20.
Elinder, E. (1965). How international can european advertising be? *Journal of Marketing*, 29, 7-11.
Haarman, H., & Waseda, M. (1985). The Use of Foreign Elements in Japanese TV Commercials: A Report. Tokyo: Hitotsubashi University.
Hoare, J., & Pares, S. (1988). *Korea: An introduction*. New York: Kegan Paul International.
Hong, Y.S. (1993). Korea's economic prospects: The next five years. *Korea's Economy*, 9, 7-8.
Hornik, J. (1980). Comparative evaluation of international vs. national advertising strategies. *Columbia Journal of World Business*, 12, 36-45.
Jain, S. (1993). *International marketing management*. Boston: PWS-Kent Publishing Company.
Kang, S.P. (1988). Korean culture, the Seoul Olympics, and world order. *Korea and World Affairs*, 12, 347-362.
Kil, S.H. (1984). Two aspects of Korea-Japan relations. *Korea and World Affairs*, 8, 505-513.

Kim C. (1988). Korea-Japan relations and Japan's security role. *Korea and World Affairs*, 12, 118-124.

Kim, H.E. (1985). *Korea: Beyond the hills*. Seoul: Samhwa Printing Co., Ltd.

Kim, K. (1988). Korea in the 1990's: Making the transition to a developed economy. *World Development*, 16, 7-18.

Kim, Y.S. (1988). Some reflections on science and technology in contemporary Korean society. *Korea Journal*, 28, 4-15.

KOBACO. (1989). *Annual report*. Seoul: Korea Broadcast Advertising Corporation.

Koo, H. (1986). The political economy of industrialization in South Korea and Taiwan. *Political Economy*. 10, 148-180.

Lee, H.B. (1987). Korea, the land of phonetic science. *Korea Journal*, 27, (February); pp. 4.

Levitt, T. (1983). The globalization of markets. *Harvard Business Review*, 61, 92-102.

McCune, S. (1966). *Korea: Land of broken calm*. New York: D. Van Nostrum Publishing.

Miracle, G.E. (1968). International advertising principles and strategies. *MSU Business Topics*, 29-36.

Miracle, G.E., Chang, K.Y., and Taylor, C.R. (1992). Culture and advertising executions: A comparison of selected characteristics of Korean and U.S. television commercials. *International Marketing Review*, 9, 5-17.

Park, U.K. (1986). Technology transfer to Korea and determinants of success. *Korea and World Affairs*, 10, 687-93.

Quelch, J.A., and Hoff, E.J. (1986). Customizing global marketing. *Harvard Business Review*, 55-69.

Ricks, D.A., Arpan, J., & Fu, M.Y. (1974). Pitfalls in advertising overseas. *Journal of Advertising Research*, 47-50.

Soon, C. (1982). The Korean-American economic relationship—1945-1982. *Korea Journal*, 22-32.

Steinberg, D.I. (1988). Sociopolitical factors and Korea's future economic policies. *World Development*, 16(1), 19-34.

Suh, C.S., & Pak, C.K. (1974). *Aspects of Korean Culture*. Seoul: Soodo Women's Teachers College Press.

Weissman, G. (1967). International expansion. In L. Adler (Ed.), *Plotting marketing strategy: A new orientation* (p. 179). New York: Simon and Schuster.

Whang, I.J. (1987). Korea toward the twenty-first century. *Korea Journal*, 27, 21-32.

Yang, W.D. (1983). *Korean ways, Korean mind*. Seoul: Tamgu Dang.

Yum, J.O. (1987). Korean philosophy and communication. In D.L. Kincaid (Ed.), *Communication theory from western and eastern perspectives* (pp. 71-86). New York: Academic Press.

PART IV

METHODOLOGICAL CONTRIBUTIONS TO THE INTERNATIONAL MARKETING LITERATURE

DIMENSIONS OF GLOBAL STRATEGY AND THEIR UTILIZATION BY EUROPEAN AND JAPANESE MNCs:
AN EXPLORATORY STUDY

Shaoming Zou and Jay L. Laughlin

ABSTRACT

Emerging literature in the area of global strategy is reviewed and Yip's five-dimension model of global strategy is expanded to 12 dimensions. A mail survey was conducted to assess the proposed dimensions and compare the use of global strategy by European and Japanese MNCs in global industries. Study results indicate that 12 dimensions have adequate reliability and capture different aspects of global strategy. Moreover, although European and Japanese MNCs appear similar in global strategy use, a few differences exist. Japanese MNCs appear to seek a higher degree of product standardization than European MNCs. Conversely, European MNCs seem to have greater global market participation and a higher degree of product development coordination activity than their Japanese counterparts. Theoretical and managerial implications of the findings are also discussed.

Advances in International Marketing, Volume 7, pages 199-210.
Copyright © 1996 by JAI Press Inc.
All rights of reproduction in any form reserved.
ISBN: 1-55938-839-0

In an era of globalization of markets, companies across the Triad (United States, Japan, and Europe) face the challenge of developing effective global strategy to gain competitive advantages in global markets. Key themes in recent discussion of international marketing strategy have been globalization and global strategy. According to Levitt (1983), markets are driven toward a converging commonality. To survive and succeed, companies must rethink their old multi-domestic posture and rationalize their global operations to attain the benefits of economies of scale. Hax (1989) argues that success or failure of a business will occur in a global setting.

Recent recognition of the importance of globalization and global strategy issues makes the identification of global strategy components an important priority for international business researchers. Companies seeking to enhance global competitiveness will be interested in both theory and empirical support which establish the strategic dimensions on which global strategy can be based. Although previous studies have begun to develop the components of global strategy (e.g., Hamel & Prahalad, 1985; Yip 1991; Yip & Johansson, 1993), formulation of a comprehensive framework has not yet been realized.

In addition to establishing preliminary strategic dimensions on which multinational corporations (MNCs) can base their competitive efforts, previous studies on global strategy have empirically compared the global strategy of U.S. MNCs with that of Japanese MNCs, and offered insight into how the U.S. and Japanese MNCs compete globally. However, no empirical study has been conducted to compare the global strategy of European and Japanese MNCs. Given the significance of the triadic competition among the United States, European, and Japanese businesses in contemporary international business, it is of interest to both the academic community and to international business practitioners to compare the global strategy of European MNCs with that of Japanese MNCs.

The purposes of the present study are to fill two gaps in the literature regarding global strategy used by MNCs. Most importantly, the study seeks to extend Yip's (1989) global strategy framework by detailing some of its existing components and by introducing additional global strategy concepts. Additionally, a measurement instrument is developed to operationalize the proposed global strategy dimensions and to provide preliminary comparison of the global strategy used by European and Japanese MNCs.

The remainder of the paper is organized in five major sections. First, the background literature on global strategy is briefly reviewed. Second, Yip's (1989) framework for global strategy is presented and evaluated, and an extended 12-dimension global strategy is proposed. Next, the research design used to collect primary data is described. Subsequently, the findings of the research are presented. Finally, the implications of the findings are discussed.

I.   A BRIEF REVIEW OF THE LITERATURE

The literature on global strategy has been characterized by a diversity of perspectives. There is no consensus as to what a global strategy is and how to compete globally. In his classic article, Levitt (1983) forcefully argues that in an era of globalization of markets, key strategic imperatives for MNCs are to attain low cost positions through the use of standardized marketing approach. Thus, companies that hold onto the old multidomestic approach, in which product and marketing programs are fully adapted to the idiosyncrasies of each individual country market, are doomed to failure, whereas global corporations that adopt product and marketing standardization will prevail.

Counter to Levitt (1983), Douglas and Wind (1987) contend that a strategy of universal standardization appears naive and oversimplistic. They argue that for a strategy of global standardization to succeed, certain conditions must be met, including the existence of a global market segment, potential synergies from standardization, and the availability of a communication and distribution infrastructure to deliver the firm's offering to target customers worldwide. Without these conditions, firms are better off pursuing a customized approach to international marketing. Douglas and Wind's (1987) contingency perspective has been reflected in Jain's (1989) conceptual framework for international marketing strategy standardization, and has been empirically verified by Cavusgil, Zou and Naidu (1993) in the context of small and medium-sized firms' export marketing strategy.

Hout, Porter and Rudden (1982), on the other hand, suggest that an effective global strategy is a bag of many tricks, not a simple standardized approach. They argue that the key to global success is to leverage the firm's competitive advantage across the interdependent country markets to change the scale and scope of competition. Hamel and Prahalad (1985) also propose a similar concept of global strategy when they contend a firm must seek cross-subsidization across product lines and markets to succeed in the global market.

Porter's (1986) view of global strategy emphasizes two dimensions of a firm's value chain activities, that is configuration and coordination. A key consideration in value chain configuration is the concentration of value-adding activities at certain strategic locations. According to Porter (1986), a particular value activity should be concentrated at those locations where the activity can be performed most efficiently and effectively. To be successful, a firm must also coordinate its worldwide value-adding activities so that interdependencies across markets and product lines can be exploited. Bartlett and Ghoshal (1988) also propose a view of global strategy. They contend that globalizing and localizing forces work together to transform many industries. Thus, a successful MNC must develop and possess "transnational capability," that is the ability to achieve global coordination and national flexibility simultaneously.

In contrast to other authors, Yip (1989) adopts a multidimensional perspective when he develops a contingency framework of global strategy. He defines a global strategy as having five major dimensions: market participation, product standardization, activity concentration, uniform marketing, and integrated competitive moves. Yip contends that a global strategy must match the globalization potential of the industry. To the extent a firm can achieve a close match, positive performance will result.

While the aforementioned studies have enriched our understanding about global strategy and the differences between the U.S. and Japanese MNCs' use of global strategy, there are at least two gaps in the literature that need to be filled. First, Yip's (1989) five-dimension model of global strategy, while significant in advancing the multidimensional perspective of global strategy, needs to be extended and modified to incorporate other dimensions of global strategy that are not captured by these five dimensions. Second, none of the studies has investigated and compared European MNCs' use of global strategy with that of Japanese MNCs or American MNCs. Since the European MNCs have a long history of international operations and since they represent a significant portion of triadic competition, it should be interesting to compare their use of global strategy with that of Japanese MNCs.

II. EXPANSION OF YIP'S GLOBAL STRATEGY FRAMEWORK

While Yip (1989) primarily intended to offer a normative framework within which MNCs can make their global strategic decisions, his work has also contributed to the literature by implicitly integrating various perspectives of global strategy. For instance, his market participation coincides with Ohmae's (1985) triadic view of global competition, his product standardization is in line with Levitt's (1983) global standardization, his activity concentration is consistent with Porter's (1986) configuration of value chain activities, his uniform marketing is similar to Jain's (1989) marketing standardization, and his integrated competitive moves implies the same logic as Hout, Porter and Rudden's (1982) competitive leverage and Hamel and Prahalad's (1985) cross-subsidization.

Yip (1991) offers some support for his multidimensional view of global strategy. Specifically, he collected primary data by interviewing 18 business units (BUs) of MNCs. Based on a bivariate rank-order correlation analysis, Yip's (1991) findings support the notion that a global strategy has five dimensions and that a global strategy has positive performance implications. In a related study, Yip and Johansson (1993) add 18 Japanese business units to Yip (1991). They found that the U.S. and Japanese MNCs differ in their perceptions of industry globalization potential. In particular, they found that Japanese BUs have a greater desire than U.S. BUs for using a global strategy, and that Japanese BUs make more use of global strategy than U.S. BUs. Yip and Johansson (1993) interpret this finding as indicating that central control from the Japanese headquarters makes integration across the globe easier.

Table 1. Dimensions of Global Strategy

The Proposed Framework of Global Strategy	Yip's (1989) Framework of Global Strategy
Global Market Participation	Market Participation
Degree of Product Standardization	Product Standardization
Standardization of Positioning	Uniform Marketing
Standardization of Promotional Campaign	Integrated Competitive Moves
Standardization of Channel/Pricing	Activity Concentration
Integration of Competitive Moves	Coordination of Manufacturing
Coordination of Product Development	
Coordination of Marketing/Service	
Concentration of Manufacturing	
Concentration of Product Development	
Concentration of Marketing/Service	

Building on Yip (1989) and the recent literature, three specific adaptations are made to Yip's framework in the proposed dimensions of global strategy. A comparison of the proposed dimensions of global strategy with those of Yip's (1989) is presented in Table 1. First, the uniform marketing component was expanded into standardization of positioning, standardization of promotional campaign, and standardization of channel/pricing. This straightforward refinement is based on the traditional managerial marketing perspective with the exception that sufficient interaction exists in distribution and pricing to combine those elements in the evaluation of global standardization. Additional sensitivity to global strategy orientation is expected as a result of this decomposition.

A second adaptation is seen in the decomposition of value-added activity concentration. Whereas Yip identifies concentration of value-added activities as a single construct, three dimensions of value-adding activities are listed in the expanded framework. These include manufacturing, product development, and marketing services. Such a refinement allows focusing on different groups of MNC activities and the identification of alternative global strategies of MNCs.

Finally, we have incorporated Porter's (1986) coordination of value-chain activities as an additional set of dimensions through which MNCs effect strategy. Just as in the case of activity concentration, the idea that coordination of value-chain activities across the three areas of manufacturing, product development, and marketing activities can contribute to differentiable strategy is included. Yip's three remaining dimensions of global market participation, degree of product standardization, and integration of competitive moves are not altered. The result of these changes is the creation of a 12-dimension framework for assessing global strategy. The operationalization and assessment of specific measures is included in the next section.

III. RESEARCH DESIGN

A cross-industry field survey of Japanese and European business units that are based in the U.S. but competing in global industries was conducted to collect the primary data. BUs rather than MNCs were selected for the study because most modern MNCs are well-diversified companies within which different BUs may pursue different worldwide strategies. Global manufacturing industries were selected for study because BUs competing in global industries are better positioned to pursue a global strategy, and because of the need to keep the sample relatively homogeneous.

Global industries were identified by a review of the globalization literature (e.g., Bartlett & Ghoshal, 1987; Hamel & Prahalad, 1985; Hout et al., 1982; Porter, 1980, 1986; Yip, 1989, 1991; Yip & Johansson, 1993). Both consumer and industrial goods industries were included in the sampling frame. Japanese and European BUs in the global manufacturing industries were identified through the database of Dun and Bradstreet Information Services, Inc.. The criteria used for identifying the BUs include (a) the BUs must be based in the United States, (b) the BUs must have international business operations in addition to their operations in the United States, (c) the BUs must have an employment level of 200 employees or more, and (d) the BUs must have total annual sales of at least $20 million. These criteria were considered necessary for further improving the relative homogeneity of the sample.

Several stages were involved in designing a structured survey questionnaire. First, the relevant literature on global strategy (e.g., Yip, 1991; Yip & Johansson, 1993) and international marketing (e.g., Cavusgil & Zou, 1994; Samiee & Roth, 1992) was employed to develop scale items that measure the 12 dimensions of a global strategy. Multiple Likert-type statements were developed for the measurement instrument. These Likert-type statements were tapped on a seven-point scale ranging from "strongly disagree" (1) to "strongly agree" (7). In addition, coordination and concentration of value-chain activities were measured by two 7-point bipolar scales ranging from "not coordinated at all" (1) to "highly coordinated" (7), and "dispersed" (1) to "concentrated" (7), respectively, with respect to 10 value chain activities.

Second, a series of personal interviews were conducted with three executives responsible for international operations of MNCs, and with four academicians familiar with global strategy literature to evaluate the validity of the list of Likert-type statements. Based on the interview feedback, some statements were dropped from the list or modified to improve the validity of the measures. The revised list of Likert-type statements were sent back to the same executives and academicians, and all of them were generally satisfied with the modified list.

Third, as a further pretest step, the Likert-type statements were put in a questionnaire format and then critiqued by two managers and three "expert researchers" in international business strategy in terms of the length of the questionnaire, time needed to complete the questionnaire, and the content of individual items. Based on the feedback, the questionnaire was finalized.

The data collection process involved two mailings. In the initial phase, a personalized cover letter, a questionnaire, and a postage-paid business reply envelope were sent to the CEO/President or Vice-President (VP) for international operations of each of the BUs. The personalized cover letter explained the purpose of the research and its significance to international business management, stated the importance of the respondent's participation in the study, described the time and effort needed to complete the questionnaire, assured the respondent's confidentiality, promised to send the respondent a summary report of the research if he/she returned a completed questionnaire with his/her business card, and thanked the respondent in advance for his/her participation.

A second phase in the data collection effort was conducted three weeks after the initial mailing. A personalized cover letter, a replacement copy of questionnaire, and a postage-paid business reply envelope were sent to those who had not responded in any way to the initial mailing. The cover letter to a respondent reminded him/her the importance of his/her participation, and urged him/her to take some time to complete and return the enclosed questionnaire. The questionnaire and the business-reply envelope were identical to that sent in the initial mailing. Four weeks after the second mailing, the data collection ended.

Overall, 40 completed questionnaires were received, 21 from Japanese BUs and 19 from European BUs. The effective response rate (after excluding undeliverable mail) is about 28 percent. The sample size achieved is similar to that of Yip (1991) and Yip and Johansson (1993), and is considered useful for the current exploratory study.

IV. FINDINGS OF THE RESEARCH

A.   Sample Characteristics

The key characteristics of the Japanese and European samples are presented in Table 2. The Japanese sample contains 21 business units, while the European sample includes 19. The average annual sales of Japanese BUs amount to $1.082 billion, which is greater than the $800 million of the European BUs. In terms of number of employees, Japanese BUs have an average of 1,174 full time employees, whereas their European counterparts have only 691. However, European BUs generally have longer international business involvement than their Japanese counterparts, operate in more country markets than the Japanese BUs, and have more foreign subsidiaries than Japanese BUs. The key informants of the Japanese sample have an average of 11.9 years of international experience, compared to the 12.5 years of their European counterparts. Overall, the Japanese BUs appear to be larger, but their European counterparts are more heavily involved in international business.

Table 2. Key Characteristics of the Samples

	Mean	
Characteristics	Japan	Europe
Annual Sales	$1,082 mil.	$800 mil.
Number of Employees	1,174	691
Years of International Business Involvement	24.2	38.2
Number of Markets Involved	11.6	34.6
Number of Foreign Subsidiaries	14.1	30.4
Years of Respondents' International Experience	11.9	12.5

Table 3. Assessment of Construct Reliability

Construct	Number of Items	Coefficient Alpha
Global Market Participation	3	.9192
Degree of Product Standardization	4	.7304
Standardization of Positioning	5	.7371
Standardization of Promotional Campaign	2	.5904
Standardization of Channel/Pricing	2	.6604
Integration of Competitive Moves	4	.6680
Coordination of Manufacturing	4	.7925
Coordination of Product Development	2	.8377
Coordination of Marketing/Services	4	.8749
Concentration of Manufacturing	4	.8669
Concentration of Product Development	2	.7777
Concentration of Marketing/Services	4	.8248

B. Assessing the Reliability of Global Strategy Dimensions

To validate the 12 dimensions of global strategy adopted in the present study, Cronbach's alpha is calculated for each of the 12 constructs across Japanese and European BUs. Cronbach's alpha, whose value falls between the interval [0,1], is a measure of the reliability of scales formed by multiple indicators (Nunnally, 1978). The larger the alpha, the more reliable the scale.

As shown in Table 3, with the exception of three constructs, all remaining nine constructs have a coefficient alpha estimate of over .700, a clear indication of good reliability of the constructs (Nunnally, 1978). Indeed, most coefficient alphas are above .800. To be specific, the coefficient alpha for global market participation is .9192, degree of product standardization .7304, standardization of positioning .7371, coordination of manufacturing .7925, coordination of product development .8377, coordination of marketing services .8749, concentration of manufacturing .8669, concentration of product development .7777, and concentration of marketing/services .8248.

As for the three constructs whose coefficient alphas are below .700, standardization of promotional campaign has an alpha of .5904, standardization of channel/pricing .6604, and integration of competitive moves .6680. Given the exploratory nature of the present study, these three constructs are judged to be adequately reliable (Nunnally 1969).

As a further assessment of the adequacy of the proposed 12-dimensions of global strategy, the correlation coefficients between the dimensions were examined. It was found that all 12 dimensions of global strategy are positively and significantly correlated. However, the correlation coefficients are not excessively high. Hence, it can be concluded that the 12 proposed dimensions are a coherent set of distinctive dimensions of a global strategy. This, plus the adequate reliability of the dimensions, supports the contention that a global strategy should have at least 12 operational dimensions.

C. Comparison of European and Japanese BUs' Use of Global Strategy

Table 4 presents the means of the 12 dimensions of global strategy for both the Japanese and European samples, and t-test results comparing the two samples on each of the 12 dimensions. Given the relatively small sample sizes, the following findings should be considered as preliminary evidence, rather than the indisputable results.

As revealed by Table 4, for Japanese BUs, there are noticeable differences in the degree of globalization across the 12 dimensions of a global strategy. For Japanese

Table 4. Comparison of Global Strategy Dimensions between Japanese and European MNCs

| | Mean | | | |
Global Strategy Dimension	Japanese	European	t-Statistic	Sig. Level
Global Market Participation	4.32	5.26	1.74	.091
Degree of Product Standardization	4.55	3.87	-1.74	.091
Standardization of Positioning	4.67	4.56	-0.31	.758
Standardization of Promotional Campaign	3.36	2.98	-0.97	.340
Standardization of Channel/Pricing	4.53	4.08	-1.09	.283
Integration of Competitive Moves	3.75	3.89	0.43	.668
Coordination of Manufacturing	4.72	4.59	-0.33	.742
Coordination of Product Development	5.50	6.03	1.82	.077
Coordination of Marketing/Services	3.80	3.93	0.26	.799
Concentration of Manufacturing	4.31	4.13	-0.38	.709
Concentration of Product Development	5.26	5.35	0.19	.850
Concentration of Marketing/Services	3.68	3.65	-0.02	.985

Note: All factors are measured on a 7-point scale.?

BUs, the degree of standardization of promotional campaign, integration of competitive moves, coordination of marketing/services, and concentration of marketing/services is generally low, since a score of 4 is the center point on a 7-point scale. In contrast, Japanese BUs appear to seek a high degree of global market participation, product standardization, standardization of positioning and channel/pricing, coordination of manufacturing and product development, and concentration of manufacturing and product development.

Similar to Japanese BUs, European BUs also seek a high degree of global market participation, standardization of positioning and channel/pricing, coordination of manufacturing and product development, and concentration of manufacturing and product development, but a low degree of standardization of promotional campaign, integration of competitive moves, coordination of marketing/services, and concentration of marketing/services. In contrast to Japanese BUs which pursue a high degree of product standardization, European BUs seem to opt for a low degree of product standardization.

When Japanese BUs are compared to European BUs on individual dimensions of a global strategy, it appears that based on the means, Japanese and European BUs do show some differences in their use of global strategy. However, except on three dimensions where the differences are marginally significant (significant at .10), these differences are not statistically significant at .05 level. Specifically, European BUs appear to participate in more markets in the world and seek a higher degree of coordination of their product development activities than their Japanese counterparts. However, Japanese BUs appear to pursue a higher degree of product standardization than European BUs. On other than these dimensions, Japanese and European BUs appear well-matched in their use of global strategy.

V. DISCUSSION

The findings of this exploratory research offer a number of insights into issues regarding the dimensions of global strategy and how Japanese and European BUs in global industries use global strategy. The findings also extend the work of Yip (1989, 1991) and Yip and Johansson (1993) by fine-tuning and expanding the number of dimensions of a global strategy.

Based on the limited evidence from 21 Japanese and 19 European BUs, it appears that a global strategy has at least 12 distinct dimensions. More specifically, Yip's (1989) five dimension model of global strategy needs to be fine-tuned to expand uniform marketing into standardization of positioning, promotional campaign and channel/pricing, and activity concentration into concentration of manufacturing, product development, and marketing/services. In addition, coordination of value chain activities (i.e., manufacturing, product development, and marketing/services), which is a key consideration in Porter's (1986) discussion of global strategy, should be added to Yip's conceptualization to offer a more complete account of various perspectives of global strategy.

This finding has both theoretical and managerial implications. Theoretically, the finding suggests researchers should take a multidimensional view of a global strategy in their investigation of global strategy. Moreover, 12 dimensions, rather than five as suggested by Yip (1989), should be adopted when developing theories of global strategy. Managerially, BUs contemplating their global strategy must consider each of the 12 dimensions carefully. They must also recognize that the 12 dimensions are closely related yet distinct aspects of a complete global strategy. The degree of globalization of each of the 12 dimensions must be determined in a way that overall global strategy is optimal.

To answer the second research question, it is found that Japanese and European BUs in global industries are pretty closely matched in their use of global strategy. Indeed, Japanese and European BUs pursue a similar degree of standardization of positioning, promotional campaign and channel/pricing, seek the similar extent of integration of competitive moves, implement similar level of coordination of manufacturing and marketing/services, and achieve similar concentrations of manufacturing, product development, and marketing/services. However, Japanese BUs seem to have a higher degree of product standardization, but a lower degree of global market participation and coordination of product development than European BUs. A managerial implication of this finding is that BUs competing in global industries should realize the formidable task of competing with Japanese and European BUs. They must develop their global strategy in a way that can outperform or at least match the Japanese and European BUs.

Another interesting finding of the current study is that although the BUs in the European sample are generally more experienced and more involved in international business than those in the Japanese sample, Japanese BUs appear to have caught up in their use of global strategy. This finding is consistent with the recent miracle of Japanese business success in global competition. It also implies that a business unit can quickly learn to compete effectively in global markets, even though its rivals may be well-established in international-business.

The findings discussed above must be interpreted in light of the limitations of this study. First, the present study investigated the Japanese and European BUs based in the United States, not in their home country. As a result, generalization of the findings to the general population of Japanese and European BUs must be made with caution. Second, though the response rate achieved in the present study is adequate compared to similar studies, the sample size is relatively small. Care must be taken when making inferences based on small-sample evidence. Nevertheless, it is the authors' opinion that the findings of the present study do contribute meaningfully to the literature by offering preliminary support for the proposed 12-dimension global strategy framework and by identifying similarities and differences between European and Japanese MNCs' use of global strategy.

REFERENCES

Bartlett, C., & Ghoshal, S. (1987). Managing across borders: New strategic requirements. *Sloan Management Review*, 7-17.

Cavusgil, S.T., & Zou, S. (1994). Marketing strategy-performance relationship: An investigation of the empirical link in export market ventures. *Journal of Marketing*, 58 (1), 1-21.

Cavusgil, S.T., Zou, S., & Naidu, G.M. (1993). Product and promotion adaptation in export ventures: An empirical investigation. *Journal of International Business Studies*, 24 (3), 479-506.

Douglas, S.P., & Wind, Y. (1987). The myth of globalization. *Columbia Journal of World Business*, 19-29.

Ghoshal, S. (1987). Global strategy: An organizing framework. *Strategic Management Journal*, 8 (5), 425-40.

Hamel, G., & Prahalad, C.K. (1985). Do you really have a global strategy? *Harvard Business Review*, 63, 139-148.

Hax, A.C. (1989). Building the firm of the future. *Sloan Management Review*, 75-82.

Hout, T., Porter, M., & Rudden, E. (1982). How global companies win out. *Harvard Business Review*, 60 98-105.

Jain, S.C. (1989). Standardization of international strategy: Some research hypotheses. *Journal of Marketing*, 53 (1), 70-79.

Levitt, T. (1983). The globalization of markets. *Harvard Business Review*, 61, 92-102.

Nunnally, J. (1969). *Psychometric theory*. New York: McGraw-Hill Book Company.

Nunnally, J. (1978). *Psychometric theory*. New York: McGraw-Hill Book Company.

Ohmae, K. (1985). *Triad power: The coming shape of global competition*. New York: Free Press.

Porter, M. (1980). *Competitive strategy*. New York: Free Press.

Porter, M. (1986). Competition in global industries: A conceptual framework. In M.E. Porter (Ed.), *Competition in Global Industries* (pp. 15-60). New York: Free Press.

Samiee, S., & Roth, K. (1992). The influence of global marketing standardization on performance. *Journal of Marketing*, 56 (2), 1-17.

Yip, G. (1989). Global strategy ... In a world of nations? *Sloan Management Review*, 29-41.

Yip, G. (1991). Do American businesses use global strategy? Marketing Science Institute, Working Paper #91-101.

Yip, G., & Johansson, J. (1993). Global market strategies of U.S. and Japanese businesses. Marketing Science Institute, Working Paper #93-102.

EVALUATING THE CYMYC COSMOPOLITANISM SCALE ON KOREAN CONSUMERS

Sung-Joon Yoon, Hugh M. Cannon and Attila Yaprak

ABSTRACT

This paper reports the results of an exploratory study evaluating the validity of the CYMYC cosmopolitanism scale (Cannon, Yoon, McGowan, & Yaprak, 1994) for Korean consumers. The results provide some support for the validity of the scale for cross-national studies. More significant, however, is the fact that an analysis of its weaknesses suggests important directions for future research regarding *cosmopolitanism*. It suggests that *cosmopolitanism* and *localism*, concepts that have tradition- ally been seen as opposite poles of a single dimension, may well be independent. Furthermore, it suggests that the interaction between the two dimensions may obscure the expression of the underlying constructs.

We live in a world where borders are becoming less significant (Ohmae, 1989). In his landmark article, "The Globalization of Markets," Levitt (1983) heralded the

Advances in International Marketing, Volume 7, pages 211-232.
Copyright © 1996 by JAI Press Inc.
All rights of reproduction in any form reserved.
ISBN: 1-55938-839-0

arrival of global thinking that encourages marketers to expand their knowledge of marketing on a global scale. Clark Kerr (1983), in predicting the convergence of future industrial societies, stated that "Lifestyles, particularly among educated youth and the professional classes, tend to become more cosmopolitan ... there comes to be an international, up-to-date style of life—what is called the new *cosmopolitan* culture"(p. 57). Levitt goes even further. He says, "*Cosmopolitanism* is no longer the monopoly of the intellectual and leisure classes; it is becoming the established property and defining characteristic of all sectors everywhere in the world. Gradually and irresistably it breaks the walls of economic insularity, nationalism, and chauvinism" (Levitt 1983, p. 101).

Does Levitt go too far? Perhaps. For all his discussion of global cosmopolitanism, it does not seem reasonable that all people are becoming more global in their orientation. Rather, we should ask, "What are the common characteristics of those who have a global, *cosmopolitan* outlook?" "Under what conditions are a person's *cosmopolitan* tendencies likely to influence behavior?" And, "How does the expression of these *cosmopolitan* tendencies change from one culture to another?"

The last of these questions is of particular interest to marketers. We may well live in a world populated by an increasing number of *cosmopolitan* citizens, but the manner in which these people express their citizenship may very well depend on their cultural heritage. *Cosmopolitan* Koreans may be different from *local* Koreans, but they may also be different from cosmopolitan Americans. From a cross-national segmentation perspective, any cultural differences must be carefully investigated to determine whether they are relevant to one's marketing program. This calls for a program of cross-cultural research.

Unfortunately, most of the studies that make cross-cultural comparisons do so primarily from the managerial rather than a marketing perspective (e.g. Hofstede, 1989; Schneider & Meyer, 1991; Kagono, Nonaka, Sakakibara, & Okumura, 1985; Tse, Lee, Vertinsky & Wehrung, 1988). These are still potentially relevant to marketing, especially in the context of industrial marketing. However, we also need to develop a tradition of cross-cultural research that focuses on marketing, and even more specifically, cross-national segmentation problems.

Cannon and Yaprak (1993) addressed this need by developing a framework for classifying marketing situations according to the degree to which consumers are *cosmopolitan* in their orientation. In order to evaluate this framework, they sought to develop a scale that captures the degree to which consumers are *cosmopolitan* in their orientation (Cannon, Yoon, McGowan, & Yaprak, 1994).

Obviously, to be useful in a global context, such a scale must be valid across cultures (Adler, 1983), not just in the United States. First, the *cosmopolitanism* it purports to measure must truly exist as a culturally independent construct. Second, the measure must be robust enough to measure this construct, regardless of the cultural context. And third, the way the construct is expressed in market behavior must be constant across cultures, or, if it is not, we must determine how its expression is conditioned by cultural factors.

The purpose of this paper will be to explore these issues. It will seek to evaluate Cannon, Yoon, McGowan and Yaprak's (1994) *Cosmopolitanism* (CYMYC) scale using a Korean sample to explore its dimensionality and psychometric properties for a non-American culture.

I. PREVIOUS RESEARCH ON COSMOPOLITANISM

The term *cosmopolitanism* was originally proposed by Merton (1957) and Gouldner (1957) to represent the tendency of people to orient themselves beyond their immediate social system. The concept has been used extensively in the sociology, geography, anthropology, and marketing literature.

In the area of business administration, research regarding the *cosmopolitanism* concept has tended to fall into one of three general categories. First, studies have tried to address the way different kinds of people relate to new market offerings. They do this by studying patterns of information exposure and the diffusion of innovations among different segments of the market. This has obvious implications for marketers, who tend to be among the most prominent contributors to this stream of research.

Second, *cosmopolitism* has been used in organizational research to address the tendency of employees to be loyal to their profession versus their individual organization. *Cosmopolitan* individuals are thought to place their professional orientation above their commitment to any individual company or organizational setting. This has profound implications for the way companies seek to manage *cosmopolitan* employees.

Third, researchers have tried to get a better understanding of the *cosmopolitan* construct itself. The primary tool in this research has been factor analysis, with the objective of determining the construct's dimensionality.

A. Cosmopolitanism, Information Exposure and Diffusion

Diffusion research suggests that *cosmopolitanism* is positively related to *innovativeness* (Robertson, 1971). By orienting themselves beyond their immediate social systems, people open themselves to new, innovative ideas. Consistent with this notion, Gatignon, Eliashberg, and Robertson (1989) note that *cosmopolitanism* has been most commonly operationalized by the level of external information activity (Coleman, Katz, & Menzel, 1966; Hage & Dewer, 1973; Kimberly, 1978).

For instance, Gatignon, Eliashberg, and Robertson (1989) used six items relating to exposure to information beyond country boundaries: (1) quantity of foreign mail received, (2) quantity of foreign mail sent, (3) international telegrams received, (4) foreign travel, (5) foreign visitors received, and (6) the number of telephones in use. They then compared *cosmopolitanism* to *innovativeness* for six consumer products. Based on these measures, Sweden was by far the most *cosmopolitan* of fourteen countries included in the study, followed by Switzerland, Denmark, Norway and Finland. Portugal, Spain, and Italy were the least *cosmopolitan* of the countries studied.

Besides the direct measures of *cosmopolitanism*, the study employed geographic mobility and the role of women in society as potentially related social factors to provide a measure of external validity. *Geographic mobility* and the presence of *working women* were expected to correlate with *cosmopolitanism*, and these, in turn, were expected to correlate with *innovativeness* and *imitativeness*. While *mobility* was correlated with *imitativeness, working women* were negatively correlated with the *imitativeness* and *innovativeness*.

Helsen, Jeddi, and Desarbo (1993) used three consumer products as a basis for their diffusion study in twelve countries, using five criteria: *mobility, health, trade, lifestyle, and cosmopolitanism*. Using variables such as foreign visitors per capita, tourist expenditures per capita, and tourist receipts per capita to measure *cosmopolitanism*, they found that Austria, Belgium, Denmark, Finland, France, Norway, and Switzerland were high on *cosmopolitanism*. Contrary to Gatignon, Eliashberg, and Robertson's (1989) findings, Helsen, Jedidi, and Desarbo's (1993) findings suggest that countries rated high on *cosmopolitanism* appear to manifest a higher *imitativeness*.

Rogers' (1983) book referred to some studies which used cosmopoliteness (*cosmopolitanism*) as an independent variable to predict diffusion-related processes. Greenberg (1964) related it to innovative decision making. Fliegel and Kivlin (1966) used it to predict innovativeness of members of a social system. Rogers and van Es (1964) used it to predict opinion leadership. And Ryan and Gross (1943) used it to predict communication channel use.

Given the fact that *comopolitanism* has tended to be operationalized in terms of communication behavior, it is not surprising that it relates to *innovativeness*. Communicative behavior has long been established as a key element in the theory of diffusion of innovations. However, the relationship is potentially misleading. *Cosmopolitanism* is a personality characteristic, not a behavior. As we have noted, several theorists have hypothesized the relationship between *cosmopolitanism* and other behaviors, with mixed results.

The behaviors involved in *imitativeness* and *working women* mentioned earlier provide good examples. While *imitativeness* involves experimentation with new behaviors, this can be driven by a desire to explore new and different ideas, or by insecurity regarding one's ability to handle these ideas without someone else to follow. The first motivation is consistent with the underlying *cosmopolitanism* construct; the second is not.

Similarly, *working women* have stepped out of traditional male-dominated sex roles by entering the work force. This can be an expression of a desire for broader and more fulfilling life experiences, but it can also be an expression of financial need or the desire to supplement a husband's income in support of traditional social norms. Again, the former is consistent with *cosmopolitanism*, while the latter is not. The reverse is also true. A woman's decision *not* to work outside the home is generally viewed as an expression of conservative, non-*cosmopolitan* values. But it might also be driven by a practical desire to make a parent more available to promote *cosmopolitan* values in the home.

Recent research in *cosmopolitanism* has sought to address the construct issue. For instance, Cannon, Yoon, McGowan and Yaprak (1994) sought to develop a *cosmopolitan* scale that would address the construct in the specific context of marketing cross-national segmentation, as proposed by Cannon and Yaprak (1993).

B.   Cosmopolitanism and Organizational Orientation

In the context of organizational behavior, research has focused on the way *cosmopolitan* versus non-*cosmopolitan* workers relate to their professions and their employers. Gouldner (1957) characterized the *cosmopolitan* people as being "low on loyalty to the employing organization, high on commitment to specialized role skill, and likely to use an outer reference group orientation." This is contrasted to *locals*, who are characterized as being "high on *loyalty to the employing organization*, low on *commitment to the specialized role skills*, and likely to use an *inner reference group orientation*." Other studies have found *cosmopolitans* high on *professional orientation and professional commitment* and low on *organizational orientation* and *organizational loyalty*, while *locals* were high on *organizational orientation* and low on professional *orientation* (Grimes & Berger, 1970; Kornhauser, 1962; Blau & Scott, 1962; Filley & House, 1969). *Cosmopolitans* were found to be more loyal to their profession, placing more value on acknowledged skills and accomplishments, while *locals* were influenced by interpersonal contacts developed over time within the community (Grimes & Berger, 1970).

Following the logic of the organizational studies, *cosmopolitanism* has also been conceptualized as a person's orientation toward community. The terms, *cosmopolitans* and *locals* were introduced by Merton (1957) who investigated community influentials in 1947. He defined *cosmopolitans* as those oriented to the world outside the local community, and locals as those oriented toward the community. Katz and Lazerfeld (1955) used a *news orientation* dimension as an operational definition of *cosmopolitans* and *locals*. *Cosmopolitans* were interested in news from outside their immediate communities, while locals were most interested in community affairs.

Note that *news orientation* is very similar to the information acquisition dimension discussed in conjunction with the diffusion of innovations literature. Of course, this makes sense. While *cosmopolitanism* has emerged from two separate research traditions, it is nevertheless a single construct.

Table 1. Summary of Cosmopolitan Taxonomy of Multidimensionality

Authors/Dimensions	Cosmopolitan	Local	Cosmopolitan and Local	Neither Cosmopolitan nor Local
Gouldner (1957)				
Organizational loyalty	Low	High		
Commitment to profession	High	Low		
External referent	High	Low		
Kornhauser (1962)				
Professional orientation	High	Low	High	Low
Organization orientation	Low	High	High	Low
Blau and Scott (1962)				
Professional commitment	High	Low	High	Low
Organization loyalty	Low	High	High	Low
Filey and House (1969)				
Professional orientation	High	Low	High	Low
Company orientation	Low	High	High	Low

Source: Grimes and Berger (1970).

C.   The Dimensionality of the Cosmopolitanism

Implicit in the discussion to this point is the notion that *cosmopolitanism* is a monolithic construct. However, numerous studies have been conducted to test this proposition in the context of organizational orientation. The empirical evidence suggests that *cosmopolitanism* is actually multidimensional (Gouldner, 1958; Blau & Scott, 1962; Kornhauser, 1962; Goldberg, Bakerm & Rubenstein, 1965; Filly & House, 1969). Grimes and Berger (1970) summarize this research in Table 1.

Gouldner (1957) saw loyalty to one's organizatoin and commitment to one's profession as polar extremes of the *cosmopolitanism* scale. However, each of the other studies mentioned in the table suggest that people can be high on both organization and professional orientation. This is illustrated in Table 2.

Grimes and Berger (1970) draw upon the work of Blau and Scott (1962) to identify the kinds of people who would naturally fall into the four categories shown in the Table. In essence, they suggest that *cosmopolitans* and *locals* may exist as polar types, but they will express their orientation differently, depending on the situation. *Cosmopolitans* will show a high organizational orientation if they see the organization as offering high professional opportunity (Cell 1). They will not show organizational loyalty if the organization does not offer relatively good professional opportunity (Cell 2). *Locals* will have no professional interest, but they will be high in organizational orientation if the opportunities are attractive within the organization (Cell 3). If not, they will have neither a professional or organizational orientation (Cell 4).

Table 2. A Classification of Professional and Organizational Orientations

Organizational Orientation	Professional Orientation	
	High	Low
High	Professional opportunity is equal to or greater in the present organization than in a competing one. . . . . Cell (1)	Low interest in professional opportunity; high interest in opportunity in the present organization . . . . Cell (2)
Low	Professional opportunity is more limited with the present organization than in a competing one . . . . Cell (3)	Low interest in opportunities in both the profession and present organization . . . . Cell (4)

Note that this analysis can still be construed to support a monolithic *cosmopolitan* dimension. However, the dimension will be masked in factor analysis by the way it interacts with the situational variables faced by different respondents to the survey instrument. The key interactive dimension appears to be organizational attractiveness.

Unfortunately, this line of research has not been extended into the marketing/diffusion-of-innovations literature. There is little research to indicate what, if any, interactive dimensions might exist when the *cosmopolitan* construct is operationalized in a marketing context. If the results are similar to those portrayed in Tables 1 and 2, *cosmopolitanism* and localism may not represent opposite poles of a single dimension. Cannon and Yaprak (1993) might be right in contrasting *cosmopolitansm* with *parochialism* rather than *localism*. Localism describes people who exhibit a strong commitment to their local culture. This is not inconsistent with a *cosmopolitan* orientation. *Locals* may appreciate other cultures as well as their own. By contrast, *parochialism* describes people whose *local* commitment comes at the expense of cosmopolitan values.

Similarly, there is virtually no research addressing how *cosmopolitanism* might interact with cultural factors. These potential interactions are one of the foci of this paper. While it is an exploratory study, aimed specifically at the Korean culture, it may provide useful insights into how cultural factors and *cosmopolitanism* interact.

II. THE CYMYC COSMOPOLITANISM SCALE

As noted earlier, the *cosmopolitanism* (CYMYC) scale developed by Cannon, Yoon, McGowan and Yaprak (1994) was constructed to investigate *cosmopolitanism* in a marketing context. It incorporates the most prominent concepts in both the communication/diffusion-of-innovations and the organizational-orientation literatures. First, the concepts were catalogued. Then, items were written to represent the concepts. Standard procedures of psychometric analysis were applied to determine which items should remain in the scale.

Because the scale is relatively new, little research has been done to evaluate its validity. However, the nature of its construction makes it a potentially useful instrument for conducting research on the *cosmopolitanism* construct. First, it includes variables representing both of the key streams of *cosmopolitanism* literature. Second, the specific variables were designed to incorporate concepts from which the apparent multi-dimensionality of the *cosmopolitanism* construct was inferred, as discussed in conjunction with Tables 1 and 2 above.

III.   THE STUDY

Adler (1983) argues that theoretical premises from which a scale is developed must be universal, if that scale is to possess cross-national validity. One way to test the validity of these premises is to administer the scale in a maximally different culture from one's own. Korean culture, with its high emphasis on group cohesion, harmony with nature, and polychronic time orientation provides such a culture, and, therefore, offers a particularly appropriate setting for evaluating the CYMYC scale.

In addition to administering the scale to a maximally dissimilar group, the study seeks to capture key elements of diversity within the Korean culture. To address this need, our research includes respondents from both large and small Korean cities. It also includes other *cosmopolitanism*-related characteristics: Information-seeking orientation, geographic mobility, education, and age (see Appendix I).

A.   Assessing the Internal Validity of the CYMYC Scale

If the CYMYC Scale is a valid, cross-culturally robust representation of the *cosmopolitanism* construct, this should be reflected in the internal structure of the scale. Each of the items was designed to represent the same construct. It follows that they should be highly correlated.

The examination of these item correlations is a standard component of psychometric procedure. However, the study has no hypotheses regarding the results because the analyses do not lend themselves to meaningful statistical tests. However, the Coefficient Alpha will be matched against general norms that have been established over the years in previous studies (Peterson, 1994).

To further investigate the nature of the construct the CYMYC Scale appears to be measuring, the study will examine its factor structure. As noted in our review of literature, many studies suggest that the *cosmopolitansm* construct is multi-dimensional. If this is the case, multiple factors should emerge from the analysis.

B.   Assessing the External Validity of the CYMYC Scale

In order to test the external validity of the CYMYC Scale, we can compare CYMYC score with other variables that have a theoretical relationship to *cosmopolitanism*. If the hypothesized relationships hold true, this would provide support for the validity of the scale as an index of *cosmopolitanism*.

Previous research on *cosmopolitanism* (Merton 1957) defines *cosmopolitans* as those persons oriented to the world outside the local community, while *locals* are those oriented toward the local community. According to Gatignon, Eliashberg, and Robertson (1989), the amount of exposure to international information, such as reading foreign magazines or communicating with overseas friends, should be linked to the level of *cosmopolitanism*. This leads to the following hypothesis:

Hypothesis 1. The level of a person's exposure to international media will be positively correlated with scores on the CYMYC Scale.

Theory would also suggest that there is a relationship between a person's geographic mobility and the amount of *cosmopolitanism* (Helsen, Jedids, & DeSarbo, 1993; Gatignon, Eliashberg & Robertson, 1989). Mobility implies a willingness to experience different environments, while international mobility implies a willingness to experience different culturers and people. Hence, we derive the following hypothesis:

Hypothesis 2. People who have spent time in a foreign country will score higher on the CYMYC Scale than those who have not.

Hill and Still (1984) argue that the level of urbanization tends to correlate with the level of economic development, as reflected in consumer lifestyles, income and purchase patterns. Helsen, Jedidi, and DeSarbo's (1993), in turn, argue that *economic development* is related to *innovativeness*. Given the relationship between *cosmopolitanism* and *innovativeness*, we may also infer that *economic development* is also related to *cosmopolitanism*. Since Korea has its major economic, political, and human resources heavily concentrated in Seoul, the proposed relationship between *economic development* and *cosmopolitanism* should be reflected in the following hypothesis:

Hypothesis 3. People residing in metropolitan cities will have higher scores on the CYMYC Scale than those who live in smaller cities.

We theorize that education plays a role in the level of *cosmopolitanism*. By its very nature, education exposes people to new ideas. Furthermore, educated people tend to have access to more economic possibilities, and with them, more media exposure and other *cosmopolitan*-related influences. This leads us to hypothesize that:

Hypothesis 4. People with relatively high levels of formal education will have higher scores on the CYMYC Scale than those with relatively low levels.

Finally, we theorize that age may be related to the level of *cosmopolitanism*. Young people tend to be less tied to cultural traditions, along with their embedded social perspectives and biases. Furthermore, they are often exposed to a broader range of diverse media influences. For instance, younger Koreans often have both access and interest in powerful cross-border media, such as MTV, CNN, and the Internet. Therefore, we hypothesize that

Hypothesis 5.   Younger consumers will score higher on the CYMYC Scale than older consumers.

IV.   METHODOLOGY

A.   Sample

Ideally, data would be gathered from a random sample of respondents that adequately and proportionately represented all the various personality types for which *cosmopolitanism* would reasonably vary. In practice, this was impossible. We would have no way of identifying respondents who represent these types if all of the types were known. In fact, they are not known. The literature offers no taxonomy of *cosmopolitan*-related personality types. The best that could be done would be to use a very large probability sample taken from a sampling frame that represented the overall Korean population, and this could not be done, given the lack of availability of sophisticated research support in Korea.

The actual data were collected from convenience samples taken from three cities in Korea, representing high and low levels of population and economic development. The fact that respondents were not randomly selected limits the generalizability of the study. However, there was sufficient variance in the measured level of *cosmopolitanism* and the various control variables (international media exposure, international travel, formal education, and age) within the respondents from each city that this was not judged to be a problem for a pilot study. The fact that samples were drawn from cities with different populations, and corresponding differences in their levels of economic development and international cultural exposure, further contributed to the diversity of respondents.

The questionnaire contained 24 questions taken from the CYMYC Scale, presented in the form of five-point Likert scale. In addition, it contained six questions addressing gender, age, household income, geographic mobility, international media exposure, and education (the Appendix). The questionnaire was administered to a total of 707 respondents—303 from a small city and 404 from two large metropolitan areas in Korea.

B.   Analysis of Internal Validity

Two analyses were performed to determine the internal validity of the scale. First, the reliability was assessed using item-to-total correlations and coefficient Alpha. These were then used to refine the scale by eliminating items with low item-to-total correlations. The item analysis was then repeated for the refined scale calculating a new coefficient Alpha.

Second, a principal components factor analysis (varimax rotation) was used to determine the underlying dimensions of the scale. The number of factors was determined by evaluating a Scree Test and Eigenvalues, combined with the authors' qualitative evaluation of the resulting factors' theoretical basis.

C.   Analysis of External Validity

In order to determine the external validity of the *cosmopolitan* scale, the total scores on the refined CYMYC scale were computed for each respondent and compared to each of the five control variables addressed in Hypotheses 1 to 5—international media exposure, international travel, city size, education, and age. The actual comparisions were based on Spearman rank-order correlations, in deference to the fact that the variables were not intervally scaled.

The international media exposure variable was operationalized by combining the frequency of watching CNN, reading foreign magazines, making international phone calls, and speaking with foreign friends. Each variable was coded "1" ("never") to "5" ("always"). The scores were then averaged across the four items included in the media exposure variable to form a single media exposure score.

V.   RESULTS

A.   Internal Validity

The results of the item-to-total analysis yielded an overall Coefficient Alpha of 0.3540 for the 24 questions in the CYMYC Scale. When the seven items showing low item-to-total correlations were dropped, the coefficient improved to 0.4930 for the reduced Scale (Table 3).

While there are no clear rules for evaluating the strength of Coefficient Alpha, these coefficients were low relative to general standards of scale development, even for the reduced Scale. Thus, the item analysis provided a relatively weak indicator of the scale's internal validity (Peterson 1994).

As discussed earlier, one explanation for a low Coefficient Alpha is the possibility that the scale is multidimensional. The results of the factor analysis suggest that this might be the case. Table 4 summarizes the results of an initial analysis.

Using a standard Scree Test, four factors appeared to best suit the data. Taken at face value, the analysis suggests dimensions that might be labeled as follows:

- **Factor 1: World-Mindedness.** The items loading on this factor appear to represent a global orientation, where respondents see themselves as citizens of a larger, global, multi-cultural society.

Table 3. Item-to-Total Correlations for the Full and
Reduced Sets of CYMYC Scale Items

Scale Items	Full[a]	Reduced[b]	Alpha if Deleted	Scale Items	Full[a]	Reduced[b]	Alpha if Deleted
Item 1	0.0847	0.1310		Item 13	0.2852	0.3693	
Item 2	−0.0197		0.3728	Item 14	0.0817	0.0132	
Item 3	0.0490	0.0030		Item 15	0.3150	0.4109	
Item 4	0.0671	0.0485		Item 16	−0.0035		0.3664
Item 5	0.1691	0.2064		Item 17	0.0210	−0.0398	
Item 6	−0.0669		0.3785	Item 18	0.2413	0.2543	
Item 7	0.0576	0.0294		Item 19	0.0727	0.1509	
Item 8	-0.0054		0.3598	Item 20	−0.0350		0.1509
Item 9	0.1910	0.1948		Item 21	0.3079	0.3759	
Item 10	0.0842	0.0870		Item 22	0.1396	0.2246	
Item 11	0.1214	0.1790		Item 23	0.0700	0.1306	
Item 12	−0.0456		0.3720	Item 24	−0.0139		0.3646

Note: [a]Coefficient Alpha for full set=0.3540
[b]Coefficient Alpha for reduced set=0.4930

- **Factor 2: Outward Orientation.** The items loading on this factor (after correcting for reverse coding) suggest a tendency to look beyond one's immediate surroundings, seeking new and varied experiences.
- **Factor 3: Interpersonal Connectedness.** The items loading on this factor (again, after correcting for reverse coding) appear to represent a lack of connection with other people.
- **Factor 4: Cultural Open-Mindedness.** The items loading on this factor suggest the tendency to seek out varied cultural experiences outside one's local community.

While the weakness of the item analysis and the emergence of factors supports the notion of multidimensionality, an analysis of the specific factors presents a number of problems. For instance, Factors 1 and 4 both appear to represent the same *cosmopolitanism* construct—the tendency to orient oneself outside of one's immediate social (cultural) system. Factors 2 and 3 seem to follow a similar theme. They address one's level of comfort/lack of comfort with new versus traditional people and experiences. Considered in this light, the factor analysis appears to offer a much less convincing case for multidimensionality in the scale.

The foregoing analysis is based on the premise that *localism* and *cosmopolitanism* represent opposite poles of a single underlying conceptual dimension. However, recall that our earlier discussion in conjunction with Table 2 offers a different perspective. A review of the literature suggests that *cosmopolitanism* may be independent of *localism*, that people might see themselves as part of a larger social sys-

Table 4. Factor Loadings for CYMYC Scale Items Based
on a Four-Factor Solution

Scale Item	Description	Factor Loading	Communality Estimates
	Factor 1		
18	World issues concern me more than the issues of any one country	0.6268	0.4316
13	I enjoy getting news from all over the world	0.6129	0.4402
15	I like to have contact with people from different cultures	0.4662	0.5192
22	When I make an important decision, I look for information from as many different sources as possible	0.3969	0.4407
	Factor 2		
12	* I appreciate the importance of following tradition	0.5384	0.3242
3	* I like to surround myself with things that are familiar to me	0.4801	0.3156
17	* I am most comfortable when I am talking to my close friends	0.3543	0.2874
11	I wish I could speak at least one foreign language	0.4661	0.3781
	Factor 3		
10	* I tend to be very loyal to my friends	0.6055	0.4087
14	* I tend to get intensively involved with the people around me	0.5181	0.4070
	Factor 4		
21	I like immersing myself in different cultural environments	0.5019	0.5013
19	I enjoy experimenting with many different kinds of foods	0.3279	0.3179

Note: *denotes reversed scale items.

tem (the world), and still be very attached to their local community and culture. This perspective calls for a slight revision in the definition of *cosmopolitanism*. *Cosmopolitanism* would connote a set of values that causes people to appreciate cultural diversity. In a sense, cosmopolitan people would orient themselves beyond their immediate social system as defined by Merton (1957) and Gouldner (1957). They would see themselves as citizens of a much larger world. But the essense of this citizenship would be to recognize and celebrate the pluralistic nature of the world. From this perspective, the opposite of *cosmopolitanism* would not be *localism*, but *narrow mindedness*, or what Cannon and Yaprak (1993) call *parochialism*.

This perspective leads us to give the factors presented in Table 4 a different interpretation. Factors 1 and 4 still appear to reflect the level of one's *cosmopolitan* orientation. However, Factors 2 and 3 appear to be more representative of *localism*. For instance, the lead items in Factor 2 are "I appreciate the importance of following tradition" and "I like to surround myself with things that are familiar to me." An appreciation of tradition can be just as characteristic of a *cosmopolitan* person as one who has a *parochial* orientation, although the motivation would be quite different. A *local* follows tradition because it is "what right-thinking people do." *Cosmopolitans* appreciate it because they value culture and the role traditions play in each cultural orientation. *Locals* like to surround themselves with familiar things because unfamiliar things make them uncomfortable. For *cosmopolitans*, surrounding oneself with familiar things provides an important means of symbolically expressing cultural values and identity.

The two items loading on Factor 3 appear to represent respondents' involvement with their immediate social system. As noted earlier, this does not preclude involvement with a larger social system as well. Indeed, as we have just noted, one of the characteristics of true *cosmopolitans* might be a commitment to appreciating the unique characteristics of their local surroundings.

The third item in Factor 2, "I am most comfortable when I am talking to my close friends," is remiscent of the items in Factor 3, except that it seems to imply a discomfort with people who are not close friends, thus reflecting a negative *cosmopolitan* orientation. The fourth item, "I wish I could speak at least one foreign language," is clearly indicative of a *cosmopolitan* orientation. This confuses the conceptual interpretation of the factors still further.

Table 5. Factor Loadings for CYMYC Scale Items Based on a Two-Factor Solution

Scale Item	Description	Factor Loadings	Communality Estimates
	Factor 1		
11	I wish I could speak at least one foreign langauge	0.7014	0.4654
21	I like immersing myself in different cultural environments	0.6300	0.4105
13	I enjoy getting news from all over the world	0.5685	0.3398
18	World issues concern me more than the issues of any one country	0.4844	0.2402
22	When I make an important decision, I look for information from as many different sources as possible	0.4124	0.2968
	Factor 2		
14	I tend to get intensively involved with the people around me	0.5122	0.2511
17	I am most comfortable when I am talking to my close friends	0.4739	0.200
13	I like to surround myself with things that are familiar to me	0.4706	0.1828
10	I tend to be very loyal to my friends	0.4451	0.2402
6	You can usually solve a lot of problems by simply doing what you are supposed to do	0.4069	0.1688
12	I appreciate the importance of following tradition	0.3688	0.2071
19	I enjoy experimenting with many different kinds of foods	0.3279	0.3179

In an effort to overcome the apparent difficulties of the four-factor solution, the factor analysis was performed a second time, this time constraining the analysis to two factors. While the two-factor solution was chosen primarily on theoretical grounds, the Scree Test and Eigenvalues provided some support for a two-factor as well as the original four-factor solution. The results of the two-factor analysis are summarized in Table 5.

The item loadings suggest the kind of *cosmopolitan* (Factor 1) and *local* (Factor 2) orientation we have just discussed.

Tables 6 and 7 show the item-to-total correlations for the *cosmopolitanism* and *localism* subscales devised from the factors illustrated in Table 5.

Note that the Coefficient Alpha is .6265 and .4995 for the two scales, respectively. While these results are still not dramatic, they do represent some improvement in internal validity over both the original and reduced CYMYC Scale. When items with low item-to-total correlations are dropped from the subscales, the Coefficients rise to 0.6975 and 0.5372, respectively, thus providing even greater support for the theorized subscale structure.

B.   External Validity

In order to evaluate the external validity of the CYMYC Scale, the five hypotheses were tested by comparing the score of the seventeen-question refined Scale items with the five control variables. In support of Hypothesis 1, the correlation between the reduced CYMYC Scale average score and international media exposure was .1083. The probability of finding a correlation this large under the null hypothesis was .007 (one-tailed test), thus supporting the hypothesis. When the test was replicated using the reduced *cosmopolitanism* subscale the correlation went up to .1757 ($p = .000$).

Hypothesis 2 posited that people who have visited a foreign country would have higher *cosmopolitanism* scores than those who have not. The correlation between

Table 6.   Item-to-Total Correlations for the CYMYC
Cosmopolitanism Scale

Scale Items	Full[a]	Reduced[b]	Alpha if Deleted	Scale Items	Full[a]	Reduced[b]	Alpha if Deleted
Item 2	0.0631		0.6498	Item 16	0.3693	0.3576	
Item 5	0.2340	0.2532		Item 18	0.3936	0.3892	
Item 8	0.1553	0.1152		Item 19	0.3410	0.3576	
Item 11	0.3642	0.3943		Item 21	0.4349	0.4611	
Item 13	0.4392	0.4717		Item 22	0.3951	0.4241	
Item 15	0.4198	0.4689		Item 24	0.2228	0.2300	

Notes: [a]Coefficient Alpha for full set=0.6265
[b]Coefficient Alpha for reduced set=0.6975

Table 7.   Item-to-Total Correlations for CYMYC
Localism Subscale

Scale Items	Full[a]	Reduced[b]	Alpha if Deleted	Scale Items	Full[a]	Reduced[b]	Alpha if Deleted
Item 1	0.0890		0.5114	Item 10	0.3121	0.3356	
Item 3	0.2709	0.2757		Item 12	0.1861	0.1816	
Item 4	0.1246	0.1444		Item 14	0.3341	0.3960	
Item 6	0.2383	0.2193		Item 17	0.2794	0.2964	
Item 7	0.1870	0.1860		Item 20	0.2262	0.2973	
Item 9	0.1110	0.0662		Item 23	0.0502		0.5162

Note: [a]Coefficient Alpha for full set=0.4995
[b]Coefficient Alpha for reduced set=0.5372

the reduced CYMYC Scale average score and foreign experience was .0305. The probability of finding a correlation this large under the null hypothesis was .232 (one-tailed test), thus failing to support the hypothesis at the traditional .05 level of significance. However, when the test was replicated using the *cosmopolitanism* subscale, the hypothesis was supported. The correlation was .0835 (p=.019).

Hypothesis 3 posits that residents of a large metropolitan area will have higher cosmopolitanism scores than will those who live in smaller cities. This hypothesis was supported. The correlation between the reduced average CYMYC Scale score and city size was .0736 (p=.038, one-tail test). When the test was replicated for the *cosmopolitanism* subscale, the correlation was .0701 (p=.040).

Hypothesis 4 posits that educated people will have higher *cosmopolitanism* scores than less educated people. This was not supported by using either the reduced Scale or the *cosmopolitanism* subscale. The correlation between the average reduced CYMYC Scale and education level was .0055 and it was .0410 for the *cosmopolitanism* subscale. The probability of finding correlations this large under the null hypothesis was .447 and .154 for the CYMYC Scale and *cosmopolitanism* subscale, respectively (one-tailed test).

Hypothesis 5 posits that young people will have higher *cosmopolitanism* scores than old people. This implies a negative correlation between age and the CYMYC Scales. In fact, the correlation between age and average scores on the reduced CYMYC Scale was -.2146 (p=.000, one-tailed test). For the *cosmopolitanism* subscale, the correlation was only -.0494 (p=.110).

Note that all of the correlations were in the hypothesized direction. Under the null hypothesis, the chance of this happening would be .5000 for each correlation. That is, if the true correlation were zero, there would be an equal chance (due to error variance) that the observed correlation would be in the hypothesized versus non-hypothesized direction. The chance of all five correlations being in the proper direction would be .0312 (the chance of five successes given p=0.5, using a binomial distribution). This provides a kind of meta-support for the external validity of the scale. In addition, three of the five individual hypotheses (Hypothesis 1, Hypothesis 3, Hypothesis 5) were supported above the .05 level using the reduced CYMYC Scale, and three (Hypothesis 1, Hypothesis 2, Hypothesis 3) were supported using the *cosmopolitanism* subscale. While the lack of agreement in findings using the two scales weakens the results, the overall strength of the findings is supportive of the scales' external validity.

VI. SUMMARY AND CONCLUSIONS

This paper sought to evaluate the validity of the Cannon, Yoon, McGowan and Yaprak (1994) *cosmopolitanism* scale (CYMYC) using Korean consumers. While the results are only those of a pilot study, they are nevertheless encouraging in many respects.

First, they are very similar to those obtained by Cannon, Yoon, McGowan and Yaprak (1994) in their pilot study of American consumers. The major weakness of both studies is the fact that their data were obtained from convenience samples. The fact that there was no basis for assessing how representative respondents were of the overall population limits the generalizability of the results. However, the fact that the samples were drawn independently by different people from two dramatically different cultures suggests that any biases the samples might have would likely be different. Thus, the fact that the results were similar provides strong evidence of convergent validity.

Second, and even more persuasive, the underlying theoretical structure of the *cosmopolitanism* construct found in this study appears to be very similar to the structure suggested by the literature on organizational behavior (Tables 1 and 2). Note that virtually all of the research from which this theory was drawn came from American cultural settings. To have the same theory borne out by a totally different kind of research design in a Korean cultural setting again provides strong evidence of convergent validity.

The theory grew out of an apparent conflict between the results regarding internal and external validity. Notwithstanding the relatively strong findings in support of external validity, the CYMYC Scale had a relatively low Coefficient Alpha, even when the items with low item-to-total correlations were dropped from the scale. This lack of internal validity presents a paradox, since one would not expect support for the hypotheses testing external validity if the scale did not provide an internally reliable measure of the construct from which the hypotheses were derived.

The proposed resolution of the paradox rests in the notion that the CYMYC Scale might represent a heterogeneous construct. While this might be due to characteristics that are unique to Korean consumers, an analysis of the factor analyses did not suggest any unique Korean cultural themes. Rather, they suggested the *cosmopolitanism* and *localism* subscales.

If these subscales are valid, we would expect the CYMYC Scale to capture some of the variance in *cosmopolitanism*, thus explaining the findings regarding external validity. We would also expect that the *cosmopolitanism* subscale would exhibit greater internal validity than the CYMYC Scale as a whole and that the subscale would exhibit greater external validity than the larger CYMYC Scale from which it was derived. In fact, both of these expectations seemed to be fulfilled. The Coefficient Alpha was substantially higher for the *cosmopolitanism* subscale (.6975 versus .4930 for the reduced item scales). With the exception of Hypothesis 5 (the relationship of age to *cosmopolitanism*), the *cosmopolitanism* subscale yielded a test that was either as strong or stronger than it was using the CYMYC scale.

The implications of this are profound. They suggest a rationale for Avery (1960) and Glaser's (1963) conclusion that pure-type *locals* and pure-type cosmopolitans are rare, that most people display some combination of the two traits. While *cosmopolitans* tend to orient themselves to a larger social system, they may also have a strong attachment to their local community. Of course, the opposite may also be the case. One may live in a community where his or her *cosmopolitan* values are antithetical to the *local* orientation, in which case the person would feel alienated from the local community. Similarly, a person's *local* culture may be seen as shallow, repressive, intolerant, or otherwise incompatible with his or her *cosmopolitan* values.

Yet another possibility is that a respondent may not be cosmopolitan in his or her orientation. She/he could still be *local* in her orientation, or perhaps s/he is neither *cosmopolitan* nor *local*.

If this analysis is correct, the results of this study can be seen as a more general version of the theory reflected in Table 2. Simply substitute *local* for *organizational orientation* and *cosmopolitan* for *professional orientation*. The result is the corresponding matrix, shown in Table 8.

Table 8 suggests a useful direction for future research. Once the basic dimensions of analysis have been established, the next step would be to begin a program of taxonomic research, classifying people according their orientation relative to the four cells of the matrix. Once this has been done, it should be pos-

Table 8. A Classification of Cosmopolitan and Local Orientations

Local Orientation	Cosmopolitan Orientation	
	High	Low
High	Local environment is supportive of cosmopolitan values....... Cell (1)	Low interest in cosmopolitan values, but high interest in local values............... Cell (2)
Low	Local environment is not supportive of cosmopolitan values .... Cell (3)	Low interest in both cosmopolitan and local .... Cell (4)

sible to identify the specific values that discriminate between one cell and another—the values that cause *cosmopolitans* to be or not to be *local* in their orientation, for instance. This, in turn, may lead us to the specific cultural factors we have been seeking.

APPENDIX

This survey is part of a university-based study of the world around us. To help us complete our study, we would very much appreciate your responses to the following questions.

I. Please circle the number that shows how much you agree or disagree with each of the following statements.

	Strongly disagree				Strongly agree
1. I don't like experimenting with things I don't enjoy.	1	2	3	4	5
2. I get uncomfortable when people suggest that there is a "right" way to do something.	1	2	3	4	5
3. I like to surround myself with things that are familiar to me.	1	2	3	4	5
4. When I make important decisions, I rely a lot on the opinions of my friends.	1	2	3	4	5
5. I tend to appreciate many different kinds of music.	1	2	3	4	5
6. You can usually solve a lot of problems by simply doing what you are supposed to do.	1	2	3	4	5
7. I pay a lot of attention to local news.	1	2	3	4	5
8. I tend to evaluate people by what they do, not who they are or what position they hold.	1	2	3	4	5
9. Foreigners often leave me uncomfortable.	1	2	3	4	5
10. I tend to be very loyal to my friends.	1	2	3	4	5
11. I wish I could speak at least one foreign language.	1	2	3	4	5
12. I appreciate the importance of following tradition.	1	2	3	4	5
13. I enjoy getting news from all over the world.	1	2	3	4	5
14. I tend to get intensively involved with the people around me.	1	2	3	4	5
15. I like to have contact with people from different cultures.	1	2	3	4	5
16. I often feel like an "outsider" in my community.	1	2	3	4	5
17. I am most comfortable when I am talking to my close friends.	1	2	3	4	5
18. World issues concern me more than the issues of any one country.	1	2	3	4	5

19. I enjoy experimenting with many different kinds
of foods.   1   2   3   4   5
20. I feel very close to the people in my community.   1   2   3   4   5
21. I like immersing myself in different cultural
environments.   1   2   3   4   5
22. When I make an important decision, I look for
information from as many different sources
as possible.   1   2   3   4   5
23. I avoid settings where people don't share my values. 1   2   3   4   5
24. I can usually make a good decision if I have the
proper information.   1   2   3   4   5

II. Please answer the following questions.
1.   What is your gender? Male _____ Female _____
2.   What is your current age?
_____ 18 - 24   _____ 45 - 54
_____ 25 - 29   _____ 55 - 64
_____ 30 - 34   _____ 65 and over
_____ 35 - 44
3.   In terms of the national average, to which quartile does your total household income belong?
_____ 1st quartile   (   )
_____ 2nd quartile   (   )
_____ 3rd quartile   (   )
_____ 4th quartile   (   )
4.   In total, approximately how long have you lived or visited abroad in your
lifetime?
_____ never
_____ less than 2 months in total
_____ more than 2 months in total
5.   How often are you exposed to each of the following?

	never	occasionally	frequently	usually	always
CNN	_____	_____	_____	_____	_____
Foreign magazines	_____	_____	_____	_____	_____
International phone calls	_____	_____	_____	_____	_____
Communicating with friends in a foreign country	_____	_____	_____	_____	_____

6.   Which of the following best describes your educational background?
_____ no high school
_____ completed high school
_____ completed college

_____ completed graduate school

THANK YOU VERY MUCH FOR YOUR COOPERATION. YOUR HELP IS GREATLY APPRECIATED.

REFERENCES

Adler, N.J. (1983). A typology of management studies involving culture. *Journal of International Business Studies,* 14, 29-47.

Avery, R. (1960). Enculturation in industrial research. *IRE Trans-Actions on Engineering Management,* 7, 20.

Blau, P.M., & Scott W. (1962). *Formal organizations.* San Francisco: Chandler.

Cannon, H.M., & Yaprak A. (1993). Paper presented at the 1993 *Annual meeting of the academy of international business.*

Cannon, H.M., et al. (1994). In search of the global consumer. Paper presented at the 1994 *Annual Meeting of the Academy of International Business.*

Coleman, J., Katz E., & Menzel H. (1966). *Medical innovation: A diffusion study.* Indianapolis, IN: Bobbs-Merrill.

Filley, A.C., & House, R.J. (1969). *Managerial process and organizational behavior.* Glenview, IL: Scott Foresman.

Fliegel, F.C., & Kivlin J.E. (1966). Attributes of innovations as factors in diffusion. *American Journal of Sociology,* 72, 235-248.

Gatignon H., Eliashberg J., & Robertson T.S.(1989). Modeling multinational diffusion patterns: An efficient methodology. *Marketing Science,* 8 (3), 231-247.

Glaser B. (1963). The local-cosmopolitan scientist. *American Journal of Sociology,* 69, 249-260.

Goldberg, L. C., Bakerm F., & Rubenstein A.H. (1965). Local-cosmopolitan: Unidimentional or multidimentional? *American Journal of Sociology,* 70, 704-710.

Gouldner, A.W (1957). Cosmopolitans and locals: Toward an analysis of latent social roles—I. *Administrative Science Quarterly,* 2, 281-306.

Greenberg, B.S. (1964). Diffusion of news about the Kennedy assassination. *Public Opinion Quarterly,* 2, 225-232.

Grimes A.J., & Berger P.K. (1970). Cosmopolitan-local: Evaluation of the construct. *Administrative Science Quarterly,* 15, 407-416.

Hage, J., & Dewar R. (1973). Elite values versus organizational structure in predicting innovation. *Administrative Science Quarterly,* 18, 279-290.

Helsen, K, Jedidi K., & Desarbo W.S. (1993). A new approach to country segmentation utilizing multinational diffusion patterns. *Journal of Marketing,* 57, 60-71.

Hill, J., & Still R. (1984). Effects of urbanization on multination product planning: Markets in LDCs. *Columbia Journal of World Business,* 19, 62-67.

Hofstede, G. (1989). Organizing for cultural diversity. *European Management Journal,* 7(4), 390-397.

Kagono, T. et al. (1985). *Strategic vs. evolutionary management: A U.S.-Japan comparison of strategy and organization.* North Holland, Elsevier Science Publishers B.V. Amsterdam.

Katz, E., & Lazarsfeld P.L. (1955). *Personal influence.* New York: Free Press.

Kimberly, J.R. (1978). Hospital adoption of innovation: The role of integration into external informational environments. *Journal of Health and Social Behavior,* 19, 361-373.

Kornhauser, W. (1962). *Scientists in industry: Conflict and accommodations.* Berkeley: University of California Press.

Levinson, D.J. (1957). Authoritarian personality and foreign policy. *Journal of Conflict Resolution,* 1, 37-47.

Levitt, T. (1983). The globalization of markets. *Harvard Business Review*, 61(3) 92-102.

Merton, R. K (1957). Patterns of influence: Local and cosmopolitan influentials. In *Social Theory and Social Structure* (pp. 387-420), New York: Free Press

Ohmae, K. (1989). Managing in a borderless world. *Harvard Business Review*, 67(2) 152-161.

Parameswaran, R., & Yaprak A. (1987). A cross-national comparison of consumer research measures. *Journal of International Business Studies*, 18 (1), 35-50.

Rogers, E.M.(1983). *Diffusion of innovations*, 3rd ed. New York: The Free Press.

Rogers, E.M., & van Es, J. (1964). *Opinion Leadership in Traditional and Modern Colombian Peasant Communities*. East Lansing, Michigan State University, Dept. of Communication. Diffusion of Innovation Research Report 2.

Ryan, B., & Gross N.(1943). The diffusion of hybrid seed corn in two Iowa communities. *Rural Sociology*, 8, 15-24.

Sampson, D.L., & Smith, H. (1957). A scale to measure world-mindedness attitudes. *Journal of Social Psychology*, 45, 99-106.

Schneider, S., & Meyer A. (1991). Interpreting and responding to strategic issues: The impact of national culture. *Strategic Management Journal*, 12, 307-320.

Shimp, T. A., & Sharma S. (1987). Consumer ethnocentrism: Construction and validation of the CETSCALE. *Journal of Marketing Research*, 24, 280-289.

Thorelli, H.B. (1990). The information seekers:Multinational strategy target. In *International Marketing Strategy*. New York: Pergamon Press.

Tse, D.K. et al. (1988). Does culture matter? A cross cultural study of executives' choice, decisiveness, and risk adjustment in international marketing. *Journal of Marketing*, 52, 81-95.

COUNTRY OF PRODUCTION/ASSEMBLY AS A NEW COUNTRY IMAGE CONSTRUCT:
A CONCEPTUAL APPLICATION TO GLOBAL TRANSPLANT DECISIONS

Dong Hwan Lee and Charles M. Schaninger

ABSTRACT

Consumers' quality perceptions of high technology and luxury products of global brands based on their country of production or assembly (COP/A) is proposed as an important new country image construct, distinctively different from the widely-studied country of origin (COO) effect. Product types and characteristics which underlie the COP/A effect are discussed and factors which are likely to moderate the COP/A effect on consumers' evaluation and purchase are identified. The authors propose a conceptual model of the global production location decision which incorporates the COP/A factor. They also propose the application of conjoint methodology to assess the COP/A effect, to estimate the market share, and to weigh the relative importance of the COP/A and price factors. Implications of the COP/A and suggestions about how their proposed model can be applied in practice are also discussed.

Advances in International Marketing, Volume 7, pages 233-254.

The recent decisions of two German auto makers to open new manufacturing facilities in the U.S. drew much media attention. BMW decided to locate a manufacturing plant for its luxury automobiles in South Carolina rather than in Mexico (*Wall Street Journal,* 1992). Daimler-Benz chose Alabama as a production site for its new Mercedes line after years of deliberation (*Business Week,* 1993). These two events occurring in the middle of the NAFTA debate caught many by surprise. Opponents of the free trade agreement claimed (and still claim) that American and foreign investment would flood into Mexico and away from the United States to take advantage of cheap Mexican labor, jeopardizing job opportunities for American workers. These two cases provide an interesting contrast with Volkswagen, another German auto maker, who has been assembling vehicles in Mexico. Given that the growing cost disadvantage against Japanese and U.S. competitors (due to higher wages) would have been a major factor in the two German auto makers' overseas production location decisions (*Business Week,* 1993), assembly facilities in Mexico would have offered substantial savings in terms of low-cost labor. However, the fact that the two companies opted for the United States despite this cost incentive suggests that other factors outweighed cheap labor.[1] Although a multitude of important factors such as transport costs, distribution, quality control (which may offset low labor costs), and manufacturing cost (the U.S. is a low-cost location by German standards) played a role in these decisions, one major marketing consideration also played an important role. As a BMW executive succinctly pointed out: "… to sell a *high-quality auto in the luxury sector, labor costs are not the determining factor… .*We have to look for *the market,* and *the U.S. is the world's largest single auto market*" (*Wall Street Journal,* 1992). American consumers might perceive the quality or prestige of a Mexican-built Mercedes or BMW as inferior to ones manufactured in the United States, even though both would be of the same German engineering design. The crux of the matter was whether consumers would be as likely to buy a luxury vehicle made in Mexico, as a Mexican-built mid-priced Volkswagen. Thus, although consumers' awareness and recognition of prestigious global brands are high, their perception of the quality of luxury products, and hence purchase decisions is likely to be influenced not only by the brand name, but also by where they are manufactured or assembled— the *country of production/assembly (COP/A)* effect. We argue that producers of image-oriented products which base their competitive advantage mainly on high technology and/or prestigious brand image must seriously consider the COP/A effect in making global transplant decisions.

In this paper, we introduce this new country image construct, the country of production and/or assembly (COP/A). Based on a review of a few emerging studies and on industry evidence, we underline the importance of the COP/A effect in the global market place and demonstrate that it is distinctively different from the more general country of origin (COO) effect, even though the two constructs share similar characteristics. Next, we develop a conceptual model which incorporates the COP/A factor and traditional cost-related factors to enhance the quality of global transplant decisions. We propose that conjoint methodology be applied to assess the importance of COP/A relative to other functional attributes. Finally, we provide suggestions about how the proposed model can be operationalized and utilized in practice.

I. COUNTRY OF PRODUCTION/ASSEMBLY

It is well documented that quality perceptions of products made in certain countries are affected by a built-in positive or negative country stereotype. The existence of the country of origin cue, to which consumers can attach meaning, has spawned a stream of consumer research on the country image effect. Although there is little consensus about the mechanism and the degree of influence, it has been generally agreed that country of origin (COO) affects consumers' product evaluations and purchase. A host of empirical studies dealing with the impact of COO on consumer perception and purchase behavior are found in the marketing literature (see Bilkey & Nes, 1982; Johansson, Douglas, & Nonaka, 1985 for reviews).

A. Evolving Country Image in Global Market Place

In general, consumers' perception of the *country of origin* (COO)—where the product is originally designed/engineered and the brand's home country—is regarded as the predominant country image factor influencing their product evaluations. That is, the brand name reflects the stereotypic image of the country where it is originally engineered and made. However, we argue that globalization trends have blurred this traditional concept, necessitating the broadening of the country image to include the new concept of country of production/assembly. Companies in industrialized nations are constantly looking for alternative production and sourcing sites around the globe due to increasing pressure to reduce the costs through joint-ventures or whole-ownership (Hibbert, 1993; Fortune, 1993). Thus, many well-known brands of a given national origin are now manufactured or assembled in other countries. Traditionally, most consumers have regarded SONY as a Japanese-made television set, Ralph Lauren "Polo" as an American-made line of casual clothing, and BMW as a German-made automobile. Consumers tend to associate the quality of each of these products with the country image of its original home base. However, the fact is that these reputed global brands are now produced or assembled in various parts of the globe away their original home countries (e.g., Malaysia, Mexico). Such products are called bi-national or hybrid products (Ettenson & Gaeth, 1991; Han & Terpstra, 1988). Global consumers are well-informed that markets are changing at a faster pace than ever before due to the communications revolution and explosion of global travel. Consequently, a consumer's purchase decision for *certain products* is influenced not only by the image of the original country of origin, but also by the country where its final work is done (COP/A). Some even suggest that as more companies develop manufacturing bases overseas, the origin of the product (i.e., COO) will become less important (Johansson, 1989). Han and Terpstra (1988) found that sourcing country image had more powerful effects than brand name on consumer evaluations of bi-national products.

B.   COP/A Effect

Although it still may be true that many U.S. consumers are unaware of where products are produced or assembled, or don't care about it, where a product's final work is done *does matter* under certain circumstances. There is ample evidence of this in the automobile industry. When Chrysler first introduced its K cars—Plymouth Reliant and Dodge Aries—assembled in Mexico in 1984, some dealers refused to sell those models and others removed the sticker showing the country of production (*Wall Street Journal,* 1984). They worried that many American consumers would be suspicious about the quality of the car and hesitant to buy one built in Mexico, which was perceived by some to be a backward, underdeveloped country.

The well-known American wristwatch BULOVA is not exclusively assembled in the United States anymore, but is now assembled in various parts of the world, including Switzerland, Germany, and France. Sales clerks at jewelry stores in New York City are frequently heard saying that certain customers are very reluctant to buy a French-assembled BULOVA, while a Swiss-made BULOVA is highly popular.[2] In less developed or developing countries, the American BULOVA image is very well established. In this case, the *country image* which influences the consumer's quality perception is not just where the product was originally engineered (i.e., COO) but where it was assembled (i.e., COP/A) as well. Thus, while such consumers were initially drawn to buy a BULOVA based on its brand name (i.e., COO effect), they did not want to buy one that was assembled in country whose reputation and prestige in watch making is either not known or negative due to higher functional and/or social risk attached to it. If they could not find a Swiss-made (or German-made) BULOVA in a store, they might switch to, say, a Japanese-made Seiko or postpone their purchase. Thus, the consumer's purchase decision resembles a two-step process using COO and COP/A at each stage. As another example, Hyundai's Excel and Sonata are the most popular car models in South Korea, and many Korean students or expatriates in the United States purchase one of these models in the States in order to bring it back to Korea when they return (these North American models are assembled in Canada), in spite of high transport costs. They do this because they consider Canadian-built models as higher in quality and prestige than Korean-built ones. Some Hyundai dealers in areas with large Korean populations sometimes maintain a waiting list for the Sonata even though that it is relatively unknown to Americans in their area.[3]

As documented in the COO literature, many factors combine to influence consumer's country of origin or production image. Country-specific factors include economic and technological level of development (Nagashima, 1970), cultural and political characteristics (Wang & Lamb, 1983), and labor quality (productivity, skill level, and workmanship—Dunning, 1981). These factors combine to influence consumers' country stereotypes. People come to develop a general perception of a country, which influences their quality perceptions of products manufactured or assembled there. Thus, even though a brand is well recognized, the perception of overall quality for *certain product categories* bearing a reputed brand name will differ depending on where they are produced or assembled. In fact, the international business literature indicates that such country-specific factors as technology and quality of labor force are not usually transferrable (Dunning, 1981). Consumers' reluctance to buy a well-known brand whose final work is done in a negatively stereotyped country appears to be due to the combined effects of perceived prestige and functional risk. Some empirical evidence supports this proposition. Han and Terpstra (1988) found that consumers' perceptions of workmanship for a given product varied according to where it was made. In general, consumer evaluations of bi-national products tend to increase as the favorableness of the country of production/assembly increases (Bilkey & Nes, 1982; Han, 1989; Cordell, 1992; Chao, 1989).

C.   Moderating Factors of COP/A Effect

The COP/A effect may not, however, be present or strong for all product types. We propose that the COP/A effect is present mainly with well-known global brands reputed for their prestigious image and/or superior functional quality. Such products have well-established national credentials or home bases (e.g., Chanel No. 5 is a *French* perfume) (Shalofsky, 1987). For an unknown or new brand whose COO and COP/A are different, consumers are most likely to regard the made-in label (i.e., COP/A) as the country of origin because they have no prior brand knowledge. If the product is a commodity, consumers probably pay little attention to where it is produced/assembled as long as it carries a reputable brand name as a quality cue. We propose that a number of environmental and individual characteristics will interact with the product type to moderate the impact of COP/A on consumers' evaluation and purchase.

First, the COP/A effect is likely to be strong for products whose perceived social and/or functional risk is high, as suggested by previous product specific COO findings (Kaynak & Cavusgil, 1983). Such products usually are image-oriented and/or technology intensive. If product consumption is publicly conspicuous and socially visible and socially desirable, consumers are likely to use the product's visibility to symbolically communicate their desired image to others (Lee, 1989; Sirgy, 1982). By publicly consuming prestigious brands, consumers express their social status and life style or indicate conformity to the norms of social groups to which they aspire acceptance. This symbolic communication is based on the premise that there is a commonly shared meaning and experience concerning the product's use in specific consumption situations (Lee, 1989). BMW's ad "why drive a *hybrid* when you can drive a *purebred*?" was intended to establish a prestige image for their German-built cars vis-à-vis Mexican- or American-built Volkswagens. Consumption as symbolic behavior may be more important in certain segments of a society than in others. We also propose that this phenomenon will be more pronounced in developing or less developed countries than in industrialized ones because in the former the gap between social strata is larger in terms of material possessions.

Functional risk refers to the risk that the product will not perform properly (Cox, 1967) and is greatest when a product is technically-complex and expensive, or when ego-related needs are involved. Consumers' concern for functional risk is also higher for expensive luxury products whose performance is highly visible socially (Lee, 1989) and when a product is technology intensive, particularly when a well-known brand is manufactured in less developed counties (Cordell, 1992).[4] In many less developed countries, well-known global brands from industrialized countries are associated with "prestige," "excellence," and "fashion." Affected product classes include luxury automobiles, luxury watches, hi-fi audio equipment, notebook computers, electronic kitchenware, high-fashion apparel, and high-priced cosmetics. We also propose that individual characteristics, including product knowledge, self-esteem, social class, and income will moderate this relationship. For example, high-knowledge consumers care less about where a product was originally engineered than do low-knowledge consumers (Maheswaran, 1994). Thus, consumers' knowledge and experience will negatively correlate with the COP/A effect. The impact of such traits as self-esteem and self-monitoring on social risk will also moderate the impact of COP/A on product evaluation and purchase. Empirical research investigating the role of such moderating variables is likely to reveal theoretically important findings with managerially relevant implications.

Finally, we suggest that for some product types, the COP/A effect may become diluted over time as consumers become accustomed to the growing trend toward global sourcing. The fact that American consumers eventually purchased Chrysler's Mexican-built K cars several years after their introduction supports this view. However, dilutions in the COP/A effect will depend on a brand's product class positioning (the K-car is a low-priced, functionally oriented car) and consumer segment characteristics (mid- to low-income, elderly). For high tech/luxury performance products (e.g., Porche, Rolex), the COP/A *is* and *should continue to be* an important product differentiation tool.

In conclusion, the COP/A effect, while under-recognized in the marketing literature, is gaining importance in the global market place. Although it is related to country of origin, it is uniquely different from the traditional country image factor. There are observations and anecdotal evidence in various industry and trade publications that some marketers are aware of this phenomenon and have undertaken actions to enhance their brand's overall prestige by associating their products with a foreign firm or country. Thus, not only should marketing managers try to better understand COP/A, but international business managers should also incorporate this concept in their transplant decision. In the next section, we expound on the application of the COP/A to the global production location decision in greater detail.

II. GLOBAL PRODUCTION LOCATION DECISION

The choice of production location is one of the most important decisions many multinational enterprises (MNE) face in today's global economy (Robock & Simmonds, 1989). Many developing countries offer highly competitive labor costs and other benefits (e.g., tax breaks and favorable financing incentives) to induce foreign investment and technology. These economic factors, especially the labor cost, traditionally have played dominant roles in MNEs' production location decisions (Moxon, 1974). However, as our previous examples demonstrate, the global transplant decision for products which base their competitive advantage primarily on high technology and well-established prestigious brand image is increasingly compounded by factors such as country image which, until recently, were secondary or marginal in MNEs' location consideration. It is interesting to note that some marketing researchers had *predicted* that the country image factor might influence a firm to establish a plant in a country that has a built-in positive production quality stereotype (White & Cundiff, 1978). Others have advocated that the COP/A effect should be one of the most important determinants of MNEs' global transplant location decision (Johansson & Nebenzahl, 1986). Considering these earlier insights and empirical evidence, it is surprising that little research in international business has examined the country image factor in the global production location model.

A.   Traditional Economic-oriented Approach

The factors emphasized in the international business literature as criteria for the production location decision can be classified into three categories: country-related, product-related, and company-related variables (Schollhammer, 1974). Country-related variables are situational characteristics and regulatory constraints that pertain to a particular country or region in which a company considers investing. Product-related variables are characteristics of a company's product line and/ or production process that have a potential impact on location decisions. Company-related variables are characteristics of a company and its management such as assets size, foreign trade volume, and strategy that may influence location choices. Although all of these factors have had significant impact on production location decisions, country-related variables have played the predominant role in locational choice decisions (Schollhammer, 1974). Traditionally, MNEs had focused on such factors as political stability, investment climate, legal aspects, and cost advantages of the prospective foreign countries (Frank, 1980). Among them, lower labor cost has been one of the most influential factors in determining foreign investment, based on the production-efficiency principle (Hibbert, 1993; Moxon, 1974; Robock & Simmonds, 1989).

Logistics has also long been another major concern for classic theories of location determinants (Greenhut, 1956; Hoover, 1948). In general, transportation is a key determinant within the logistics mix because the location of a plant with respect to markets and raw material sources affects the total cost of transport and hence, profitability (Ballou, 1992). Many location analyses emphasize a selection that minimizes inbound and outbound transportation costs to maximize profits (Coyle & Bardi, 1992).

B. Modern Consumer-Oriented Approach

Although the traditional approach has guided MNEs' production location decisions for decades, it has a serious weakness from a modern marketing perspective. Even though a host of factors considered in the traditional approach are very important in production location decisions, most of them are not directly considered in consumers' purchase decisions. The possible exception to this is cost, where there is a significantly large price sensitive consumer segment and significant cost savings which result in lower consumer prices. This is particularly salient for low-value goods (e.g., soft drinks). While the *market* has been recognized as an important determinant of foreign direct investment, the focus of international business researchers (e.g., Schollhammer, 1974; Tong & Walker, 1980) has not been on consumer responses, but on economic and logistics concerns such as market size and proximity to the market. Few international business researchers emphasize the market from a consumer orientation. It is well documented that modern consumers are increasingly more concerned with the total value of a product based on *quality* rather than with a single factor for most purchase decisions. The quality perception and purchase decision based on country image has been identified as an important factor influencing consumer choice (Erickson, Johansson, & Chao, 1984; Johansson et al., 1985; Han, 1989). Like country of origin, we argue that country of production/assembly (COP/A) is becoming increasingly more important as consumers become more sophisticated in this age of globalization. As we discussed earlier, these trends have made managers of well-established global brands more sensitive not only to their brand image, but also to the consumer's growing awareness and perception of the country where the product is manufactured or assembled (Lee & Park, 1995).

III. MODEL OF THE GLOBAL TRANSPLANT DECISION

In this section, a conceptual model is proposed in which country of production/ assembly (COP/A) is incorporated with traditional economic variables into the global production location decision. We *assume* that other important variables such as economic, political, legal, logistics, social, and cultural factors are already considered at the initial screening stage of selecting the candidates of the production location. We also assume that the firm's objective is profit maximization. (A firm can pursue other objectives, such as revenue or market share maximization.) We propose the application of conjoint analysis to quantify the COP/A effect, with the COP/A utility used to estimate market share. The proposed conceptual model takes the COP/A price, and cost factors into consideration in the production location decision. Price and the production cost factors are considered because the former is one of the most important attributes in the consumer's purchase decision (Monroe & Della Bitta, 1978; Rao & Monroe, 1989), whereas the latter has a direct impact on the price as the most important economic factor (Frank, 1980; Moxon, 1974). Moreover, where a product is produced or assembled directly influences both production costs and price.

A. A Location Decision Scenario

Let us assume that a hypothetical U.S. notebook computer company in California named "Prime" (also assume it is a reputed global brand) is planning to expand its market penetration into the rapidly growing Far East Asian market, while reducing cost pressures to counter strong Japanese and European competition. The company is targeting five markets in the region, including China, South Korea, Japan, Taiwan, and Hong Kong. It seriously examined the possibility of building one manufacturing facility in the Far East to lower production and logistics costs (assume only one Asian plant is economically feasible due to company resources). Assume that based on an initial screening model which used traditional economic and political factors, the company has selected two candidate countries—China and South Korea, having eliminated Japan due to high labor and plant acquisition costs and Taiwan and Hong Kong for long term political considerations.

Notebook computers require high-level technology and a skilled work force. This product also represents a highly socially visible item (e.g., travel, business meetings, presentations) and its typical users are in the upper socio-economic echelon (this is especially true in Asian countries). Thus, the country of production/ assembly effect (or even "state" or "province" of production for domestic consumption), not to mention of country of origin, would be salient on consumers' decision criteria, particularly in Asia. It is likely, if other things are equal, that a product manufactured in the United States would be evaluated more favorably by Asian consumers because they know that the product is developed and pioneered by U.S. technology and "Prime" is a highly recognized global brand among Asian consumers. One alternative for "Prime" is to expand the current facility in California. However, from the cost-economics point of view, California is not the most advantageous location. South Korean labor costs are lower than in California, skilled labor is readily available, and key components can readily be supplied from Japan at adequate prices. In addition, Asian consumers are already familiar with electronic products from South Korea (e.g., Samsung, Gold Star, Leading Edge) as reasonable alternatives to expensive Western products. The most attractive aspects of manufacturing in China includes low wages, minimal logistics, and transportation costs. However, the Chinese labor force is not regarded as skilled, and its technology is still perceived as primitive as evidenced by the absence of Chinese electronics brands. Thus, consumers' quality perceptions of such a high-tech product as a notebook computer, produced or assembled in China are likely to be less favorable, even though it carries a well-established brand name.

Since Prime's brand recognition is already established in Asia, the company believes that the *tradeoffs* between the COP/A effect and price in consumers' minds will influence their evaluation and purchase of the product. Thus, this tradeoff relationship and its impact on profits should be carefully considered in the final stage of the location transplant decision process. If notebook computers are already manufactured in any of those Far East Asian countries, "Prime" should also take the competitive factor into account, because sales volume, market share, and profits are subject to competitive forces. Thus, the company needs to investigate the following issues to make an optimal global production location decision:

1. The evaluation of the COP/A effect in each of the five markets.
2. Tradeoff relationships between COP/A and price factors.
3. Projection of market share and demand in each of the five countries.
4. Impact of COP/A, price, production costs, and market share on the overall profit in each of the two location candidates.

The model we propose considers each of these issues step by step in order to facilitate the company's choice of optimal production location.

B.   Proposed Conjoint Methodology

To assess the COP/A effect, we propose to apply the conjoint method. Conjoint analysis is one of the most widely used techniques for new product development and concept evaluation of multiattribute products and services (Green & Srinivasan, 1990). We first describe this technique's application, and then propose a basic research design and data collection method. Finally, we explain how to derive the utility (part-worth) of COP/A factor in the context of the described scenario.

1. Conjoint Analysis

A major objective of conjoint measurement is to derive information about the trade-offs consumers make among various attributes. Trade-off values are used to assess the part-worth and relative importance of each attribute. Conjoint methodology is based on a decompositional approach that estimates a set of part-worths for individual attributes that, given some type of compositional rule (e.g., an additive rule), are most consistent with the respondent's overall evaluations of a set of alternatives that are pre-specified in terms of levels of different attributes (Green & Rao, 1971, Green and Srinivasan 1978, 1990). The data are obtained by an indirect process in which respondents make judgments (preference ratings or rankings) about various alternatives, each of which is characterized by a complete set of attributes (full-profile approach), or by sets of partial stimuli described in terms of varied levels on two attributes (two-factor-at-a-time approach). These input judgments are converted into interval-scaled values (part-worths) which represent the importance an individual assigns to each attribute, and the trade-offs the individual would make among them. Typically, the conjoint method generates robust parameter estimates with the main effects only model, and inclusion of interaction terms is usually not recommended (Green & Srinivasan, 1990). However, a modified design can be used to measure selected two-way interaction effects (Carmone & Green, 1981).

Various algorithms can be employed to measure the effects of each level of every attribute such that the additive combination of each effect optimally maintains the rank order of input preferences. The part-worth function model provides the greatest flexibility in allowing different preference function shapes along each of the attributes (Green & Srinivasan, 1978). The model and its parameters are formally stated as follows (Green & Rao, 1971):

$$R'_{hj} = \sum_i \sum_k \lambda_{hik} \, d_{jik} + \varepsilon$$

where R'_{hj} = transformed rank order of alternative j by subject h
   i = the number of attribute
   k = level of an attribute
   λ_{hik} = part-worth of attribute i at level k assessed by subject h
   d_{jik} = 1 if alternative j has attribute i at level k; 0 otherwise
   ε = error term

The full-profile approach works well when six or fewer attributes are included. With a large number of attributes (over six), parameter estimation is problematic due to reduced degrees of freedom (Green & Srinivasan, 1990). Fractional factorial designs used in more advanced conjoint analysis can alleviate this problem. The use of conjoint analysis in product evaluation rests on several assumptions.

Consumer decision making models based on the conjoint method posit that consumers' evaluation (or purchase decision) is only determined by the utility of the product, even though other variables may influence purchase behavior (Green & Srinivasan, 1978). Further, it is assumed that consumers make comparison judgments across alternatives on the basis of information provided in the stimuli set (including inferred quality or prestige related to brand name, COO, or COP/A) (Szybillo & Jacoby, 1974). Our approach is also built on these assumptions.

2. Conjoint vs. Self-Explication Approaches

Some may question why we propose a rather complex conjoint analysis instead of simply collecting attribute importance ratings directly. There is good reason to question the validity of what people tell us about the attribute importance. It is well documented that self-reports are often unreliable due to their potential biases and demand artifacts in some situations (see Nisbett & Wilson, 1977 and Sawyer, 1975). When people have difficulty reporting their stimulus responses, they are often motivated to confirm what they believe to be the experimental hypothesis. While respondents tend to *react rationally* when their views on an object are directly asked, there is ample evidence that consumers' value perceptions and product evaluations are not necessarily rational. A classic example demonstrates this view. In the early 1940s, GM conducted large-scale surveys asking people to rate the relative importance of various car attributes. The results showed that dependability and safety scored very high, whereas appearance and performance produced very low ratings. However, researchers knew that appearance and styling played a major determinant role in their actual purchase decisions. It was clear that survey participants wanted to be viewed as sober, rational drivers, not interested in such juvenile fripperies as styling and fast pickup. Fortunately for GM, they discounted the survey results in their final product design (Semon 1995).

The question "how important is attribute X?" is ambiguous because respondents may answer on the basis of their own range of experience over existing products, rather than on a broader experimentally defined range of attribute levels.[5] With the conjoint method, respondents provide an overall evaluation of each alternative holistically, in the context of given attributes, without worrying about the importance/value of each attribute. By decomposing the overall rating, each attribute's importance can be more accurately isolated, reflecting natural ecological correlations among attributes.

3. Research Design and Stimulus Construction

The conjoint method utilizes a within-subjects experimental design. The evaluation task created under this design is similar to real world situations in which consumers simultaneously evaluate multiple alternatives of the same brand manufactured in different countries. Going back to our scenario, important

Table 1. Notebook Computer and Key Attributes

Attribute	Level			
Processor	—	—	—	
Warranty	—	—	—	
Battery Life	—	—	—	
Weight	—	—	—	
Price*	ℜ20203	ℜ23600	ℜ26130	
COP/A	U.S.	S. Korea	China	Local Brand**

Notes: *Prices are given in Chinese currency Renminbi (ℜ). The respective country's currency should be used where data are collected.
**If there is a local brand, it can be included.

attributes that significantly affect consumers' evaluations and purchase decisions for a notebook computer can be identified through exploratory research. To illustrate this application, we present five attributes along with the COP/A factor which are considered important for consumers' evaluation of notebook computers in Table 1.[6]

Previous studies indicate that six is a reasonable and workable number of attributes to measure consumers' product evaluations. The range of each attribute may vary from two to four levels, depending on that attribute's nature. The competitive market environment can also be considered by including existing local brands, if any, as part of COP/A. Utilizing the full-profile approach, a fractional factorial design allows use of a subset of the maximum 24 alternatives (see Table 1) to reduce respondents' information overload in the evaluation task. A set of profile cards for each alternative would consist of some predetermined combination of attributes (five attributes and COP/A in this case). Unacceptable and unrealistic combinations would be eliminated. Thus, each alternative notebook computer would be composed of a unique combination of six attributes' levels (including the COP/A), and would be presented by a terse attribute profile as shown in one example in Table 2.

4. Sample and Data Collection

Particular care must be taken in properly defining the appropriate population and the sampling plan used to recruit potential notebook purchasers in each of the five Asian markets based on careful exploratory research. Although conjoint data should be collected from each country to assess the market share and total demand, we use only China in our illustration. In China, this product is most likely to be purchased by high level business managers and government officials, and is unlikely to be purchased by college students due to its high cost relative to their disposable

Table 2.   Task Instructions, Stimulus, and Measurement Scale

Instructions

Prime is a very well known notebook computer brand in the United States. It plans to sell *Prime* notebook computers in China*. The company is considering various models for introduction to China*. After examining each alternative as described in the profile card, evaluate it on the provided scale according to your preference.

A Sample Alternative

This model has Intel's 486DX2 microprocessor, weighs 3 pounds, and lasts 3 hours on a single charge. The model, assembled in South Korea, is 23600 Renminbi with one year warranty.

Preference Measure

Based on the above information, what is your evaluation of the product?

Place a check mark below the word that closely describes your reaction.

extremely	very	somewhat	neither good	somewhat	very bad	extremely
good	good	good	nor bad	bad		bad

Note: *The respective country name should be used in which data are collected.

income. The sample size would be determined by the statistical power necessary for the situation. Respondents would be asked to provide their preferences for each of the alternatives, and the order of the presentation should be rotated systematically across respondents to eliminate order biases. We recommend that overall *preference judgement* for each alternative be measured, instead of purchase intention because situational factors might intervene between preference and purchase action. Sample task instructions and measurement scales are presented in Table 2. Detailed guides for data collection forms and procedures are available from relevant sources (e.g., Urban & Hauser, 1980, Green & Wind, 1973).

5.   Estimation of Factor Part-worths and Product Utility

Let us assume that we obtained the "part-worths" of COP/A and price as shown in Table 3. While only two factors are considered for simplicity's sake, this procedure can be applied when the number of attributes are increased without loss of generality. There are several other reasons for presenting COP/A and price. First, the price level will be significantly influenced by the locational decision (which is usually not the case with other functional attributes). Second, as discussed previously, price is not only an important attribute for consumers' purchase decisions in general, but is a conspicuous selling tool for many IBM clone notebook computers.

The respective values in Table 3 can be generated for each respondent because the data are collected individually. Conjoint analysis is usually carried out at the individual level because of substantial among-person variation in individual preferences. Each part-worth in Table 3 may be interpreted as the *importance weight* the consumer places on a specific level of a particular attribute (Green & Rao,

Table 3. Part-worths Of COP/A and Price

Country of Production/Assembly	$U_{COP/A}$	Price*	U_{Price}
Prime	3.3	ℜ20230	3.8
made in the U.S.		($2400)	
Prime	2.8	ℜ23600	3.1
made in South Korea		($2800)	
Prime	2.4	ℜ26130	2.6
made in China		($3100)	
Local Brand	2.1		
in China			

Note: *The exchange rate between U.S. Dollar ($) and Chinese Renminbi (ℜ) is about 1: 8.84 as of February 1995.

1971). The utility of the low priced local brand is 5.9, which is obtained by $U_{Local/ℜ20230} = 2.1 + 3.8 = 5.9$, whereas the utilities of medium priced South Korean made ($U_{SK/ℜ23600} = 2.8 + 3.1$) and highest priced U.S. made ($U_{US/ℜ26130} = 3.3 + 2.6$) alternatives are also 5.9. Thus, we can infer that the Chinese consumer who evaluated the same brand of notebook computers made in different countries is willing to pay an additional ℜ5900 or ℜ3370 to buy an expensive U.S. built notebook computer or a medium priced South Korean built one instead of the local product, signifying the *country of production/assembly effect*. The part-worths of COP/A and price serve as key inputs to the model described next.

C.   The Global Production Location Model

As discussed, profit maximization is assumed to be the main objective of the firm. The relationships among COP/A, price, and cost can be examined through the following profit function proposed:

$$\Pi_i = \sum_k [Q_k \, f(P_k, COP/A_k) \times P_k] - VC_i \times \sum_k [Q_k \, f(P_k, COP/A_k)] - FC_i$$

where Π_i = profit at i_{th} candidate location
       Q_k = quantity demanded at k_{th} market (country)
       COP/A_k = COP/A factor at k_{th} market (country)
       P_k = price factor at k_{th} market (country)
       VC_i = variable cost at i_{th} candidate location
       FC_i = fixed cost at i_{th} candidate location

i $= i_{th}$ candidate country (i = 3 in our example)

k = the number of markets (k = 5 in our example)

In the model, the functional relationship between demand, COP/A, and price is described as: $Qf(P, COP/A)$—the quantity demanded (Q) is a function of not only the price (P) but the consumer's perception of country of production/ assembly (COP/A). This relationship can be used to confirm the COP/A effect using price as an anchor. For instance, with a constant price (P), if the quantities demanded (Q) show the following relationship: $Qf(P, COP/A_{SK}) > Qf(P, COP/A_{China})$, it signifies the existence of the COP/A effect. Thus, the evidence of trade-off relationships between country of production/assembly (COP/A) and price (P) can be assessed. It is also likely that variable (e.g., labor, logistics, and raw materials) and fixed (e.g., land and construction) costs in different countries show the following relations: $VC_{China} < VC_{SK}$ and $FC_{China} < FC_{SK}$. This indicates that although a decision to locate a factory in South Korea instead in China would result in a increase in quantity demanded (due to the COP/A effect), it would also increase the production cost. Thus, the final decision about the country of production/ assembly should be made based on the comparison of *overall profits* in candidate locations (i.e., Π_{China}, Π_{SK}, Π_{US}).

6.   Estimation of Market Share (MS)

The part-worths of each of the attributes obtained by conjoint analysis can also be used to estimate the market share (MS_k) of each alternative made in different locations in each market. Using our example in Table 3, we can project the market share of each alternative. If individual utility data of 60 participants out of 200 in a representative sample yielded the highest product utility for Prime$_{SK/\Re23600}$, then the expected market share of the alternative will be 30 percent in Chinese market. In the same way, the expected market shares for other alternative versions can be calculated. (We acknowledge the potential confounding effects of marketing mix variables and competitive reaction, and hence assume they are held constant.) The market share information (MS_k) of the most popular version is used to estimate the demand in each market (Q_k), which is then used with price information (P_k) as input to calculate the combined profit across all five markets as described in the next section.

7.   Assessment of Demand (Q), Costs (VC & FC), and Profit (Π)

The expected total quantity demanded in each market (Q_k) can be calculated as follows: $Q_k f(P_k, COP/A_k) = PMS_k \times MS_k$ The information about the projected market size in each country (PMS_k) can be obtained from secondary data sources (see Discussion) and how the market share (MS_k) is estimated was described in the previous section. Next, the total revenue generated from each candidate location country can be calculated as follows. Total demand in each market (Q_k) is multiplied by the price (P_k) in each market, and then the amount is aggregated across the five markets ($\Sigma[Q_k \times P_k]$). We already know the anchor prices of alternatives which were selected as input because each of those selected yielded the highest product utility in each market when individual data were aggregated. These input prices can be adjusted realistically at the final stage by management. Once the aggregated revenue is calculated, cost information should be estimated to assess overall profit to be generated from each candidate location (Π_i). Because the major portion of costs (VC_i and FC_i) can be determined by the country of production/assembly location, the company should be able to obtain the relevant cost information (e.g., labor costs, transport, distribution, and locally supplied materials) from the secondary data sources (see Discussion) to estimate the costs in each candidate location country. After obtaining the aggregated revenue and cost information, management is in a position to make an overall assessment about the impact of all the factors on profit (Π_i) for each of the candidate location countries. Following the profit maximization principle, the company should select the country of production/assembly which generates the highest overall profit.

VII. DISCUSSION

Although consumers' quality perceptions based on where a product is originally designed/engineered (*country of origin or COO effect*) have been extensively studied, those based on where the product is manufactured or assembled (*COP/A effect*) have attracted very little attention. We highlighted the COP/A as new country image construct, an outgrowth of traditional country image (i.e., COO) in the global market place, but uniquely different from it. The COP/A effect should receive more attention by researchers in our increasingly global economy because intense pressure to reduce production costs forces more companies in industrialized countries to seek alternative production and sourcing sites around the globe. At the same time, today's consumers are more knowledgeable about technological advances/backwardness and quality control levels of many countries due to advances in communications and transportation. Future research should identify and empirically examine previously discussed moderating factors. Also, cross-cultural studies contrasting consumers in industrialized western countries with those in developing countries are likely to reveal some interesting differences, which can be used to guide international marketers' decision making. We also recognize that a negative COP/A effect may be diluted over time as consumers become more aware of improved quality in brands produced in a given country. As the earlier example of Chrysler's K car demonstrated, a negative COP/A effect can be overcome by maintaining tight quality control and production engineering and emphasizing this in the firm's communication strategies for mid to low price range segments of non-luxury products. Future research should investigate empirically whether various tactics identified in the COO literature can be adopted to deal with an adverse COP/A effect, taking into account product category factors and individual characteristics. In spite of the possibility of diluting negative COP/A effects over time, we believe that this potential is less likely for products with high symbolic expressive value and/or high functional risk. Thus, we strongly recommend that international marketers of such products incorporate the COP/A factor in their location decision rather than battle a negative COP/A effect and risk lower sales and diminished profits should that dilution effect not develop.

Although the COP/A construct is clearly applicable to global production location decisions, international business researchers have neglected this consumer-oriented market factor. We proposed a conceptual model that incorporates the COP/A effect into these decisions. The part-worths for the country of production/assembly effect estimated by conjoint analysis can be used to project the market share of alternative versions in the proposed model. Furthermore, this model incorporates traditional cost factors that can be obtained from the secondary data and/or historical data along with price and the COP/A factors. Finally, COP/A and cost information can be used to estimate the projected overall profit from multiple markets from each of the candidate locations. We recommend that this approach be used at the advanced stage of a location decision based on a thorough initial investigation of economic, political, logistics, and legal factors.

Although our illustration focused primarily on price and COP/A, extension of our approach/model to complex situations is feasible, although it is beyond the scope of this article. Company resource constraints could be built into the model, and the conjoint results could be used to compare the overall profitabilities of offering different lines, and even different COP/A versions of the products to different markets, thus permitting more of a locally adapted product assortment in each country market. This would clearly add to the complexity of the model, and would require examination of separate demand estimates, markets shares, and logistics and distribution costs for all product x COP/A combinations considered for each market. This approach could also be extended to fit the needs of multinational enterprises with multiple related product lines sharing common production and distribution facilities. However, it would be feasible only for companies with strong market research and information systems departments which are capable of supplying all the required information to operationalize the proposed model.

Although our model requires external data to operationalize such variables as cost and total market demand, it is not difficult to identify such data for a given product category. Relevant cost information should be available through a company's internal and/or external sources. Many excellent external secondary sources are readily available to draw upon. For example, information about manufacturing wages in foreign countries can be obtained from the "Yearbook of Labor Statistics" published by the International Labor Office in Geneva. The market size of foreign countries can be estimated by combining information from general economic statistics (e.g., the "Indicators of Market Size for 117 Countries" published by Business International) with industry-specific statistics (e.g., for the personal computer industry, the "Source Book" published by International Data Corp.). Recent information on modes of transportation and how to estimate freight costs can also be obtained by consulting such publications as "Inbound Logistics" by Thomas Publishing. Many practical guides and computer software programs are available for assessing consumers' image of country of production/assembly through conjoint analysis (see Green & Srinivasan, 1990; Urban & Hauser, 1980, Wittink & Cattin, 1989).

The main thrust of this paper was *not* to propose a comprehensive model of the global production location decision. Our intent, rather, was to provide the impetus for future research focusing on the consumer's subjective image of country of production/assembly, which has been neglected in global production location decisions. There are several limitations of our proposed approach. First, it does not explicitly incorporate other factors which are input to the global production location decision. However, we don't regard this as a serious deficiency, because we recommend that it be used at the advanced stage of location decision making, after having taken other such factors into account. It should also be emphasized that a verbal response or preference based on a hypothetical situation might differ from actual behavior in real world decisions. Tracing the effects of a location shift on the final choice using a test market approach, although expensive, is recommended when substantial investment and future market opportunity costs are at stake. Finally, profit maximization and utility-based consumer decision making are the underlying assumptions of our conceptualization.

In spite of these potential limitations to the applicability of the COP/A construct, we believe that it is time to get some data and test this approach. Our proposed approach makes an incremental contribution to the global production location decision by introducing the consumer image factor of country of production/assembly. Although imperfect, consumers' preferences with respect to purchases of such products as luxury automobiles, luxury watches, high fashion apparels, and high-priced cosmetics should be an important input to the global transplant decision. We believe that our approach has strong practical application potential as a consumer-oriented decision aid to *supplement* the traditional economic-based location model. Empirical refinement of the COP/A construct and our proposed approach would benefit by the use of other techniques in addition to conjoint analysis. Such empirical research should improve measurement of the construct and its applicability, and overcome some of the initial limitations discussed. Future research is needed to empirically test the proposed model of global locational decisions in selected industries to evaluate its validity, applicability, and value in the real world.

NOTES

1.   For some products in which low-cost labor is less important than such factors as a high skilled work force, access to supporting technology, and quality of the transportation, Mexico may not prove to be the cheapest solution. However, for the auto industry, in which assembly labor accounts for a significant portion of cost structure, Mexico is still very attractive. As of 1992, the average hourly wage in transportation equipment manufacturing was $2.51 (7804 pesos) in Mexico vs. $11.93 in the United States. Full time workers' compensation (including fringe benefits) was $4.30 (13029 pesos) in Mexico vs. $22.20 in the U.S. (Yearbook of Labor Statistics, 1993). The Big Three U.S. auto makers, Volkswagen of Germany, and Nissan of Japan are all assembling medium/low priced cars in Mexico and expanding their capacity (National Trade Data Bank, 1994). Although one reason was a rapidly growing Mexican market, cheap labor was one of the important factors behind their location decisions. The low cost labor in Lain America is especially attractive to German auto makers who have the highest cost structure in EC. Volkswagen has another manufacturing plant in Brazil.

2.   This observation is based upon anecdotal evidence provided to the senior author by a proprietor of a jewelry shop in Manhattan.

3.   In the process of further developing our understanding of this phenomenon, the senior author conducted personal and telephone interviews with Korean residents from several different states and metropolitan areas. This was augmented by visits to Hyundai dealers in the greater New York metropolitan area, who acknowledged that awareness of this phenomenon sometimes led them to no longer give substantial price discounts on these models to Korean customers (especially *Sonata*). While foreign cars are virtually inaccessible to ordinary consumers in Korea due to prohibitively high tariffs, Hyundai cars assembled in Canada are classified as South Korean origin by Korean Customs Services and are exempt from import duties.

4.   We employ the term "luxury" here in the sense that it is used in the reference group literature to represent a publicly consumed/visible product which is not a necessity or a staple good (Bearden & Etzel, 1982). While this reference group concept is similar to the economic theory concept of a "luxury good," the latter often implies a kinked demand curve due to the prestige component. Thus, a luxury good may have an inherently different demand function from that of a high technology good (e.g., hi-fi audio equipment, notebook computer) where the COP/A effect may exist for other reasons.

5.   See Green and Srinivasan 1990 for a more complete discussion of problems of the self-explicated approach to measure the importance of multiple attributes, as well as Neslin (1981) for an empirical comparison of Conjoint versus Self-Explication approaches.

6.   These attributes were actually used in a consumer research study in which consumers' preference and evaluations for portable computers were measured (Lee & Olshavsky, 1995).

REFERENCES

Ballou, R.H. (1992). *Business logistics management*, 3rd ed. Englewood Cliff, NJ: Prentice-Hall.
Bearden, W.O., & Etzel, M.J. (1982). Reference group influence on product and brand purchase decisions. *Journal of Consumer Research*, 9 (2), 183-194.
Bilkey, W.J., & Nes, E. (1982). Country of origin effects on product evaluations. *Journal of International Business Studies*, Spring/Summer, 89 -99.
Business Week. (1993). Why Mercedes is Alabama bound. October 11.
Carmon, F.J., & Green, P.E. (1981). Model misspecification in multiattribute parameter estimation. *Journal of Marketing Research*, 18, 87-93.
Cordell, V.V. (1992). Effects of consumer preference for foreign products. *Journal of International Business Studies*, (2), 251-269.
Cox, D.F. (1967). Clues for advertising strategies. In D.F. Cox (Ed.), *Risk Taking and Information Handling in Consumer Behavior* (pp. 112-151). Boston, MA: Harvard University Press.

Coyle, J.J., & Bardi, E.J. (1992). *The management of business logistics*, 5th ed. St. Paul, MN: West Publishing Co.

Dunning, J.H. (1981). *International production and the multinational enterprise*. London, UK: George Allen and Unwin.

Erickson, G.M., Johansson, J.K., & Chao, P. (1984). Image variables in multi-attribute production evaluations: Country of origin effects. *Journal of Consumer Research*, 11 (September), 694-699.

Fortune. (1993). The modular corporation. February 8.

Frank, I. (1980). *Foreign enterprise in developing countries*. Baltimore, MD: Johns Hopkins University.

Green, P.E., & Rao, V.R. (1971). Conjoint measurement for quantifying judgmental data. *Journal of Marketing Research*, 8 (August), 355-363.

Green, P.E., & Srinivasan, V. (1978). Conjoint analysis in consumer research: Issues and outlook. *Journal of Consumer Research*, 5 (September), 103-123.

Green, P.E., & Srinivasan, V. (1990). Conjoint analysis in marketing: New developments with implications for research and practice. *Journal of Marketing*, 54 (October), 3-19.

Green, P.E., & Wind, Y. (1973). *Multivariate decisions in marketing: A measurement approach*. Chicago, IL: Dryden Press.

Greenhut, M.I. (1956). *Plant location in theory and in practice*. Chapel Hill, NC: University of North Carolina.

Han, C.M. (1989). Country image: Halo or summary construct? *Journal of Marketing Research*, 26 (May), 222-229.

Han, C.M., & Terpstra, V. (1988). Country of origin effects for uni-national and bi-national products. *Journal of International Business Studies*, 16 (Summer), 235-256.

Hibbert, E.P. (1993). Global make-or-buy decisions. *Industrial Marketing Management*, 22 (May), 67-77.

Hoover, E.H. (1948). *The Location of Economic Activity*. New York, NY: McGraw-Hill.

Jacoby, J., & Kaplan, L.B. (1972). The components of perceived risk. In M. Venkatesan (Ed.), *Proceedings of Association for Consumer Research* (pp. 382-393). Chicago, IL: University of Chicago.

Johansson, J.K., Douglas, S.P., & Nonaka, I. (1985). Assessing the impact of country of origin on product evaluations: A new methodological perspective. *Journal of Marketing Research*, 22 (November), 388-396.

Johansson, J.K., & Nebenzahl, I.D. (1986). Multinational production: Effect on brand value. *Journal of International Business Studies*, Fall, 101-126.

Johansson, J.K., & Thorelli, H.B. (1985). International product positioning. *Journal of International Business Studies*, Fall, 57-75.

Kaynak, E., & Cavusgil, T. (1983). Consumer attitudes towards products of foreign origin: Do they vary across product classes? *International Journal of Advertising*, 2, 147-157.

Lee, D.H. (1989). Symbolic interactionism: Some implications for consumer self-concept and product symbolism research. In M.E. Goldberg, G. Gorn & R.W. Pollay (Eds.), *Advances in Consumer Research* (Vol. 17, pp. 386-393). Provo, UT: Association for Consumer Research.

Lee, D.H., & Olshavsky, R.W. (1995). Conditions and consequences of spontaneous inference generation: A concurrent protocol approach. *Organizational Behavior and Human Decision Processes*, 61 (2).

Lee, D.H., & Park, C.W. (1995). A conceptual model of global production location decision: A consumer-oriented approach. In S. Tamer Cavusgil & J.W. Lim, (Eds.), *Proceedings of American Marketing Association and Korean Marketing Association Joint Conference,* 338-354.

Maheswaran, D. (1994). Country of origin as a stereotype: Effects of consumer expertise and attribute strength on product evaluations. *Journal of Consumer Research*, 21 (September), 354-365.

Monroe, K.B., & Della Bitta, A.J. (1978). Models for pricing decisions. *Journal of Marketing Research*, 15 (August), 413-428.

Moxon, R.W. (1974). Offshore production in the less developed countries. In *The Bulletin*, July, 98-99.

Nagashima, A. (1977). A comparative 'made in' product image survey among Japanese businessmen. *Journal of Marketing*, 41, 95-100.

National Trade Data Bank. (1994). *Market research report, "Mexico - auto industry profile.* International Trade Administration, Department of Commerce.

Neslin, S.A. (1981). Linking product features to perceptions: Self-stated versus statistically revealed importance weights. *Journal of Marketing Research*, 18 (February), 80-86.

Nisbett, R.E., & Wilson, T.D. (1977). Telling more than we can know: Verbal reports on mental processes. *Psychological Review*, 84 (May), 231-258.

Rao, A., & Monroe, K. (1989). The effect of price, brand name, and store name on buyers' perception of product quality: An integrative review. *Journal of Marketing Research*, 26 (August), 351-357.

Robock, S.H., & Simmonds, K. (1989). *International Business and Multinational Enterprises*, 4th ed. Homewood, IL: Irwin.

Semon, T.T. (1995). Asking simple question to improve analysis of value perception. *Marketing News*. 29 (5).

Sawyer, A.G. (1975). Demand artifacts in laboratory experiments in consumer research. *Journal of Consumer Research*, 1, 20-30.

Schollhammer, H. (1974). *Locational strategies of multinational firms*. Los Angeles, CA: Pepperdine University.

Shalofsky, I. (1987). Research for global brands. *European Research*, May, 88-93.

Sirgy, M.J. (1982). Self-concept in consumer behavior: A critical review. *Journal of Consumer Research*, 9 (December), 287-300.

Szybillo, G.J., & Jacoby, J. (1974). Intrinsic versus extrinsic cues as determinants of perceived product quality. *Journal of Applied Psychology*, 59 (1), 74-78.

Tong, H.M., & Walker, C.K. (1980). An empirical study of plant location decisions of foreign manufacturing investors in the United States. *Columbia Journal of World Business*, Spring, 66-73.

Urban, G.L., & Hauser, J.R. (1980). *Designing and marketing new products*. Englewood Cliffs, NJ: Prentice-Hall.

Wall Street Journal. (1992). Luxury-auto makers considers Mexico: Its low-cost labor vs. image perception. November 27.

White, P.D., & Cundiff, E.W. (1978). Assessing the quality of industrial products. *Journal of Marketing*, 42 (January), 80-86.

Wittink, D.R., & Cattin, P. (1989). Commercial use of conjoint analysis: An update. *Journal of Marketing*, 53 (July), 91-97.

Yearbook of Labor Statistics. (1993). 52nd Issue, International Labour Office, Geneva, Switzerland.

AN INVESTIGATION OF THE OPTIMUM NUMBER OF RESPONSE CATEGORIES FOR KOREAN CONSUMERS

Kyung Hoon Kim

ABSTRACT

This study examines the relationship between number of response categories and the reliability and validity of data. Using data from a study of Korean consumer satisfaction, 3-,5-, 7- and 9-point scales were analyzed. The 3-point scale showed low reliability while the 5-, 7- and 9-point scales exhibited a reasonable level of reliability. In terms of validity, the 3-point scale ranked lowest, the 7-point scale was at a medium level, and the 5- and 9-point scales ranked the highest. Implications of these findings for research conducted in Asian countries are discussed.

I. INTRODUCTION

An important question facing marketing researchers is the number of response categories that should be used to capture a subject's response to a question. Deter-

Advances in International Marketing, Volume 7, pages 255-272.
ISBN: 1-55938-839-0

mining the optimum number of response categories is especially important in constructing scales commonly used by marketers (e.g., rating scales, interval scales, and Likert scales). As a result, prior researchers have devoted considerable attention to this issue. Jacoby and Matell (1971), for example, noted that too few response categories can result in too coarse a scale and a loss of much of the raters' discriminatory powers, while too fine a scale may go beyond the raters' limited powers of discrimination. While some researchers have advocated the use of as many categories as the subject can discriminate (e.g., a 12 or 20 point scale), others recommend the use of a 2- or 3-point scale based on the ease of coding or opinions about the respondents' limited discriminating ability (Benson, 1971).

The relationship between number of response categories and data reliability and validity has been investigated by many researchers (Cicchetti, Showalter, & Tyrer, 1985; Aiken, 1983; Lissitz & Green, 1975). However, it should be noted that these studies have been performed in Western countries using data from Western subjects. For international marketing scholars and practitioners, it is important to investigate whether a similar number of response categories can be used in Western countries and Asia.

The purposes of this study are: (1) to review past research on the relationship between number of response categories and the reliability and validity of data, (2) to investigate the relationship between the number of response categories and reliability and validity by using data collected from Korean consumers, and (3) to draw practical implications for marketers interested in doing research in Asia.

II. NUMBER OF RESPONSE CATEGORIES, RELIABILITY, AND VALIDITY

A. Optimum Number of Response Categories

In exploring the optimum number of response categories, Miller (1956) suggested that a subject's accuracy of perception of unidimensional stimuli is limited to seven bits. A later study by Bevan and Avant (1968) found that mean response latency was lowest in the 2 category situation and increased with each increase in number of categories to 64. These authors also found that response uncertainty increased as the number of available categories increased to 32 but did not change substantially beyond this point.

Green and Rao (1970) approached the problem of determining the appropriate number of rating scales and response categories by using the sensitivity of solution recovery method. They reported that little information appeared to be gained by increasing the number of rating scales beyond eight or the number of response categories beyond six. Thus, they recommended that 6- or 7-point scales are appropriate in marketing research. Benson (1971) argued for the use of even less scale points, noting that the frequent applicability and practical convenience of 2- or 3-point scales are strong points in their favor.

Lehmann and Hulbert (1972) delineated the conditions under which a 2- or 3-point scale may be sufficient by examining simulated data. They found that if the researcher is interested in averages across people (or will aggregate several individual scales to produce a new scale), then two or three scale points are acceptable. Their findings indicated that if the focus of the study is on individual behavior, 5- to 7-point scales should be used.

Matell and Jacoby (1972) recommended that if the primary consideration of a study is information recovery and reproduction of the original data matrix, (especially in situations where several instruments are used), then 6- or 7-point scales are the best choice.

Martin (1973) demonstrated that the correlation coefficient decreases as the number of response categories grows smaller. He concluded that the amount of information lost by collapsing scales is greater when the original variables are highly correlated. His study indicated that, when it is justifiable, one should use 10- to 20-point scales. Martin (1978) also found that the information loss can be substantial for correlations computed from variables which both have fewer than 10 scaling points.

Cox (1980) made some recommendations for applied researchers. First, scales with two or three response alternatives are generally inadequate in that: (a) they are incapable of transmitting much information; and (b) they tend to frustrate and stifle respondents. Second, he noted that the the marginal returns from using more than nine response alternatives are minimal. Cox's third recommendation was that an odd rather than an even number of response alternatives is preferable under circumstances in which the respondent can legitimately adopt a neutral position. In his review paper, he suggested that the range of five to nine is appropriate for applied research.

The research mentioned above tried to delineate general rules for the optimum number of response categories. However, some researchers have argued that the optimum number of response categories depends on subject characteristics. Guilford (1954), for example, suggested that the optimal number of scale intervals varies with the situation and that the appropriate number should be empirically determined. This approach is very rigorous, since it requires extensive pretesting before an instrument can be used. In fact, in most marketing research situations this is unrealistic. However, Hartel (1993) did find that differences in rating accuracy associated with different rating formats is contingent upon rater characteristics.

B. Number of Response Categories, Reliability and Validity

Many studies have examined the relationship between the number of response categories and data reliability and validity (e.g., Cronbach, 1950; Bending, 1954; Komorita, 1963; Komorita & Graham, 1965). Peabody (1962) and Matell and Jacoby (1971) found that reliability is generally independent of the number of scale points used for Likert-type items. However, Symonds (1924) and Champney and Marshall (1939) offered the opinion that they are not independent. Jahoda, Deutsch and Cook (1951) and Ferguson (1941) agreed, suggesting that the reliability of a scale increases as the number of scale points increases. Komorita and Graham's (1965) study indicated that, with relatively homogeneous items, reliability increases with an increase in the number of scale points.

Jacoby and Matell (1971) found no systematic relationship between number of response categories and: (a) predictive validity; (b) concurrent validity; (c) internal consistency reliability; and (d) test-retest reliability. They suggested that it would be desirable to allow a subject to select the rating format which best suits his needs. Data collected in this fashion could then be collapsed into dichotomous or trichotomous measures, which would not lead to any deleterious effects vis-a-vis reliability or validity.

Lissitz and Green (1975) argued that the reason why most past studies indicated that no particular number of scale points yielded maximum reliability was based on the sizes of the standard deviations in comparison to the differences in magnitudes of the reliability coefficients from one particular number of scale points to another. They gave strong support for rejection of 7-point scales as an optimal number.

Cicchetti, Showalter and Tyrer (1985) found that the extent of inter-rater reliability on a clinical scale is affected by the number of categories or scale points. Their results indicated that reliability increased steadily up to 7-point scale, beyond which no substantial increases occur, even when the number of scale points was increased to as many as 100.

Aiken (1983) found that means of item responses increased linearly and item variances increased curvilinearly with number of response categories. However, the study indicated that internal consistency reliability coefficients (alpha) of total scores did not change systematically with increases in the number of response categories.

III. NUMBER OF RESPONSE CATEGORIES, RELIABILITY, AND VALIDITY IN KOREAN MARKETING STUDIES

Prior to analyzing the optimal number of response categories for data collected in Korea, the number and types of response categories which have been used in recent Korean marketing studies is examined. The issue of how Korean marketing researchers measure reliability and validity is also explored. Marketing research papers published in the two main Korean marketing journals and one Korean management journal from 1990 to 1994 were reviewed. The journals were *Korean Marketing Review, Journal of Marketing Studies*, and *Korean Management Review*. Survey research which used rating scales, interval scales, and Likert scales to collect data were reviewed. In sum, 54 articles were examined.

Table 1 shows that the 5-point scale was used most often. The second most frequently used scale was the 7-point scale. 3-, 4- and 9-point scales were also used,

Table 1.   Number of Response Categories Used in Korean Marketing Studies

	Number of Response Categories						Total
	3	4	5	7	9	n.a.*	
Number of Studies	2	1	28	14	4	11	54

Note: *n.a.: Not available

Table 2.   Reliability Measures Used in Korean Marketing Studies

	Reliability Measure						Total
	α Cronbach's Coefficient	Split-half Reliability	Test-retest Reliability	Interjudge Reliability	Alternative Form Reliability	n.a.	
Number of Studies	36	1	1	2	1	15	54

Table 3.   Validity Measures in Korean Marketing Studies

	Validity Measure			Total
	Factor Analysis	Correlation	n.a.	
Number of Studies	16	3	33	54

but their importance was minimal. Eleven out of 54 papers did not indicate what kind of response category they used.

Table 2 shows that Cronbach's alpha was the most commonly used measure of reliability. Split-half coefficient and test-retest reliability were used in only two studies. Two studies used interjudge reliability. Fifteen out of 54 studies did not indicate whether they checked reliability of their data.

As shown in Table 3, factor analysis is the most frequently used method to check validity in recent Korean marketing studies. There were also three studies which used correlation to check the validity of their data. However, 33 out of 54 studies did not indicate how they checked the validity of their data.

IV.   METHOD

A.   Sample

Sampling units used in this study consisted of four independent samples using 3-, 5-, 7-, and 9-point scales. The three independent samples for the 3-, 5- and 7-point scales consisted of three groups of graduate and undergraduate students from a Korean university. Data for three types of response categories (3-, 5- and 7-point scales) were collected during the fall of 1994. 111 questionnaires for the 3-point scale, 134 questionnaires for the 5-point scale, and 134 questionnaires for the 7-point scale were usable for analysis. A sample for a 9-point scale was collected in fall of 1990. One-hundred-eighty-nine questionnaires from this sample were usable. The sampling units for this study consisted of individuals who owned personal computers.

B.   Measurement

Consumer satisfaction was measured by nine constructs including (1) sales method and ability of sales force, (2) delivery and installation of the product, (3) quality of manual, (4) education, (5) customer support and service, (6) hardware, (7) software, (8) price vs. performance, and (9) advertising. Scales used in this study were originally developed by Kim and Chu (1991). Four different forms of questionnaires were prepared for the four different response categories.

Specific variables to measure each construct were: (1) sales method and ability of sales force: easiness of meeting salesman, understanding customer's needs, proper recommendation, technical knowledge, observing promises, providing a new product information, kindness and sincerity; (2) delivery and installation of product: on-time delivery, observing delivery condition, help for installation, spare parts and documents; (3) manual: packaging and appearance, ease of understanding contents, useful information, comprehensiveness, technical accuracy, proper graphs and examples; (4) education: opportunity for education, various educational programs, self-learning materials, quality of education, and convenient location; (5) customer support and service: support and service, real-time response, on-time solution, correct service, and assistance in using; (6) hardware: right application, right solution, speed, response and resource, compatibility, easy to use, reliability, upgradability, conformity to local standard; (7) software: right solution, speed, response and resource, compatibility, easy to use, reliability; (8) price vs. performance: competitive price, economy in upgrading, economy in service, and maintenance cost; (9) advertising: frequency, interest, and getting the message across. These variables were measured by 3-, 5-, 7- and 9-point Likert type scales.

C.   Statistical Procedure

Since Cronbach's alpha was found to be the most frequently used method in the previous section, it was calculated for each construct. The split-half reliability coefficient was also used to measure reliability in this study. To understand the relationship between reliability and number of response categories, the nine Cronbach's alphas and nine split-half reliability coefficients were compared across four types of response categories.

Factor analysis was used to measure the validity of data in this study. The factor extraction method employed in this study was maximum likelihood for the 5-, 7- and 9-point scale data. Factor analysis using maximum likelihood was not able to extract any factor from 3-point scale data. Thus, the principle components method was used to extract factors from 3-point scale data. Varimax rotation was used for the 5-, 7-, and 9-point scale data. No method of rotation was possible for the 3-point scale data. To understand the relationship between validity and response categories, results of the rotated factor analysis except for the 3-point scale data were compared.

V. ANALYSIS

To understand the relationship between reliability and number of response categories, Cronbach's alpha and split-half reliability coefficients were calculated for each satisfaction construct across the different response categories.

Table 4 shows the standardized Cronbach's alpha's. All of the four different scales had an acceptable level of reliability by Nunnally's reliability standard. The highest Cronbach's alpha was .9214 and the lowest was .6752. Nunnally (1967) suggested that, in early stages of research, modest reliability in the range of .5 to .6 will suffice. For basic research, he argued that reliability above .8 was necessary

Table 4. Cronbach's α and Split-half Coefficients

Satisfaction Construct	Cronbach's α**				Split-half Coefficients			
	Response Category				Response Category			
	3	5	7	9	3	5	7	9
Sales Method and Ability of Sales Force	.8052	.8619	.8654*	.8551	.8010	.8428*	.7665	.7884
Delivery and Installation of Product	.6752	.8245*	.7840	.7658	.5579	.7356*	.6521	.7266
Manual	.7171	.7833	.8225	.8803*	.7065	.7085	.7896	.8450*
Educational Service	.7210	.8725	.8850	.8908*	.8017	.8486	.8820*	.8628
Customer Support and Service	.7904	.9116	.9108	.9214*	.7374	.8936	.8504	.9012*
Hardware	.7826	.8906	.8754	.8952*	.7114	.8873*	.8070	.8645
Software	.7152	.7871	.8629*	.8478	.6698	.7216	.8142	.8409*
Price vs. Performance	.6666	.6944	.8226*	.7955	.6157	.7340*	.7297	.7299
Advertising	.7718	.8820	.9103*	.8544	.7546	.8912	.9195*	.8506

Note: *Highest among the four different response categories.
**Standardized Item Alpha.

because at that level correlations were attenuated very little by measurement error. Nunnally also said that in applied settings, reliability of .9 was the minimum that should be tolerated and a reliability of .95 should be considered as the desirable standard. However, Peter (1979) has argued that Nunnally's reliability standard was too much rigid for marketing settings.

The four Cronbach's alphas calculated for the same construct for the four different response categories were compared to determine the relative level of reliability of each. The 9-point scale data had four of the highest alpha's (among the four types of response categories) and three of the second highest alpha's. The 7-point scale data had four of the highest alpha's and three of the second highest alpha's. The 5-point scale data had only one of highest alpha's and three of second highest Cronbach's alpha's. The 3-point scale data did not have any of the highest Cronbach's alphas. Thus, 7- and 9-point scales had the highest reliability as measured by Cronbach's alpha and the 5-point scale data had a medium level of reliability. The 3-point scale data had the lowest reliability level.

The Spearman-Brown reliability coefficient for split-half reliability was calculated for each satisfaction construct across the four types of scales and then compared. As can be seen from Table 5, the 9-point scale data had three of the highest coefficients and four of the second highest coefficients. The 7-point scale data had two of the highest coefficients and two of the second highest coefficients. The 5-point scale data had four of the highest coefficients and two of the second highest coefficients. However, the 3-point scale data had only one of the second highest coefficients. Thus, in terms of split-half reliability coefficient, the 5-point scale data had highest level of reliability, followed by the 9-point scale, the 7-point scale, and the 3-point scale data.

Table 5 also shows the results of a rotated factor analysis for the data used in this study. For the 5-, 7- and 9-point scales, the maximum likelihood extraction and varimax rotation methods were used. 9 factors explained 62.8 percent of total variance for the 9-point scale data. Factor analysis for 9-point scale data revealed that satisfaction for hardware and software might be one construct. The factor analysis could discriminate most of the constructs correctly and with reasonable accuracy. However, factor analysis for the 9-point scale data had difficulty in discriminating variables for certain constructs (e.g., sales method, ability of sales force and hardware). Thus, the 9-point scale data had a high level of validity.

Ten factors explained 66.8 percent of the total variance for the 7-point scale data. Satisfaction with hardware and software were also found to be one construct for the 7-point scale. Factor analysis for the 7-point scale data could discriminate the variables into the 6 constructs correctly, (e.g., sales method, ability of sales force, manual, education, software, price vs. performance, and advertising). The factor analysis had difficulties in discriminating variables for the other three constructs (e.g., delivery and installation of product, customer support and service, and hardware). Thus, in terms of factor analysis, the 7-point scale data showed a reasonable level of validity.

Table 5. Factor Analysis Results for Different Response Categories

Satisfaction Construct	Variable	*Response Category*																
		3 — Factor							5 — Factor									
		1	2	3	4	5	6	7	1	2	3	4	5	6	7	8	9	10
Sales Method and Ability of Sales Force	Ease of Meeting Salesman	—																
	Understanding Customer's Needs		—															
	Proper Recommendation	—								—								
	Technical Knowledge	—								—								
	Observing Promises	—								—								
	New Product Information							—		—								
	Kindness and Sincerity	—																
Delivery and Installation of Product	On-time Delivery	—						—							—			
	Observing Delivery Condition	—					—								—			
	Help for Installation	—													—			
	Spare Parts and Documents	—				—									—			
Manual	Packaging and Appearance	—														—		
	Ease of Understanding Contents			—												—		
	Useful Information			—												—		
	Comprehensiveness		—													—		
	Technical Accuracy			—												—		
	Proper Graphs and Examples	—														—		
Education	Opportunity for Education	—	—									—						
	Various Educational Programs		—									—						
	Self Learning Materials		—									—						
	Quality of Education	—	—									—						
	Convenient Location	—										—						
Customer Support and Service	Support and Service	—									—							
	Real-time Response	—									—							
	On-time Solution	—									—							
	Correct Service	—									—							
	Assistance in Using	—									—							

(continued)

Table 5. (Continued)

Satisfaction Construct	Variable	3-Factor 1	2	3	4	5	6	7	5-Factor 1	2	3	4	5	6	7	8	9	10
Hardware	Right Application	■							■									
	Right Solution	■							■									
	Speed, Response and Resources		■						■									
	Compatibility	■															■	
	Ease of Use	■							■									
	Reliability	■							■									
	Upgradability	■							■									
	Conformity to Local Standard	■							■									
Software	Right Solution	■																■
	Speed, Response and Resources	■															■	
	Compatibility	■							■									
	Ease of Use					■												
	Reliability						■										■	■
Price vs. Performance	Competitive Price		■													■		
	Economy in Upgrading					■										■		
	Economy in Service					■										■		
	Maintenance Cost	■							■									
Advertising	Frequency				■								■					
	Interest				■								■					
	Get the Message Across	■											■					

Note: ■ : Factor Loading > 0.4
**The principle component method for 3-point scale data and maximum likelihood method for 5-point scale data were used to extract factors. Rotation for the 3-point scale data was not possible. Varimax rotation was tried for 5-point scale data.

Table 5. Factor Analysis Results for Different Response Categories

Satisfaction Construct	Variable	7 Factor										9 Factor									
		1	2	3	4	5	6	7	8	9	10	1	2	3	4	5	6	7	8	9	10
Sales Method and Ability of Sales Force	Ease of Meeting Salesman		—										—								
	Understanding Customer's Needs		—										—								
	Proper Recommendation		—										—								
	Technical Knowledge			—												—					
	Observing Promises		—													—					
	New Product Information		—										—								
	Kindness and Sincerity		—													—					
Delivery and Installation of Product	On-time Delivery								—										—		
	Observing Delivery Condition								—										—		
	Help for Installation	—																	—		
	Spare Parts and Documents																				
Manual	Packaging and Appearance				—										—						
	Ease of Understanding Contents				—										—						
	Useful Information				—										—						
	Comprehensiveness				—										—						
	Technical Accuracy				—										—						
	Proper Graphs and Examples				—										—						
Education	Opportunity for Education			—										—							
	Various Educational Programs			—										—							
	Self Learning Materials				—									—							
	Quality of Education			—										—							
	Convenient Location		—													—					
Customer Support and Service	Support and Service								—							—					
	Real-time Response								—							—					
	On-time Solution	—														—					
	Correct Service										—					—					
	Assistance in Using									—						—					

(continued)

265

Table 5. (Continued)

Satisfaction Construct	Variable	7 Factor 1	2	3	4	5	6	7	8	9	10	9 Factor 1	2	3	4	5	6	7	8	9	10
Hardware	Right Application					I															I
	Right Solution					I															I
	Speed, Response and Resources	I										I									
	Compatibility	I										I									
	Ease of Use	I										I									
	Reliability	I										I									
	Upgradability	I																		I	
	Conformity to Local Standard	I																		I	
Software	Right Solution					I						I									
	Speed, Response and Resources	I										I									
	Compatibility	I										I									
	Ease of Use	I										I									
	Reliability	I										I									
Price vs. Performance	Competitive Price							I										I			
	Economy in Upgrading							I										I			
	Economy in Service							I										I			
	Maintenance Cost																				
Advertising	Frequency						I										I				
	Interest						I										I				
	Get the Message Across						I										I				

Note: *I : Factor Loading> 0.4
**Maximum likelihood method and varimax rotation were used for 7- and 9-point scales data.

266

For 5-point scale data, 10 factors explained 62 percent of total variance. Factor analysis for the 5-point scale data was able to correctly discriminate variables for the hardware construct and the software construct. With reasonable accuracy, factor analysis could correctly discriminate variables for 7 constructs. Factor analysis had difficulties in discriminating variables for two constructs (manual and software). Overall, the 5-point scale data showed a high level of validity.

For the 3-point scale, the principle component method extracted 15 factors which had eigenvalues of more than 1. Seven factors explained 52.1 percent of the total variance. The highest eigenvalue was 10.1 for factor 1. The second highest eigenvalue was 3.7 for factor 2, indicating a big difference in eigenvalue between factor 1 and factor 2. The factor loading pattern for the 3-point scale data is shown in Table 6. These factor loadings reveal that too many variables were related to only factor 1. Differences in factor loadings between constructs for the 3-point scale data were neglibible. Only the variables of education and advertising were related to their own constructs correctly. The factor analysis could not discriminate between constructs correctly. Thus, there was almost no validity associated with the 3-point scale data used in this study.

To summarize, if factor analysis is used to measure validity of the data, the 5-point scale and the 9-point scale data had the highest levels of validity. The 7-point scale had a medium level of validity, while the 3-point scale had the lowest level of validity. The 5-point scale had better ability to discriminate variables for constructs than any other scale.

VI. CONCLUSION AND IMPLICATIONS

Conclusions from this study are as follows:

First, in terms of reliability level, the 3-point scale ranked low while the 5-, 7-, and 9-point scales showed a reasonable level of reliability. The study found that 9- and 7-point scales had the highest levels of reliability as measured by Cronbach's alpha and the 5-point scale had the highest level of accuracy as measured by the split-half reliability coefficient. The 3-point scale had the lowest Cronbach's alpha and split-half coefficient. This finding is in partial agreement with the Komorita and Graham (1965) study, which concluded that reliability increases with an increase of the number of scale points. Meanwhile, these findings disagree with Aiken's (1983) research finding that Cronbach's alpha is independent of the number of response categories. However, this study failed to find evidence of a significant difference in reliability level between 5-,7- and 9-point scale data.

In terms of validity level, the 3-point scale ranked low, the 7-point scale at a medium level, and the 5- and 9-point scales had highest level of validity. This finding disagrees with Jacoby and Matell's (1971) research finding that the level of validity is independent of the number of response categories.

Overall, the 3-point scale was found to have the lowest level of reliability and validity. Thus, the 3-point scale may be less capable of transmitting information and more likely to stifle respondents compared to the other scale point levels used in this study (Cox, 1980).

In general, the 5-, 7- and 9-point scales performed at a reasonable level in terms of reliability and validity. However, this study could not determine which was best among these three types of response categories. This finding agrees with the results of some previous studies (Miller, 1956; Green & Rao, 1970; Lehman & Hulbert, 1972; Matell & Jacoby, 1972; Cox, 1980), but disagrees with the results of others (Benson, 1971; Jacoby & Matell, 1971).

Implications from conclusions mentioned above are as follows.

First, When Korean consumer behavior is examined, marketing researchers should note that using 5-,7- and 9-point response categories can enhance the validity and reliability of their measuring instruments. The use of 3-point scales without careful pretests should be avoided in studies of Korean consumers.

Second, marketing researchers in Korea should carefully pretest scales. Guilford (1954) suggests that the appropriate number of response categories should be empirically determined. Since survey research using various numbers of response categories in Korean marketing practice is still in the developing stage, it is especially important to monitor scale effectiveness.

Third, the findings from this study may call into question the use of 3-point scales in other Asian countries, including Japan, Hong Kong, and Singapore which share similar basic cultural roots as well as developed economies. It may be the case that the response behavior patterns of consumers in these Asian countries toward response categories are similar.

Limitations of this study are: First, the data used in this study were gathered to assess consumer satisfaction with personal computers in Korea. It may be difficult to safely generalize findings from this study into other situations in Korea. Second, four different samples were analyzed in this study. Ideally, it would be better to use one sample for comparing response patterns among different scale points. Third, the research is limited in that only four types of response categories were used. Response categories beyond the scale points used here should also be tested.

REFERENCES

Ahn, G.S. (1993). An empirical investigation of influence of market maven in energy conservation. *Korean Marketing Review*, 8 (September), 19-46.

Ahn, K.H., & Choi, S.I. (1993). An investigation of store choice behavior using a mutinomial logit model. *Korean Management Review*, 12 (June), 101-120.

Aiken, L.R. (1983). Number of response categories and statistics on a teacher rating scale. *Educational and Psychological Measurement*. 43, 397-401.

Bending, A.W. (1954). Reliability and the number of rating categories. *Journal of Applied Psychology*, 38 (February), 38-40.

Benson, P.H. (1971). How many scales and how many categories shall we use in consumer research?— A comment. *Journal of Marketing*, 35 (October), 59-61.

Bevan, W., & Avant, L.L. (1968). Response latency, response uncertainty, information transmitted and the number of available judgemental categories. *Journal of Experimental Psychology*, 76 (3), 394-397.

Chaiy, S., & Kim, J.H. (1993). Brand strategies of Korean export companies. *Korean Marketing Review*, 8 (September), 65-79.

Champney, H., & Marshall, H. (1939). Optimal refinement of the rating scale. *Journal of Applied Psychology*, 23, 323-331.

Cho, N.K. (1991). A study on the consumer's store image perception. *Korean Management Review*, 20 (May), 325-352.

Ciccchetti, D.V., Showalter, D., & Tyrer, P.J. (1985). The effect of number of rating scale categories on levels of interrater reliability: A Monte Carlo investigation. *Applied Psychological Measurement*, 9 (March), 31-36.

Cox, E.P., III (1980). The optimal number of response alternatives for a scale: A review. *Journal of Marketing Research*, 17 (November), 407-422.

Cronbach, L.J. (1950). Further evidence on response sets and test design. *Educational and Psychological Measurement*, 10 (Spring), 3-31.

Ferguson, L.W. (1941). A study of the Likert technique of attitude scale construction. *Journal of Social Psychology*, 13, 51-57.

Green P., & Rao, V. (1970). Rating scales and information recovery—How many scales and response categories to use. *Journal of Marketing*, 34 (July), 33-39.

Guilford, J. P. (1954). *Psychometric methods*. New York: McGraw-Hill.

Hah, N.I. (1992). A study of the relationship between conflict and power in marketing channel. *Korean Marketing Review*, 7 (March), 146-167.

Han, C.M. (1990). The role of country of origin and brand name in U.S consumers' product evaluation. *Korean Marketing Review*, 5 (March), 261-276.

Han, C.M., & Lee, B.W. (1992). Country images for foreign products in Europe: An analysis of Korean, Japanese, U.S., and German automobiles. *Korean Management Review*, 21 (May), 223-248.

Hwang, M.T. (1993). An examination of the validity of the behavioral intention model-applied on smoking cessation behavior. *Korean Marketing Review*, 8 (September), 189-198.

Hartel, C.E.J. (1993). Rating format research revisited: Format effectiveness and acceptability depend on rater characteristics. *Journal of Applied Psychology*, 78 (2), 212-217.

Jacoby, J., & Matell, M. (1971). Three-point Likert scales are good enough. *Journal of Marketing Research*, 8 (November), 495-500.

Jahoda, M., Deutsch, M., & Cook, S.W. (1951). *Research methods in social relations*. New York: Dryden Press.

Jeon, I.S., & Han, J.Y. (1994). The effect of market orientation on business performance. *Korean Marketing Review*, 9 (March), 75-91.

Jun, S., Lee, S., & Gentry, J.W. (1994). Acculturation of American expatriates in Korea: Delineation of the behavioral and attitudinal dimension. *Journal of Marketing Studies*, 3 (February), 141-152.

Kim, B.J., & Chaiy, S. (1991). Impact of strategic marketing effort and market environment on performance. *Korean Marketing Review*, 6 (March), 43-69.

Kim, D.K., Bae, S.H., & Park, J.W. (1993). Effects of the consumer's involvement and product knowledge on attitudes and behaviors. *Korean Marketing Review*, 8 (September), 1-17.

Kim, J.I. (1993). Effects of purchase situation and organizational characteristics on the importance of information sources and decision criteria. *Korean Marketing Review*, 8 (April), 70-81.

Kim, J.B. (1992). An empirical study on the key factors influencing new product performance. *Korean Marketing Review*, 7 (March), 121-145.

Kim, J.M., & Park, M.H. (1994). The working relationship's effect between franchise strategy and performance. *Journal of Marketing Studies*, 4 (August), 17-24.

Kim, K.H. (1991). Consumer attributes of brand loyalty for low-involvement products. *Korean Marketing Review*, 6 (March), 82-111.

Kim, K.H. (1993). Reliability: A review of recent marketing practices and problems. *Korean Marketing Review*, 8 (September), 199-230.

Kim, K.H. (1994). Determinants of industrial consumers' PC purchasing decision. *Journal of Marketing Studies*, 4 (August), 85-93.

Kim, K.H. (1994a). Effects of outliers on transformation of consumer satisfaction data. *Journal of Marketing Studies*, 3 (February), 1-17.

Kim, K.H., & Chu, K.W. (1991). Limitations of factor analysis in the research of consumer satisfaction. *Journal of Marketing Studies*, 1 (October), 1-26.

Kim, M.K., & Cho, J.W. (1993). A study on strategy development of service marketing mix of hotel enterprises. *Journal of Marketing Studies*, 3 (August), 17-37.

Kim, M.J. (1993). Objective and subjective well-being according to life-cycle. *Journal of Marketing Studies*, 3 (August), 39-63.

Kim, S.H. (1992). A study on the shopping propensity of Korean consumers. *Korean Marketing Review*, 7 (March), 11-33.

Kim, Y.K. (1992). A study on the influence of the peripheral cues in an ad on the consumer's attitude toward products. *Korean Marketing Review*, 7 (March), 102-120.

Komorita, A.W., & Graham, W.K. (1965). Number of scale points and the reliability of scales. *Educational and Psychological Measurement*, 25 (November), 987-995.

Komorita, S.S. (1963). Attitude content, intensity, and the neutral point on a likert scale. *Journal of Social Psychology*, 61 (December), 327-334.

Lee, C.R., & Kim, C.S. (1993). An empirical study on the evaluation and the measurement of a bank's service quality. *Korean Marketing Review*, 8 (September), 163-188.

Lee, C.H., & Oh, S. (1991). Environmental dynamism effects on bureaucratic structuring and conflict in marketing channels. *Korean Marketing Review*, 6 (March), 26-42.

Lee, C. (1990). A modification of the Fishbein behavioral intention model for Korean consumers. *Korean Marketing Review*, 5 (March), 182-209.

Lee, D.H. (1993). An empirical study of brand awareness caused by advertisements: Intensity effects and valence effect. *Korean Management Review*, 23 (November), 1-20.

Lee, D.H., & Lim, T.K. (1993). A cornerstone of Korean advertising theory building. *Korean Marketing Review*, 8 (September), 231-258.

Lee, H. (1991). Emotional responses as mediator of advertising effects: Moderating roles of product experiences and involvement. *Korean Management Review*, 21 (November), 345-367.

Lee, H., Chae, K.H., & Lee, H.B. (1992). Influences of personality and life style on consumption communication. *Korean Marketing Review*, 7 (March), 65-79.

Lee, J.W. (1994). A study on measuring service value. *Journal of Marketing Studies*, 4 (August), 41-66.

Lee, J.H. (1994). Traits of environmentally conscious consumers in lifestyle research. *Journal of Marketing Studies*, 3, 97-114.

Lee, S.H. (1992). Bank selection attributes and segmenting a bank's customer set. *Journal of Marketing Studies*, 1 (February), 73-82.

Lee, S.T. (1993). An empirical study on product involvement for the change of consumer attitude-with special reference to the attitude change of university students. *Korean Marketing Review*, 8 (April), 97-122.

Lee, W.I. (1993). The effects of perceived crowding and cognitive control on consumer in-store exploratory behavior. *Korean Management Review*, 23 (November), 173-199.

Lehmann, D.R., & Hulbert, J. (1972). Are three-point scales always good enough? *Journal of Marketing Research*, 9 (November), 444-446.

Lissitz, R.W., & Green, S.B. (1975). Effect of the number of scale points on reliability: A Monte Carlo approach. *Journal of Applied Psychology*, 60 (1), 10-13.

Martin, W.S. (1973). The effect of scaling on the correlation coefficient: A test of validity. *Journal of Marketing Research*, 10 (August), 316-318.

Martin, W.S. (1978). Effects of Scaling on the correlation coefficient: Additional considerations. *Journal of Marketing Research*, (May), 304-307.

Matell, M.S., & Jacoby, J. (1972). Is there an optimal number of alternatives for Likert-scale items? Effects of testing time and scale properties. *Journal of Applied Psychology*, 56 (6), 506-509.

Miller, G.A. (1956). The magical number seven, plus or minus two: Some limits on our capacity for processing information. *The Psychological Review*, 63 (March), 81-97.

Noh, J.P. (1991). The effect of perceived risk on industrial buyer's different preferences for risk handling strategies. *Korean Marketing Review*, 6 (March), 131-145.

Nunnally, J. (1967). *Psychometric methods*. New York: McGraw-Hill Book Co..

Oh, S., Rhim, B.S., & Kim, S.I. (1993). Effects of relational norms and bureaucratic structuring on conflict in industrial buyer-seller relationships. *Korean Marketing Review*, 8 (April), 1-11.

Oh, S., Park, J., & Kang, H. (1994). Relational norms, bureaucratic structuring and power structures in industrial buyer-seller relationships. *Korean Management Review*, 23 (November), 1-16.

Oh, S., Park, K.D., & Kim, S.I. (1992). The effects of environmental munificence and channel configuration on internal economic structures in marketing channels. *Korean Management Review*, 21 (May), 29-53.

Oh, S., Kim, S.I., & Choi, D.H. (1994). The effects of bureaucratic structuring and relational norms on opportunism and trust in marketing channels. *Korean Marketing Review*, 9 (March), 57-74.

Pahng, S. (1993). A content analysis of message cues in Korean, U.S and Japanese television advertising. *Korean Marketing Review*, 8 (April), 84-95.

Park, C.W., & Hyun, Y.J. (1994). The memory of newspaper ads as affected by ad size and article involvement. *Korean Marketing Review*, 9 (March), 39-56.

Park, I.S. (1994). A study on R&D and marketing cooperation. *Journal of Marketing Studies*, 3 (February), 55-76.

Park, J.H. (1993). The effects of environmental dynamism and interchannel competition on internal political economy in franchise channels of distribution. *Korean Management Review*, 23 (November), 391-422.

Park, J. (1993). A study of influences on export expansion strategy. *Journal of Marketing Studies*, 3 (August), 65-75.

Park, M.H. (1993). A study on the buying behavior of credit card users. *Korean Marketing Review*, 8 (April), 123-144.

Park, Y.K. (1994). Logistics strategy of manufacturing firms. *Journal of Marketing Studies*, 3 (February), 35-53.

Peabody, D. (1962). Two components in bipolar scales: Direction and extremeness. *Psychological Review*, 69, 65-73.

Peter, J. P. (1979). Reliability: A review of psychometric basics and recent marketing practices. *Journal of Marketing Research*, 16 (February), 6-17.

Shin, B.D. (1994). A study on influence determinants of buying center members. *Journal of Marketing Studies*, 3 (February); pp. 77-95.

Shin, J.Y. (1992). Influential factor analysis on consumer satisfaction in distribution channels of electric home appliance. *Journal of Marketing Studies*, 1 (February), 83-117.

Song, Y.S. (1994). An alternative direction for restructuring marketing curricula in Korea. *Korean Marketing Review*, 9 (March), 1-22.

Sung, S.K., Choi, J.H., & Lee, J.C. (1993). Statistical errors in research papers in *Korean Management Review*. *Korean Management Review*, 22 (June), 163-198.

Symonds, P.M. (1924). On the loss of reliability in ratings due to coarseness of the scale. *Journal of Experimental Psychology*, 7, 456-461.

Whang, E.R. (1993). An empirical study of the multi-stage brand evaluation model. *Korean Management Review*, 23 (November), 233-260.

Yae, J.S., & Kim, M.K. (1992). A study on the actual conditions of marketing applications in Korean firms. *Korean Marketing Review*, 7 (March), 80-101.

Yoon. M.H. (1993). A cross-cultural investigation of the reliability of LOV (list of values). *Journal of Marketing Studies*, 2 (February), 87-105.

Advances in International Marketing

Edited by **S. Tamer Cavusgil,** *The Eli Broad Graduate School of Management, Michigan State University*

A collection of original, high-quality essays in international marketing. Both theoretical/conceptual and empirical contributions are included. Written by scholars from all over the world, these essays address various aspects of export and multinational marketing. While some authors focus on managerial issues in international marketing, others take a public policy or comparative perspective. Similarly, while some authors may confine their analyses to well-established concepts or methodologies in international marketing, others have the opportunity to incorporate new and innovative perspectives.

Volume 6, Export Marketing:
International Perspectives
1993, 229 pp. $73.25
ISBN 1-55938-645-2

Edited by **Catherine N. Axinn,** *College of Business Administration, Ohio University*

CONTENTS: Preface. Introduction: International Perspectives on Export Marketing, *Catherine N. Axinn.* PART I. CONCEPTUAL ADVANCES. A Conceptual Framework for Country Selection in Cross-National Export Studies, *Hartmut H. Holzmüller and Barbara Stöllnberger.* A Contingency Approach to Export Performance Research, *Tage Koed Madsen.* Entrepreneurship and Export Promotion: A Proposed Conceptual Model, *Poh-Lin Yeoh.* International Marketing and Market Orientation: An Early Attempt at Conceptual Integration, *Tevfik Dalgic.* PART II. EMPIRICAL INSIGHTS FROM AROUND THE WORLD. The "Exporting" Process: The Evolution of Small and Medium Sized Firms Towards Internationalization, *Daniele Dalli.* The Export Experience of a Developing Country: A Review of Empirical Studies of Export Behavior and the Performance of Brazilian Firms, *Angela da Rocha and Carl H. Christensen.* Linking Distribution Strategy Choice to Context and Implementation in Export Markets, *Catherine N. Axinn, James M. Sinkula and Sharon V. Thach.* Linking Export Manpower to Export Performance: A Canonical Regression Analysis of European and U.S. Data, *A. Diamantopoulos and B.B. Schlegelmilch.* Foreign Market Indicators, Structural Resources and Marketing Strategies as Determinants of Export Performance, *Muzaffer Bodur.* Export Performance of Australian Manufacturing Companies, *Felicitas U. Evangelista.*

Also Available:
Volumes 1-5 (1986-1993) $73.25 each

J
A
I

P
R
E
S
S

Research in Marketing

Edited by **Jagdish N. Sheth,** *College of Business, Emory University*

Volume 12, 1995, 293 pp. $73.25
ISBN 1-55938-653-3

CONTENTS: List of Contributors. Preface, *Jagdish Sheth.* Franchising Coordination with Brand Name Considerations, *Abraham Charnes, Zhimin Huang, and Vijay Mahajan.* An integrative Review of Nonresponse Errors in Survey Research: Major Influences and Strategies, *Nejdet Delener.* Can Advanced Marketing Transfer to Manufacturing Firms in Developing Countries? The Venuzuelan Experience as an Empirical Test of Current Assumptions, *Luis V. Dominguez and Ronald A. Fullerton.* The Effect of Specific Human Capital on Compensation and Sales Force Turnover, *Khalid M. Dubas and James T. Strong.* Facet Analysis: A Metatheory for Marketing Research and Theory, *Jacob Hornik and Joseph Cherian.* Battles for Market Share in Hyperselective Markets, *F. Xavier Olleros.* Quick Choices as Targetable Units of the Consumer Decision Process, *Robert M. Schindler.* Forming Perceptions of Overall Product Quality in Consumer Goods: A Process of Quality Element Integration, *Steven N. Silverman and Rajiv Grover.*

Also Available:
Volumes 1-11 (1979-1992)
   + Supplements 1-6 (1982-1994) $73.25 each

JAI PRESS INC.
55 Old Post Road No. 2 - P.O. Box 1678
Greenwich, Connecticut 06836-1678
Tel: (203) 661- 7602   Fax: (203) 661-0792

Advances in Services Marketing and Management
Research and Practice

Edited by **Teresa A. Swartz**, *California Polytechnic State University—San Luis Obispo,* **David E. Bowen**, *Arizona State University-West*, and **Stephen W. Brown,** *Arizona State University*

Advances in Services Marketing and Management: Research and Practice is an interdisciplinary series on the latest research and practice in services. The series focuses on new, fresh ideas in services marketing and management and is committed to encouraging scholars new to the area of services to pursue innovative and interdisciplinary services-related research. Also encouraged is work that crosses the boundaries between academic research and business practice. Leading scholars will delve into services issues such as service quality, internal marketing, service design, human resources in services, services operations, etc. Included are directions for future research and managerial implications.

Volume 4, 1995, 376 pp. $73.25
ISBN 1-55938-885-2

CONTENTS: Preface, *Teresa A. Swartz, David E. Bowen and Stephen W. Brown.* Acknowledgments. About the First Interstate Center for Services Marketing. Executive Summaries of Articles. Service Quality and Consumer Attitudes: Reconciling Theory and Measurement, *Steven A. Taylor.* Exploring the Quality of the Service Experience: A Theoretical and Empirical Analysis, *Julie E. Otto and J.R. Brent Ritchie.* Technology: Servant or Master in the Delivery of Services?, *Christopher H. Lovelock.* Process Factors in Service Delivery: What Employee Effort Means to Customers, *Lois A. Mohr and Mary Jo Bitner.* Linking Customer Intelligence to Service Operations: Exploiting the Connection at GTE, *James H. Drew and Ruth N. Bolton.* The Nature of Customer Relationships in Services, *Veronica Liljander and Tore Strandvik.* A Conceptual Model of Customer Satisfaction for Business-to-Business, Professional Services, *Paul G. Patterson.* Factors Influencing Customers Assessments of Service Quality and Their Invocation of a Service Warranty, *Ruth N. Bolton and James Drew.* Service Failure and Recovery: Impact, Attributes and Process, *Robert Johnston.* Strategic Investment in Service Quality: Protecting Profitable Customer Relationships, *Judith A. Cumby and James G. Barnes.* Signalling and Monitoring Strategies of Service Firms: Interdisciplinary Perspectives, *Debra Prasad Mishra.* Systems Theoretic Perspectives in Services Management, *Ravi S. Behara.* Perspectives on International Services Marketing and Management, *Frank Bradley.* About the Editors. About the Contributors.

Also Available:
Volumes 1-3 (1992-1994) $73.25 each

J A I P R E S S

J A I   P R E S S

Advances in Nonprofit Marketing

Edited by **Richard J. Semenik,** *David Eccles School of Business, University of Utah* and **Gary J. Bamossy,** *Econmics Faculty, Vrije University*

Volume 4, 1993, 147 pp. $73.25
ISBN 1-55938-363-1

CONTENTS: Preface, *Richard J. Semenik and Gary J. Bamossy.* Using Strategic Groups to Understand Your Industry and Competition: A Study of Hospitals, *Deepika Nath.* Vertical Relationships Among Health Care Organizations: Strategic Options, *Debra L. Scammon and Dan A. Fuller.* Sustaining Helping Behavior: A Field Test of Empathetic, Labeling, and Dependency Appeals, *Chris T. Allen, Robert J. Kent, and Terri F. Barr.* From Community Workshop to Professional Theatre: Audience Development and the Consumption of Art, *Annamma Joy and Clarence Bayne.* The Electronic Group Discussion: A New Tool in Higher Education Marketing, *Jeromee D. Williams, Daniel R. Toy, and John J. Gormley.*

Also Available:
Volumes 1-3 (1985-1990) $73.25 each

JAI PRESS INC.
55 Old Post Road No. 2 - P.O. Box 1678
Greenwich, Connecticut 06836-1678
Tel: (203) 661- 7602   Fax: (203) 661-0792

Advances in Business Marketing and Purchasing

Edited by **Arch G. Woodside**, *A.B. Freeman School of Business, Tulane University*

Volume 6, Handbook of Business-to-Business Marketing Management
1995, 333 pp. $73.25
ISBN 1-55938-735-1

CONTENTS: Preface, *Arch G. Woodside*. Strategic Management and Business Marketing, *Daryl McKee and Arch G. Woodside*. Organizational Buying in the Quality Revolution, *Elizabeth J. Wilson*. Segmenting Industrial Markets, *Yoram Wind and Robert J. Thomas*. Effective Product Decision-Making in the Industrial Environment, *George J. Avlonitis and Athanassios G. Kouremenos*. Making Better Pricing Decisions in Business Marketing, *Arch G. Woodside*. Business-to-Business Selling and Sales Force Management, *Wesley J. Johnson and James S. Boles*. Industrial Advertising Decisions, *J. David Litchenthal and Robert H. Ducoffe*. Industrial Publicity, *Jerome D. Williams and Srinath Gopalakrishna*. Marketing Strategies in Manufacturer-Distributor Relationships, *Roger J. Calantone and Jule Gassenheimer*.

Also Available:
Volumes 1-5 (1986-1992) $73.25 each

JAI PRESS INC.
55 Old Post Road No. 2 - P.O. Box 1678
Greenwich, Connecticut 06836-1678
Tel: (203) 661- 7602   Fax: (203) 661-0792

J A I   P R E S S

Research in Consumer Behavior

Edited by Clifford J. Shultz II, *Business Programs, Arizona State University,* **Russell W. Belk,** *School of Business, University of Utah* and **Güliz Ger,** *Faculty of Business Administration, Bilkent University*

Volume 7, Consumption in Marketing Behavior
1994, 292 pp. $73.25
ISBN 1-55938-783-1

Also Available:
Volumes 1-6 (1985-1993) $73.25 each

JAI PRESS INC.
55 Old Post Road No. 2 - P.O. Box 1678
Greenwich, Connecticut 06836-1678
Tel: (203) 661- 7602   Fax: (203) 661-0792